# HOW TO WIN AT JUST ABOUT EVERYTHING

# HOW TO WIN
# AT JUST ABOUT
# EVERYTHING
## David Feldman

Illustrations by Kas Schwan

WILLIAM MORROW AND COMPANY, INC.
*New York*

*158.1*
*Feldman*

**Library of Congress Cataloging-in-Publication Data**

Feldman, David.
    How to win at just about everything.

    1. Success.   I. Title.
BJ1611.2.F42   1987    158′.1       86-31252
    ISBN 0-688-06465-5

Printed in the United States of America

First Edition

1 2 3 4 5 6 7 8 9 10

BOOK DESIGN BY BERNARD SCHLEIFER

*In memory of*
EUNICE RIEDEL

# Acknowledgments

WE WRITERS LOVE nothing more than complaining about all the horrible people who prevent our deathless prose from reaching the millions of folks clamoring to read it. We must, at all times, be armed with handy rationalizations for our failures, both aesthetic and commercial.

But my ungenerous collaborators provide me with no excuse for screwing up. My agent, Jim Trupin, does nothing but help and encourage me. My editor, Eunice Riedel, has altogether too much respect for my opinions, is suspiciously good-humored, and has the audacity to improve my work. When Eunice isn't available, her assistant, Randy Ladenheim, is too darn helpful and supportive to be a decent scapegoat. Perhaps if this book bombs, I can blame its illustrator, Kas Schwan. Her drawings were so great, I could convincingly argue, that I subconsciously slacked off in my writing after seeing them. Of course, if *How to Win at Just About Everything* becomes a best-seller, her wonderful drawings were inspired solely by my great wit.

Come to think of it, if this book fails, it is the fault of the publicity department of William Morrow and Company. If Lela Rolontz, Lori Ames, Ann Whitney, and Diana Faust's dedication and skill hadn't kept me hopping promoting my last book, I would have had more time to make this book perfect instead of merely brilliant and spellbinding. And Mark Kohut, in Morrow's sales department, is no better. How dare he lull me away from my word processor by actually listening to an author's input, compounding his crime by sharing his knowledge about marketing and sales with me?

Then there were those especially valuable people who

either served as sources for the book or led me to other sources. I take *all* of the credit for their perspicacity, since *I* found them; of course, if you have any complaints about their statements, please contact *them*: Jeff Bayone, Phil Feldman, Bonnie Gellas, Dan Gordon, Christal Henner, Francois Martine, Stan Newman, Robert E. O'Neill, Merrill Perlman, Karen Puro, Neil Puro, Paul Rosenbaum, and Tom Rugg.

Of course, a writer does not live by work alone. Since my friends and family were so crucial in bolstering my spirits while writing this book, they are at least as responsible as the author for its shortcomings.

# Contents

## Winning for Yourself

# Introduction

I FIRST THOUGHT ABOUT WRITING this book one gray afternoon, as I stood fuming during an endless wait at a checkout
line at my local supermarket. I consider myself a reasonably
intelligent person. I have a college education. I even read a
book on occasion. But as I watched shoppers on both sides of
me breeze through with their purchases, I was full of self-
loathing: Why do I *always* choose the wrong checkout line?

The law of averages would dictate that I would occasionally
stumble into the right checkout line, so I knew that I was
doing *something* consistently wrong. At that very moment, I
was determined to be a winner in the supermarket checkout-
line game and to impart my newfound wisdom to other losers
suffering from this affliction rarely discussed in polite company.

All of us feel like losers some of the time. Perhaps you are
not a Wall Street wizard. Even the dimmest stockbroker
can make you feel like a dunce with his prattle about price-
earnings ratios, straddles, and betas. But you are unbeatable
on the tennis court. Although you don't have the athletic talent
of a John McEnroe or a Martina Navratilova, you instinctively
know where to place the ball to befuddle your opponent.
Without consciously thinking about it, you seize upon your
opponent's weaknesses.

In the stock market, you are Don Knotts. Inside the tennis
court, you are Superman. If only you could feel in command
in the world of bears and bulls . . .

How do we propose to turn you Don Knotts feel-alikes
into men and women of steel? We want you to look at each
of the subjects in this book as a game. Games can be serious

or they can be frivolous, but they all contain a conflict of interest (some players win, others lose) and an agreed-upon set of rules. Some games, such as chess or bridge, have rules you can read. Other games, like getting a good table at a fancy restaurant or doing well in a job interview, have unwritten rules that only experienced winners seem to know. We'll explain the ground rules of each subject to you, so you will at least be on equal footing with the other players in the game.

Two underlying themes unify every chapter in this book, despite the diverse subject matter. If you understand these two concepts, it is unlikely that even Kryptonite can keep you from winning:

1. *In any conflict situation, there is an explicit or implicit opponent or enemy. Determine who your opponent is, and learn how your opponent thinks.* In many situations, such as negotiations, an understanding of your opponent's needs and emotional state is crucial to success, yet nervous employees asking for a raise are more likely to view a boss as a cash machine rather than a human being with his or her own ego problems.

If there is one consistent trait in losers, it is their preoccupation with their own problems rather than their ability to empathize with the opponent. When you are performing well at tennis, you can't be overly concerned with the fact that your last backhand shot went awry. You are too busy anticipating the shots of your opponents. You probably aren't thinking at all—your body and mind are fused.

This is not a book about how to intimidate the opponent but rather about how to understand the opponent. We do not expect our tennis foe to hand us a victory (we would be insulted if he did). Neither should we expect the used-car salesperson to hand us a "steal." We will have to learn how a salesperson thinks and how we can satisfy his or her needs as well as our own.

Most of the time, when we look at a game from our opponents' point of view, we learn that they are people much like ourselves. It is reassuring to note that when we see an IRS tax audit from the point of view of the auditor, we learn that screwing you out of your pennies is probably not going to make her day. She has her own problems, not the least of which is why she is confronting you over hundreds of dollars, when her colleagues are extracting millions from crooked tax shelters, the kind of work that gains recognition within the IRS. Chances are, your audit bores her as much as it scares you.

We'll show you how to solve a crossword puzzle by concentrating on the problems of the crossword constructor. You think solving a crossword is hard? Try constructing one. We'll show you the toughest hurdles in creating a crossword. When you learn these problems, solving the puzzles will be a lot easier.

2. *Learn how losers act. Then act in the opposite way.* Losers are much more consistent in their behavior than winners. A person may think of one brilliant idea and then never produce another one. In the case of Hugh Hefner and *Playboy*, that one epiphany can sustain a fortune. But most of us never come up with one brilliant idea, and it is senseless to squander our time waiting for such an inspiration to occur. If we want to learn, for example, how to win at poker, it is far more productive to study why losers lose than to try to decipher the arcane musings of an instinctive poker genius. Surprisingly, bad poker players share more methods in common than great players anyway. *How to Win at Just About Everything* is going to teach you how bad players play, and thus how you can win by not playing like the losers.

The purpose of *How to Win at Just About Everything* is to make you think like a winner, so that you will stop feeling like a Don Knotts character when playing many of life's games. By avoiding the conventional wisdom of the crowd (crowds are, by definition, mediocre), you will change from a loser to a winner. If you can't always feel like an instant Superman in every possible situation, you'll feel at least a notch more confident than Clark Kent.

# WINNING
## AGAINST
# THE CROWD

# The Crowd—And Why You Should Run Away from It

*Or How to Win at Football Betting, Horse Racing, and the Stock Market*

WALK INTO ANY serious poker game. The atmosphere is tense, heavy. Most of the players are, appropriately enough, poker-faced. Next to them, Charles Bronson is expressive.

You may find one joker or loudmouth, as volatile as the others are stone-faced. Chances are, the joker is trying to intimidate the opponents or trying to convince them that he is a fool. If he is telegraphing his actual emotions while playing a hand, he is probably drunk, and certainly will leave the table poorer than when he sat down.

Poker players may respect, even like, their adversaries at the table, but gambling is neither group therapy nor the family dinner table. That nice woman check-raising you is trying to take your money. She is—until you rise from the table—your enemy.

Now walk over to your nearest brokerage house. Or to your local racetrack. Or your favorite bar where football bettors congregate. Engage the nearest friendly face in conversation. You will hear tales of woe:

- of the stock that was sold at 14 for a loss and then went up to 38 two months later.

- of the 19-to-1 longshot that was closing fast at the finish but got boxed out in the stretch.
- of the 14-point favorite who jumped to a 27-point lead and gave up two "meaningless" touchdowns at the end of the game, failing to cover the spread.
- of the longshot who won the first part of the daily double and was wheeled to a can't-miss favorite—who missed.

You will also hear inspiring stories about rare courage and blinding insight:

- of the nifty computer stock that his brother Bernie's friend Arthur recommended that has split three times and quintupled in price.
- of the 15-point underdog that not only covered the spread but won outright.
- of the winning 55-to-1 shot picked because of its fabulous breeding despite its poor racing history.

Once they complete the cycle of complaining and/or bragging about their past record, football plungers, stock pickers, and horse bettors will get down to the nitty-gritty:

- Who do you like in the fourth race?
- What do you think of the May IBM puts?
- Should I take Buffalo plus 8 points against Miami?

Your newfound pals are trying to make money as surely as the sharks in the poker game, yet in the world of stocks, horses, and football, most players are more than willing to exchange information not only with friends but also with casual acquaintances. They are pleased not only to tell you what they are planning to bet on but to offer their rationale as well. After all, in a poker game, if Joe wins, he is taking your money. But in football, stocks, or horse racing, you are betting against the house, right?

Wrong! If I can convince you of anything in the next few chapters, I hope it will be that *in any games with odds, your* "opponents" are the fellow bettors who help establish the odds, even if you don't literally take your winnings from their pocket. Let's see how this principle applies to each "game."

## FOOTBALL BETTING

When football betting started, linesmakers would simply lay odds on the chances of either team winning outright. Fans were reluctant to bet on certain underdogs at any price. So the "line" was instituted. The line provides an underdog with a handicap of a certain number of points. If the Jets are favored by 7 over the Oilers, it indicates that an Oiler bettor will win if his team wins outright or loses by 6 points or less. If the Oilers lose by 7, it is a tie, and no money changes hands. The Las Vegas casino (or the bookie) makes its profit by charging 11-to-10 odds when the bettor loses. Although this profit margin is relatively small (a football bettor need win only 52.37 percent of his bets to break even), it has proven to be more than sufficient to make sports books lucrative propositions.

By Monday the Vegas line for the next week's games (excluding the participants in that Monday night's game) are released. The linesmaker is not necessarily predicting what he thinks the final score will be. Although the official line might favor the Jets by 7 over the Oilers, the linesmaker might personally think the Jets will win by only 3 points. His job is to split the betting populace—to make 50 percent of the betting money side on the Jets and 50 percent on Houston. If he succeeds in splitting the pool, he is guaranteeing that sports books will make money. When billions of dollars are wagered on football betting every year, those 11-to-10 odds start adding up to fortunes for bookmakers.

The only problem for the house comes when the betting is uneven. The only way it can guarantee a split in the betting money when there is an imbalance is by adjusting the line. For example, if the public decides that the Oilers are a bargain at plus 7, the oddsmakers will move the line to plus 6½. If this fails to stir enough action on the Jets, the line could move to 6 or even lower, to 5½ or 5. At this point, presumably, much more money will come in on New York. Moving the line is not without dangers, however, since if New York wins by 6 points, the book loses not only to players who took Houston at the original plus 7 points but also to the new bettors who sniffed a bargain and took New York giving only 5½. In some cases, individuals might have made bets on both teams, trying to achieve this "middle."

Since setting the line is a precarious and financially crucial decision for the bookmakers, it is not surprising that the linesmakers are truly expert at their work. There have been weeks when not one NFL number has deviated by more than one point from the opening line until game time. The Las Vegas linesmakers are privy to the most esoteric information about football teams from all over the country. It is highly unlikely that you know more about football than the linesmaker.

So how can you win if you know less about football than the people setting the line? You might not be able to win betting against the linesmakers themselves, but luckily, you don't have to. You can win because you know more about football *betting* than your true opponents, your fellow bettors, whose cash decides the final line. Remember I said that the linesmaker's goal is not so much to predict the score at the end of the game as to predict the line that will split bettors down the middle. If the linesmaker gave out what he thought was the true line, the betting would be uneven. In order to beat football, you must learn about the characteristics of the football bettor and where he goes wrong in calculating what the spread should be in a football game. If you can find patterns in how the crowd bets football games incorrectly, and loses, you can bet against the crowd and win. In the chapter on football, I will show you how I have consistently won by betting against men who know much more about football than I will ever know.

That friendly guy at the bar assuring you that the Jets are a steal at minus 7 against the Oilers is no doubt sincere. He has already gotten his bet down. He can't, for the life of him, see how spreading his genius can hurt him financially, because your bet will not affect his chances of winning or the odds he will be paid if he does win. And in the narrow sense, he's right. If you follow his advice and bet the Jets, he won't win more or less money regardless of how the game turns out. Obviously, though, the more people who agree with his side in the game, the more likely that the spread will move against him if he decides to wager additional money. And because you want to win at football betting, you are not looking for games in which the spread is moving against you. You are looking for opportunities to get more generous odds than the game merits, to pick teams that the crowd undervalues. By studying how the gambling crowd thinks, we'll discover the specific reasons why the 11-to-10 spread beats all but the most intrepid football bettors.

## HORSE RACING

Of our three "games," here's the easiest in which to analyze how and why your fellow plungers are the enemy. The totalizator board is tangible evidence of how the other bettors affect your profit potential. In football betting, the books collect money in two ways. First, they skim their 11-to-10 profit off the top. But they also can make additional revenue if more than half of the bettors lose their bets. In fact, in most weeks, bettors do achieve less than a 50 percent success rate. The definition of a perfect line, from a bookmaker's point of view, is one that splits the money fairly well between each team but has attracted slightly more money on the team that loses against the spread.

The owners of racetracks, on the other hand, couldn't care less which horse wins a race. The racetrack counts the gross receipts for each race, takes its cut, takes out tax revenues for the state, and then splits the rest of the pool among the supporters of the three top horses in each race. Although racetracks want to maximize the amount bet, they have no vested interest in which horses win.

Between the racetrack's profit and taxes, bettors start at a disadvantage of about 17 percent (this figure varies depending mostly on the tax rates of each state) and have one other strike against them. Most racetracks pay off in increments of twenty cents. If a horse's true odds would pay $2.95 to show, at most tracks in North America you would receive only $2.80. This rounding out to the next *lower* twenty-cent increment is called *breakage*. Breakage can add several more percent to a bettor's disadvantage and can be especially troublesome to place and show bettors, for whom a loss of ten cents per $2 wagered can cut profit margins by more than 20 percent.

To give you some idea of how poor a proposition horserace betting is: The house's take in horse racing is actually greater than for casino slot machines. If you are to overcome an almost 20 percent handicap to the house, it is clear that you must be a great deal smarter than the crowd at the track in order to show a net profit. But slot machines are inanimate objects that relentlessly grind out profits for their owners. At the racetrack, you have a chance to make money because you are betting not against the house but against the other horse players. You can't make a profit simply by betting on the horse that you think has the best chance to win each race. These horses invariably are also the favorites of the crowd. Many mathematical studies have proven conclusively that the crowd does an excellent job of picking favorites in horse racing. Favorites consistently win more than second favorites, who win more than third favorites, and so on. Even when favorites win more than a third of the time, their return is not enough to turn a profit.

Obviously, the only way you can overcome the cards stacked against you is by not only finding the right horses but also finding the situations in which these horses' chances have been greatly underestimated by the crowd. So your fellow horse bettors are your opponents in two ways. First, if they agree with your selection, they are lessening your potential reward if you are right. Second, by constantly making mistakes in evaluating horses, the crowd can entice you to pick not only the wrong horse but an overvalued horse.

But by being so consistently wrongheaded in its thinking, the crowd is your adviser as well as your enemy. You will find your solutions, as you do in football betting, not so much by a study of the sport but by a study of crowd psychology. When you figure out how the crowd goes wrong in its thinking, you'll know how to go right and when to disregard horses with which the crowd falls in love.

## THE STOCK MARKET

Although I will be discussing many of the similarities between playing the stock market and playing the horses or football, there are several notable differences. (I am not referring to the relative morality or to the status of undertaking these pursuits as a vocation or avocation; for our purposes, the stock market or buying a car is just another game.) One of these differences is that a football or horse bet is a one-shot opportunity. Except in options or futures trading, one ordinarily has unlimited time to buy and hold a stock. In football or horse racing if the crowd agrees with your selection, it lowers your odds and decreases your financial payback when you win. The crowd then becomes your enemy unless you and the crowd are on different sides of the fence. Ironically, when the crowd disagrees with your selection, the crowd has become your friend because its money has increased the odds on your selection.

In the stock market you want the crowd to agree with you in your estimation of a stock, but *only after you've bought the stock.* Before you buy a stock, you hope that the company has fallen out of favor or is obscure, for a stock ignored by the crowd obivously can be bought at a cheaper level. If your coveted stock, Widget Inc., has been selling in a trading range of $11 to $13 for the past few weeks, you have no reason not to prefer nabbing it for $11. Once you own Widget, you are rooting for Widget to break out of its trading range and zoom upward. The only way it will zoom is if the crowd (or *a* crowd, because the stock market is as full of as many crowd subcultures as any high school) discovers your stock as well. One of the reasons why everyone from casual acquaintances to investment advisers on national television shows are so willing and eager to share their enthusiasm about companies in which they already own stock is that by motivating others to buy, their holdings are more likely to rise in value.

The only way a football or horse bettor can be dissuaded from placing a bet on his favored team or horse is if the spread or odds become so low that the risk of the bet is not worth the potential reward. The stock-market model is a little different, resembling a free market. For one of the salient features of the stock market is that *every time you decide to buy a stock, someone else has decided to sell those shares.* You have decided that this is exactly the right time to buy. Someone else has decided that this is the perfect time to sell. One of you is wrong.

You and the seller are on opposite sides, with opposite positions, yet one can hardly say that you are opponents. After all, he has been nice enough to sell you his shares at a price you think is fair. And he feels affection for the buyer he will never meet for being kind enough to pay *that* much money for the stock he was looking to unload.

Since a stock-market purchase is not a one-shot action, there will be no bell to signify when the "bet" is over. At any given time, you might not know whether or not you have "won" your bet. There is no game, no race to observe. Sure, you can follow earnings reports, look for dividend increases, and most important, watch the fluctuations in the price of the stock. But there is always someone willing to unload a widely traded stock at the right place. Your real opponents in the stock game are the other players who own your stock, who can jeopardize the price of the stock by deciding to sell regardless of how well Widget Inc. as a company is performing.

There are times in the stock market when all stocks seem to go up or down. Even a company that is in serious financial danger can be swept along in a tide of mass euphoria among investors. During periods of extreme bearishness and bullishness, all investors are your opponents, for it takes great discipline to maintain your confidence in your evaluation of the proper price of Widget Inc. when everyone else thinks you are crazy.

Your opponent, then, in all three games, is "the crowd." Luckily for you, you can depend on one thing. The crowd is almost always wrong. The crowd is a loser.

The average football or horse bettor loses a tremendous amount of money. And while the average stock-market investor "makes" money, he underperforms the popular stock-market averages.

If the crowd always loses, your strategy is simple. You are going to study how the crowd behaves in game situations. And then you are going to do the opposite of what the crowd does.

The word *crowd* has a negative connotation. You wouldn't describe the members of the Constitutional Conventions as a crowd; the fans at a wrestling match are more what you may have in mind. Crowds tend to mask the individual identity of their constituents. In matters of strategy the crowd seems to fall into the same traps regardless of the game. In the following three chapters you will see how the crowd consistently uses bad strategy in each particular game. For now, let's look at the general tendencies of the crowd in betting strategy. By studying what the losing crowd does, you will know what *not* to do.

## The Ten Fatal Betting Mistakes of Crowds

1. *The crowd overbets favorites.* The crowd loves favorites. Almost every year in football, more underdogs than favorites win against the spread, yet every year the public wagers more on favorites than underdogs. In the stock market, favorites,

with high price-earnings ratios, seem to gain favor as they get more expensive. Yet, consistently, low P-E stocks outperform high P-E stocks. Only in horse racing is there a tendency to undervalue favorites, yet many people at the racetrack bet favorites exclusively—a proposition doomed to failure.

The crowd, dubious of its own ability to distinguish quality, is not a confident group. By picking a team, a stock, a horse that is esteemed by the majority, the loser feels that his position must be worthy, must be logical. The favorite-picker is likely to survive longer than the random-stabber in any game but is unlikely to win at any of them.

2. *The crowd relies too much on the last performance.* The crowd is always looking for the next hot proposition. As a result, it overestimates the importance of the last game, the last race, the last earnings report, figuring that the most recent performance must be a signal of an impending trend. In some cases it may be a trend, but in other cases the last performance may have been a fluke.

The crowd is lazy and registers only what can be stated in round figures on a scorecard or in stock tables. The loser is unlikely to bother finding out *why* a football team was upset last week, why a horse who had won on five straight outings ran out of the money, or why a high-growth stock suddenly incurred a loss. If you can come up with a legitimate reason to disregard the last performance of an otherwise admirable investment, you are likely to come out a winner, for you can be sure that the crowd will have soured on it. On the other hand, if an otherwise losing team, horse, or stock suddenly emerges with a great success and you can divine a reason why that one performance was a fluke, you have been given a wonderful opportunity to beat the crowd, which is sure that it has found the golden egg.

3. *The crowd relies too much on "expert" advice.* Losers in almost any endeavor are convinced that somewhere out there are unidentified geniuses who have tapped the secrets

of winning. And losers are more than happy to pay for the privilege of hearing out the experts. It always astonishes me that folks are willing to pay big money to horse-racing and football touts for advice in a betting proposition in which everyone knows there are so few winners. The same people who scoff at investing money in a bank CD because the interest rate is too low are willing to shell out hundreds of dollars a week for dubious advice in a field where, at best, 2 percent of the serious players are winners over the long haul. But never underestimate the lack of confidence of the crowd member, and never underestimate the number of people willing to take advantage of this lack of confidence.

Although several stock advisers have outperformed the stock-market averages over the long haul, advisers as a group have done shabbily, underperforming no-load mutual funds. Yet even experienced stock-market devotees are willing to pay hundreds of dollars for information from a tipster, simply because he has had one hot year or, in some cases, one hot month. Stock-market advisers have performed so poorly as a group that they have become a valid contrary indicator: When a strong majority of advisers are bullish, it is one of the most reliable indicators available that we are due for a bear market. When the advisers are at their most bearish, the market tends to erupt on the upside.

The crowd is unwilling to face the scary truth: Nobody knows for certain what is going to happen in any game. The winners just play the percentages and let nature take its course.

4. *The crowd forgets the odds of the game they are playing.* Many of us buy a house not only to provide a place to live but also as an investment. We might find a house that seems ideal, one that we can afford but that we think is overpriced. The sellers are asking $130,000 for the house, but we think it is worth $110,000 at most. So we make a counteroffer of $100,000, hoping to smoke the seller down. The seller barely budges, informing the broker that $125,000 is as low as he is willing to go.

Most of us put in this situation would be sad and would reluctantly but firmly reject buying the house. It is too expensive. *It is not a good value*, regardless of how much we love the house.

And yet put the same person in a game situation and he will fall in love so much with a team, a horse, or a stock, that he will disregard the odds, which determine his potential risks and reward. This makes no sense at all. At least if you buy an overpriced house, you can enjoy it. You can sit by the wood-burning fireplace or lie down in your family room while you worry about the house's resale value.

If you are sure a horse is going to win a race, but it is going off at odds of 2-to-5 (returning a mere eighty cents for every $2 invested), you have to contemplate seriously whether the potential payoff justifies the outlay of money. There are no tangible compensations if you lose your bet on the horse.

Why was our loser analyzing his house purchase so logically and his bet so myopically? Probably because the down payment and mortgage payments involve so much more money than his bet. But the principle of value remains the same for both investments, and if you are going to win money at the racetrack, regardless of the size of your bet, you are going to have to win money from losers such as this who worry only over which horse is going to win the race and not at all about whether or not there is enough value in the odds on that horse to risk a bet.

Most reasonable people can agree on which companies are best managed and which have the rosiest prospects for increased earnings in the near future. There is not nearly as much agreement, however, on what the proper price evaluation for the stock should be at the present time. It is just as silly to buy the stock of a wonderful company whose stock is overpriced as it is to buy a dream house whose owner refuses to budge from an inflated asking price. Just because you retain only a scant ownership position when you buy one hundred shares of General Motors doesn't negate the fact that a one-millionth share of a bad value is no better as an investment than 100 percent ownership of a bad value. And you can't sit and watch television and munch popcorn in your safe-deposit box.

The importance of value is even easier to understand in football betting. Even if you think that the Jets are a mortal lock to beat the Oilers on Sunday, the linesmaker can set a number that you will find impossible to bet. If you are sure the Jets are going to win, maybe it is worth giving 7 points. But are the Jets worth giving 10 points or 14 points?

While you may care about beating the spread, the football coach is unlikely to worry about it. If his team is ahead by 17 points late in the game, the coach won't think twice about resting his starters. If the Oilers score a meaningless touchdown late in the game, you have lost your bet but the coach has won his game and rested his battered stars to boot. No football bet is worth taking, regardless of the relative merits of the team, if you don't receive a line that you think is a bargain.

5. *The crowd believes in the power of "inside information."* The crowd believes that there is a group of insiders who have access to information to which mere mortals are not privy. These insiders are usually friends of a friend's cousin. At best, they are a friend's cousin.

Why is it you never meet the actual cousin? Probably because he doesn't really exist. Oh sure, there is a cousin, but the cousin himself doesn't think he is an insider. It's just that he heard an interesting piece of information from the groomer of a top trainer. Or from the secretary of a computer software company. Or from the sound technician at the radio station that carries the Bengals game.

Information spreads. The chances that you will receive valuable information that the marketplace has not already factored into the odds is quite small. By the time your friend's cousin has heard the information, hundreds already have. If he hears a rumor that a favored horse has a bone spur, everyone else at the track has, too.

The alluring feature of most inside information is that it is unverifiable and, therefore, glamorous and attractive because it gives its possessor a feeling of superiority ("I know what the riffraff doesn't know") and also gives him an excuse not to do his homework and check out the rumor ("there's no way the Dolphins will admit Marino has arm trouble").

The most crucial thing to consider is that *inside information is not necessarily valuable even if it is true.* One of the most popular academic theories about the stock market is called the "efficient-market theory." Those who believe in an efficient market feel that at any given time, all of the relevant information about a stock has been factored into its price. By the time you learn about any inside information, they believe, the price reflects what you thought was semi-exclusive information. Market players who believe in an efficient market feel that it is impossible to beat the averages over the long haul and that excellence in stock picking is more likely to be the result of random variation than of a reflection of ability. When the efficient-market theorists were in vogue, they were successful at marketing index mutual funds, which merely held a position, say, in every Standard & Poor's industrial stock. The fund wasn't trying to beat the averages but merely to match them.

The efficient-market thesis was particularly popular with academic economists, but few professionals on Wall Street believed in it because there simply are some money managers who consistently (but not always) do surpass the market averages. And with all of the new financial toys introduced into the stock market—particularly the dazzling array of options and futures—it is clear that the stock market is only semi-efficient. Some people *can* consistently make money by straddling and hedging among calls, puts, futures, and the underlying stocks. Eventually, however, it is likely that the market, by osmosis, will absorb these lessons and become more efficient, making it harder even for currently successful traders to make what are essentially mathematical rather than evaluative decisions.

Much evidence suggests that both the football and horse-racing games are also semi-efficient markets. As noted, the crowd consistently deems the right horses as favorites, second favorites, and so on. Invariably, the football spread manages to split the betting down the middle. If there were true hot information, spreads would tend to swing more wildly than they do during the week.

If you can't uncover inside information unknown to the public, then you can't assume that you can beat any of these games by knowing more than your opponents. You will have to work from the same data. You will make your money by interpreting the same data differently from your opponents.

6. *The crowd relies on trends and streaks to continue indefinitely.* If a football team or a horse has won five times in a row, or if a publicly traded company reports five sharp earnings increases in a row, they are perceived to be hot. Everyone loves having an investment in a hot commodity, but the crowd seems unwilling to analyze why its bet got hot in the first place and why it might cool off in the near- or long-term future. Perhaps the horse has been winning against distinctly inferior competition compared to today's race; perhaps the football team just happened to play five lousy teams in a row; maybe the company's burgeoning profits were caused by a temporarily low cost for its raw commodities. You can't place a bet on the future of an investment without knowing the reasons for its success in the past and without being confident that the elements are still in place for the prosperity to continue.

The crowd has a pack mentality. When the crowd sees a positive article about a football team in the newspaper or sees a stock featured on *Wall Street Week*, it jumps in, little realizing that in a semi-efficient market such as we have just discussed, chances are this news has already been factored into the odds. The public loves a hot streak, and chances are the odds are more than what is justified for what you will have to lay down to invest in a hot horse, football team, or stock.

There is a mathematical principle called "reversion to the mean." Simply stated, reversion to the mean posits that most streaks have a tendency to overdo themselves. If a stock soars, the public reacts with euphoria, projecting that profit gains will continue and that the price of the stock will be limitless on the upside. The crowd figures that if earnings have risen from $1 to $10 in one year, why wouldn't earnings increase tenfold again to $100 a share next year? Reversion to the mean argues that it is far more likely that the stock will fall back to earth, in a pendulumlike effect. The first time the company stumbles, it is likely to be hit very hard, because its investors have expectations of uninterrupted growth. Buyers of the stock at astronomical P-E ratios will unload it, until the stock becomes undervalued. And then bargain hunters will become interested in the stock, figuring that the sellers have become like spurned lovers, betrayed at one misstep, blind to the strengths of the company.

Reversion to the mean is a crucial concept to keep in mind when playing any game with odds. There will always be doomsayers while the stock market is going down, proclaiming that we are headed for the next Depression. When the stock market is going up, the same people tack on another thousand or two to the Dow Jones Index's near-term potential. These extreme occurrences are possible. But it is far more likely that the stock market, after a roaring bull or grinding bear market, will return to historical levels of evaluation, if only because a swinging pendulum crosses middle ground far more often and for much longer a time than it does at either extreme. This is why it is crucial for a player in any of these games to stress the odds, the value he is offered as a reward for risking his money.

7. *The crowd bets on the past rather than on the future.* The crowd tends to forget that although a study of past performance might be the primary means of evaluating an investment opportunity, the fate of the wager it lays down today will be based on *future* events. The odds you are offered are

usually determined largely by past performance, so in order to get good value, the prudent investor looks to see how this race, this game, this earnings period might be different from the past one.

Betting propositions that have been consistently successful in the past carry a surcharge. Football teams popular with the crowd are favored by up to several points more than they deserve strictly on merit precisely because the linesmakers know that the team will be overvalued by the public. Stocks with impeccable growth records, such as Walgreen, sell at a much higher P-E premium to other retailers in their sectors precisely because their past performance has been reliable. But to justify these premiums, the investor had better be certain that a rosy future lies ahead—for one poor earnings performance, or even one flat quarter of earnings, is enough to turn the crowd against the stock.

We see all around us in many fields the insanity of projecting the future based strictly on past performance. Much has been written about jinxes in sports. People who appear on the cover of *Sports Illustrated* seem to collapse in performance immediately after this notoriety. In baseball, Cy Young winners seem to fall apart the season after they win the award. In the business world, no worse fate can befall a company than to be touted on the cover of *Fortune*. Shortly thereafter, the company's performance always seems to stumble.

Is there a jinx? Probably not. More likely, the successful company gets profiled at the peak of its success, at the point where the pendulum is at one extreme waiting to swing downward. Although we would like to think that peak performances in sports or business are manifestations of genius and planning, they are often accidents. Sure, a pitcher must be an excellent athlete to win the Cy Young Award, but he also needs his team to hit well when he gives up runs and he needs a good defense to protect him. In other words, he needs some luck. Perhaps the touted star is as overrated at the top of the pendulum as he is unfairly disparaged at the bottom.

The problem with investing in the company profiled on

the cover of *Fortune* is that its accomplishments have already been factored into the price of the stock. If you are reading about the wonders of Widget Inc. in *Fortune*, you don't have inside information. You have information shared by millions of others and, even worse, information that might have already been acted on faster by others. In that famous Super Bowl game where Joe Namath led his Jets to victory over the Baltimore Colts, all of the sportswriters "knew" that the Jets couldn't win, and they let the crowd know about their moral certainty in countless articles bewailing the supposed mismatch. But the crowd became oblivious to how many points Baltimore would have to score to beat the spread, refusing to back the Jets at plus 17 points. The line moved higher, until bargain hunters realized the value they were offered.

In the individual chapters on each game, I will talk about how you can make an educated guess about whether the future of a stock, football team, or horse is likely to coincide with its past. But for now, it is enough to remember that the biggest mistake the crowd makes is projecting future results when the pendulum is at one of its extremes.

8. *The crowd confuses the quality of a bet with the quality of what it is betting on.* John Q. Public picks up his copy of *Business Week*. There is a profile on a retail chain called Widgets R Us. Widgets R Us is well managed, has excellent growth potential, and has had an uninterrupted series of quarterly earnings increases. John Q. calls his broker and says, "Get me one hundred shares of Widgets R Us at the market price."

Jenny L. Public looks at the *Daily Racing Form* for tomorrow's handicap race and sees that one horse, Penguin Feet, has never lost a race in eight attempts. The other horses have posted good times but don't seem to have the killer instinct necessary to finish first. Jenny circles Penguin Feet, a sure bet for tomorrow.

Joe K. Public watches an NFL doubleheader on Sunday:

the Jets versus the Browns at 1:00 P.M. and the Oilers versus the Bengals at 4:00 P.M. Joe feels lucky to see these particular games because the Oilers are playing the Jets next Sunday, and Joe is being given an opportunity to compare the two teams. The Jets whomp the Browns and the Oilers are humiliated by the Bengals, who Joe doesn't even think are as good a team as the Browns. Joe makes a mental note that the Jets are a sure bet next Sunday.

It might turn out that John, Jenny, and Joe are all going to make money on their bets, but there is reason for pessimism. All three are guilty of confusing a proven quantity with a good investment. John's enthusiasm about buying Widgets R Us is the most misplaced. As we have just discussed, he is likely to have to pay a premium for this stock whose virtues are well known but whose potential dangers are likely to be underrepresented in an enthusiastic article. The best of companies, even ones with outstanding records such as IBM throughout most of the 1970s, can be laggards as stocks. Some of the 1960s high-growth stocks, including IBM, were spurned by investors for not being able to sustain the growth rates they had when they were much smaller companies. Anyone would be proud to own, manage, or work for a company like IBM, but this is not reason enough to think that IBM is therefore a good investment. That judgment depends upon whether conditions are likely to change in the future and, most of all, whether IBM is at present a good value, whether the pendulum has swung toward making IBM undervalued or overvalued.

✓     Because Penguin Feet has won all of his previous races, Jenny can't assume that his "will to win" will carry the day again. Perhaps his victories were against inferior competition. Perhaps the horse has sustained a minor injury, one that could only be detected by seeing Penguin Feet parade in the paddock. Perhaps Penguin Feet's odds will be so onerous that a show bet would pay as much as a win bet, with much less risk involved. Jenny's work is hardly over after she determines that, based on prior performance, Penguin Feet is the best horse in the race. She still has to figure out whether Penguin Feet is the best *bet* in the race, or indeed whether *any* bet is a good value in the race.

Joe, of course, is falling into the same trap as the bettors who refused to back the Jets as the line became more and more generous. He hasn't sat back and thought about whether conditions might change this week so that the Oilers would not be pushovers for the Jets. Perhaps the Oilers might want to avenge a trouncing from the Jets earlier in the season— some losing teams point emotionally toward one game late in the season, even when they have no chance of getting to the playoffs. Perhaps a key player for the Oilers is coming back after an injury. Perhaps the Jets will be pointing toward the game the week after they meet the Oilers. The Jets could be a great *team*, but still be a lousy *investment* this particular week.

9. *The crowd views an entity that falters as a bad investment.* Why should I invest in a depressed industry, thinks the crowd, when there are so many successful companies in burgeoning industries?

There are two reasons. The first and most obvious reason is that stocks in the halycon industries are likely to be over-valued and, as I have just discussed, at the top of their pendulum swing. But a second reason is that an industry or an individual company that has nothing but rosy prospects can only receive bad news. If everyone expects 35 percent a year earnings growth and that expectation is built into the price of the stock, the good news that the company has achieved this excellent growth will not cause the stock to rise. And worse, the first piece of troubling news will knock the stock's price down emphatically, even if the bad news is beyond the control of the company. When Widgets R Us becomes a roaring success, how can it prevent a new company, McWidgets, from opening up shop and competing? Widgets R Us might face a soaring rise in raw parts for widgets, dampening its profit margin. Many troubling events for successful companies cannot be foreseen.

After the first Arab oil embargo, the shares of domestic oil companies zoomed. While consumers bellyached about the ascending prices at the pump, investors saw visions of never-ending gas price rises, with OPEC artificially keeping the cost of imported oil high and finite North American oil reserves assuring low supplies and high prices. The stock prices of companies involved in the drilling and servicing of oil ran up even higher, because high oil prices would motivate more exploration for oil reserves.

In hindsight, we can see that most of us were guilty of projecting the future as a replica of the past. Many of the high-rolling oil drillers have gone bankrupt; crude oil, at the time this is being written, sells for less than one-third of its peak price. Even the valuation of the oil companies that can maintain a healthy profit by refining and marketing oil at these lower prices has been hit hard in the stock market. The Exxons of the world are not guilty of mismanagement but of having been part of a glamor industry that crumbled in the perception of the crowd at the discovery of bad news.

Similarly, a horse that is clearly superior to the competition can be bumped right at the start of a race, never gain its proper stride, and lose badly. A physically superior football team can have an emotional letdown, or have a bum referee-call against them cost the game. No investor can control these unforeseen events, but he can assure himself that the odds on his investment are comfortable enough to leave room for a few bumpy spots along the road.

Luckily, the tendency of the crowd to see an entity that falters as a bad investment leaves open one of the most powerful areas in betting. There are seldom better undervalued opportunities than companies, horses, or football teams that have recently encountered trouble (the more recent the trouble, the better, for as you have learned, the crowd tends to

focus disproportionately on the most recent past performance).

Your focus will be on trying to find entities that have been
successful in the past and whose current trouble might only
be temporary. You will seek to find reasons why the poor
performance might change. If you can discover legitimate
reasons to throw out the recent performance as a fluke, or at
least a nonrecurring problem, you will almost always find
attractive odds on your proposition.

10. *The crowd thinks that there is safety in numbers.* Here
is the crux of the crowd's problem. Whether it tries to find
guidance from insiders, professional advisers, cousin Bernie,
magazines, or friends, the crowd wants to be part of a pack,
to be one of the winners.

The crowd's image of "the winners" is of a group of like-
minded nabobs, spending winters together in Palm Beach or
chomping cigars together in tony nightclubs, sharing their
strategies and laughing at the losers.

Actually, there are probably no such groups of winners.
For winners in games tend to be solitary types, not just socially
but in their investment thinking. If the pack, if the big, so-
called smart money, is going in one direction, the only way
anyone is going to outperform them is to go in the contrary
direction. Some football bettors concentrate only on one NCAA
conference and win consistently. They must be tempted to
branch out and apply some of their precepts to NFL games
or games outside their geographical area of expertise. But they
are content to carve out a small but profitable niche for themselves, to be superior, in one small area, to the competition.

If you are going to win at football, horse racing, or the
stock market, you are going to have to analyze your strengths
and weaknesses as a bettor and be willing to pass up what the
stockbroker, the railbird tout, or Bernie's cousin at the bar
will assure you is a foolproof opportunity. It isn't easy to
separate yourself from the crowd that used to be your guide

and to look now at the crowd as your friendly enemy. The crowd has become your enemy because you will presently, more often than not, have to take opposite sides from it. But the crowd has also become your friend, because by being so consistently wrong, it has shown you how to invest rightly.

# How to Win at NFL Football Betting

IF YOU NEVER INTEND to make a bet on football in your life, I hope you will read this chapter. If you don't care about football betting, or even if you don't care about the sport of football, I still hope you will read this chapter. Because the key to winning at football betting isn't caring about whether the Vikings beat the Rams. The key to winning at football betting isn't even *knowing* anything about football—the secret is in applying the principles discussed in more general terms in the previous chapter. And since football betting is one of the simplest and most decisive illustrations of how my "betting against the crowd" approach can make you money, you can apply what you learn in this chapter to almost every other subject in the book.

I am a baseball fan, and I know something about the game. I don't know very much about football. I couldn't name more than five NFL linemen off the top of my head. No matter how many times I hear explanations of nickel defenses or stunting, their meanings remain as elusive to me as quantum physics.

I get bored watching football games on television. I'd rather watch seven hours of bowling than a football doubleheader on Sunday. On Monday nights I don't watch the NFL game until after *Cagney and Lacey* and the local news are over, and then only because *Monday Night Football* preempts *Nightline*. I am more interested in finding out the results of the games than in watching them.

But I've always been interested in football betting and why it seems so hard for gamblers to beat the relatively small 11-to-10 odds that are against them. To turn a profit, a football bettor must win 52.37 percent of the time. Comparing this with the horse-race bettor's staggering 17 percent disadvantage, I wondered why football bettors didn't seem to fare much better. Could I do better?

In 1977 one of the New York daily newspapers, the *New York Post*, started a full-page feature every week called "Bettor's Guide to the NFL." In my research on the stock market and horse racing, I always looked for the recommendations of experts, mostly to see how they would fare if actual money were bet on their picks. In the *Post*'s "Bettor's Guide to the NFL," each participating sportswriter was asked to pick which team would win every NFL game that week against the Las Vegas spread, and to indicate which three games he considered best bets.

From the inception of the "Bettor's Guide," a pattern became crystal clear. You would lose money if you systematically followed the betting suggestions of the panel consensus every single year since its inception. In fact, the panel's picks, as a group, have broken .500 only once—during the unusual strike-shortened 1981 season, when many betting patterns were disrupted. Even during that year, the panel's .519 record would not pay out enough to cover the 11-to-10 odds.

And you would lose money if you followed the advice of any one of the writers, although some obviously did better than others. Except for the strike year, not more than one of the panelists has ever won against the spread in *any* season.

The performance of these panelists was *so* consistently poor that I wondered whether a system could be developed based on using them as a contrary indicator. Would simply betting against the majority choices of the panelists work?

Here are the year-end percentages of the panel. We have excluded the strike-shortened season (which is hard to compare to other seasons because of the fewer games picked and the unprecedented conditions), which would have boosted slightly the overall averages, and we have excluded some of the choices of "The Computer," a panelist whose totals were not officially included in the *Post* rankings at first and whose bad performance would bring down the total averages as much as the strike-season would add.

1977—.481
1978—.481
1979—.477
1980—.470
1981—.465
1983—.487
1984—.498
1985—.499
Average percentage—.482

If you did nothing but bet against every pick of the *New York Post* consensus, then, you would have achieved a .518 percentage, only an elusive .005 away from the break-even point. Could you find some angles to improve your chances? Were there characteristics of individual selectors that might guide you to a winning system?

There is a tendency in all gambling toward reversion to the mean. Teams with spectacular winning streaks tend to compensate with losing streaks later in that season or in the next year. The same is true for gamblers. The odds of probability favor any gambler betting on a fifty-fifty proposition to have protracted hot streaks and cold streaks. After all, if you flip a coin often enough, heads is going to come up seven times in a row every 128 times. So you have to be careful in evaluating football prognosticators as potential contrary indicators, to be sure that their losing streaks are indeed manifestations of faulty reasoning.

After reading the *Post* column every Friday for several years, it became clear to me that several of the panelists were consistent losers, and that money could be made simply by betting against their picks not only because their records were inferior to their competition on the panel but because they repeatedly followed the same patterns in making their (wrong) selections.

Over the eight years of the "Bettor's Guide," an excellent sportswriter, Jerry Lisker, consistently demonstrated that he had made a wise decision to write about rather than bet on sports. In one year besides the shortened 1982 season, 1981, Lisker posted a 114-to-103 record, exactly one game more than needed to break even against the 11-to-10. Otherwise, his record was not overwhelming:

> 1977—.492
> 1978—.430
> 1979—.411
> 1980—.450
> 1981—.525
> 1983—.465
> 1984—.430
> 1985—.502

Despite Lisker's "comeback" in 1985, his average success rate against the spread was a poor .463. Betting against him in every game would yield a .537 win total, a healthy profit.

We are so accustomed to *following* the investment advice of experts that it may seem cruel to recommend that you can make money by listening to sincerely offered advice and then running out to bet on the *other* side, especially when the adviser is a writer as respected and knowledgeable as Lisker. But knowledge of football is a different matter from knowledge of football betting, and it is Lisker and his fellow panelists' lack of betting expertise that make them such extraordinarily valuable contrary indicators.

A computer program generated by Bud Goode became my second negative indicator. Although year-end records were not kept on The Computer until 1983, its performance was on about the same level as Jerry Lisker's.

Ralph Blumenfeld became a panelist in 1979, and his picks

became especially important to me because he was the only member who gave the rationale for his pick, along with a roundup of injuries and observations about each game. Although his record has not been as consistently bad as Lisker's or The Computer's (.487), I have found Blumenfeld to be an important negative indicator when used along with the other two.

I also found three positive indicators, and discovered that when the "positive three" all disagreed in a game with a united "negative three," I had my strongest configuration. The positive three were the Odd Couple (who have changed over the years but whose current occupants have an average success rate of .519), Hank Gola (.517) and Bill Gallo (.479). Note that Gallo's cumulative winning percentage is actually lower than negative indicator, Ralph Blumenfeld's. The reason is that Gallo is the only panel member whose betting strategy has noticeably improved over the years. Maybe he spent the time during the strike season learning how to bet. Since 1977, here is his record:

1977—.443
1978—.457
1979—.493
1980—.455
1981—.444
1983—.521
1984—.489
1985—.530

The rest of the panel I view as mildly negative indicators. I feel better when the other two writers, Steve Serby and Peter Finney, Jr., go against my pick, but their sentiments are not enough to keep me from placing a bet.

So, how have I done? Pretty well. In 1984 I had a spectacular season, going 66-to-38 for 63 percent. Although in 1985 I managed only a .504, not enough to make a profit, my 1983 59 percent success rate (98–71) enabled me to "post" a three-year record of .577, a three-year average *superior to any one season* of any of the *Post's* thirteen panelists who have participated in the "Bettor's Guide to the NFL" since it debuted in 1977.

Here is my system, which will admittedly only be directly helpful to those of you who have access to the Friday *New York Post* during the football season. Even if you can't use these sportswriters to bet against, we'll follow our outline of the system with a discussion of *why* we think this particular "crowd" of sportswriters are so uncannily wrong and how you can apply these principles in places where you can't bet against these particular negative indicators.

## *The Anti-*Post *System*

The Negative Indicators: Lisker, The Computer, Blumenfeld
The Positive Indicators: Gallo, Odd Couple, Gola
Neutral/Mildly Negative Indicators: Finney, Serby

### THE GOLDEN RULES

1. *Never* bet on a team favored by Jerry Lisker. I have tried betting Lisker picks when literally every other indicator points to the conclusion that his pick is correct, and although these selections do much better than Lisker's usual choices, they are still not profitable. When you are given as good a benchmark as Jerry Lisker, don't mess with it.

2. If all three of the negative indicators (Lisker, The Computer, and Blumenfeld) favor the same team, regardless of any of the other prognostications, you have an automatic bet on the other team. This system alone has been mildly but consistently profitable over the last two years,* hitting about

*The success rate for each golden rule is based on twenty-seven weeks of regular season games. On weeks that I was out of town and a *New York Post* was not available, no bets were made.

54 percent (compared to an overall 57 percent on my total picks).

3. If all of the panelists, including the positive indicators, predict the same team will win a given game, you have a mandatory bet according to Rule #2. Don't worry about going against the positive indicators, for picking against a unanimous panel is one of the strongest selections, hitting over 57 percent for the two years, and at a higher percentage in previous years. When you gather together eight knowledgeable football people and all of them agree on a game, it is amazing how often they are wrong. Invariably, the unanimous pick is a favorite, and the crowd sees only the athletic superiority of the favorite and not the lack of value offered by the point spread. These are the types of bets that will provoke your friends to laugh at you, but we already warned you that winning is a lonely business.

4. If the three negative indicators all go for the same team, and the three positive indicators pick the other, you have the single strongest configuration of the panel (feel even more secure if the two neutral pickers agree with the negative indicators). This lineup occurred only nine times in the last two years, and it won six times. Although the .667 percentage is impressive, it must be remembered that nine games is hardly a huge sample. Nevertheless, this system also worked over 60 percent of the time in 1984 and before, when Gallo was not yet a positive indicator.

5. If the negative indicators make their unanimous picks best bets, you should be more confident about your bet. One of the most amazing characteristics of the panelists is how consistently they did worse on their three best-bet selections each week than they did on their other selections. In the last eight full seasons, the panelists averaged .483 on their regular games, but a pathetic .470 on their best bets. Yes, one could

have scraped a small profit simply by betting against the best bets of all of the panelists.

If you increase your bets when all three negative indicators agree on the same team but at least two of the three make the selection a best bet, you could greatly increase your total winnings, because you would have won just under 60 percent of your bets (13-to-9, or .591) using Rule #5.

There is one other strange pattern for which I have no logical explanation. When *all* three negative indicators pick a game as a best-bet selection, but they split 2-to-1 on which team will win, the majority has been wrong all six times over the last two years. Although this configuration is consistent with our general theory (when in doubt, go against the majority picks of the negative indicators), I can't think of any reason why they would be particularly awful at selecting games in which all three have strong but differing feelings about who will win. You may have wondered how the negative indicators fared when all three picked one team as a best bet. It has only happened twice in the last two years, and they won one and lost one. Still, the next time it occurs, I will be eager to bet against them.

At the very end of this chapter, after I try to explain *why* the crowd always seems to go wrong at picking football games against the spread, I will discuss a few fine-tuning variations on these five golden rules; but these five alone should be enough to make you profitable or at least to keep you around .500 during a streak of bad luck. Luckily for us, the performance of the *New York Post* writers is more predictable than the football teams they are writing about.

You could flip a coin to determine your selections and achieve a higher success rate than these knowledgeable sportswriters. The sportswriters at the *New York Post* are not the only group who consistently fall below .500 in picking against the spread. In fact, it is hard to find *any* group that *does* hit .500, let alone a profitable rate.

Because all crowds seem to lose at football betting, here's

an optional system for winning. Find ten people you know who are most knowledgeable about football. Ask them to pick the week's line-up against the spread. If a strong majority (at least eight) of them like one team, *bet on the other team.* Although I have not personally used this approach, I am sure it will at least beat .500 over the long haul, for it seems that for people unsophisticated about betting strategy, the *more they know about football, the worse they do as bettors.* They know just enough to parrot the conventional wisdom. Conventional wisdom always loses.

Crowds, by definition, are not outstanding thinkers. Outstanding thinkers, to achieve superior performance over the long haul, must ponder areas we mortals are ignoring or misjudging. Over the years, I have observed the *New York Post* panelists' mistakes, and those of other crowds (in particular, office pools) and acquaintances who spew the conventional wisdom at parties and sporting events. Most of these crowd members know much more about football and the teams themselves than I do, but they make the same betting mistakes over and over again, and they are all variations on the general principles of errors that crowds make in betting other kinds of games. By studying why the crowd goes wrong, you'll know how and why to run away from their selections.

### The Fourteen Most Common Errors the Crowd Makes in Betting Football

1. *The crowd overestimates the importance of the last game.* The crowd loves nothing more than streaks, and tends to see cosmic implications in the results of the last game. When a team wins a game during a mediocre season, you start hearing such statements as:

"They've finally hit their stride."

"Now they know they can win."

"If they play as well as they did last week, they've got to win."

Any of these comments *might* be true, but the crowd assumes that the last game must be more significant than previous games in assessing the chances of a team to win this week. There is no evidence to support this belief.

The winning bettor is always looking for a good reason to throw out the results of the last game, because he knows that the crowd will be placing too much emphasis on it. Often, he is looking for a reason why the winning team last week might have been at an emotional high then (a revenge game? an intradivisional game last week and an interdivisional game this week? a home game last week and an away game this week?) and at an emotional low now (are they playing a weak interdivisional opponent this week after playing a tough intradivisional rival last week?).

Yes, occasionally a team does find its bearings after one inspirational win or a team becomes demoralized after a poor performance, ruining their spirits (and results) for the rest of the season. More often, however, the last game is not more important in determining the team's fate this week than was the game before last. The winning bettor capitalizes on the crowd's obsession with the results of the last game by not stressing its importance in his handicapping.

2. *The crowd overemphasizes the importance of injuries to the prospects of a team.* You will see later that the crowd inflates the importance of the backfield, particularly the quarterback, in determining the chances of a team. Every week the NFL releases an injury list, and bettors pore over it, wondering whether a "probable" will be a "definite," or a "possible" will become a "probable." The crowd is less inclined to bet a team whose star player is out.

Usually the crowd is wrong, for three important reasons. First, there is usually an able replacement for most NFL players. Second, the crowd gets concerned about injuries for the wrong positions. Although quarterbacks and running backs are the most visible starters on any football team, they are rarely the most difficult to replace. Much more crucial are safeties and cornerbacks, who can be picked apart by the opposition's passing game if they can't succeed in one-on-one confrontations. When the O. J. Simpsons and Walter Paytons of the world share their glory with their offensive linemen, they are not being modest. If a key offensive lineman is injured, and one defensive lineman can consistently penetrate the backfield, a whole offense can be crippled. The third and most important reason injuries should not be stressed when handicapping a football game is that injuries are already factored into the line of every game; and injuries to key players are usually overstressed in the line, because the linesmakers are aware that the crowd is wary of playing a team with, say, an injured quarterback. This leaves the winning player an opportunity to receive good value for a bet on the team *with* the key injuries.

3. *When the opening line moves against the crowd's team, the crowd gets more enthusiastic about the team.* Let's say the crowd favors Miami over New England, and the line is set at Miami minus 6 (i.e., Miami is favored by 6 points). If the line moves to Miami minus 7, the crowd sees the shift as proof that it has the right side, because the smart money is also behind Miami. What the crowd has ignored, of course, is that there is a big difference between laying 6 points and laying 7 points. Many games are decided in the range between 6 and 7 points, and the person who lays 7 will lose or tie many bets he might have won if laying 6 points. If you are going to win at football, or any other game with odds, it is imperative to have confidence in your own assessment of each betting situation. If you pick Miami, you should hope to receive the most generous odds possible. If the line moves from Miami minus 6 to minus 5, you should see this as a positive sign. The fact that the line has moved has not made Miami a better team or a worse team. It has simply provided you with a better value.

4. *The crowd tends to bet on what it thinks is the best team, rather than the best value.* In the last chapter we discussed the crowd's mistake of assuming that a good company is necessarily a good stock to buy, forgetting that everyone else also knows that the company is a good one and that assessment is built into the current price of the stock. Many football bettors make the parallel mistake: They confuse a good team with a good bet.

The linesmakers know better than you do not only which football teams are superior but also how that advantage is best translated into point spreads. The crowd has also read the standings and has a general sense of the football superiority of each team. You can't beat the spread without comprehending off the field factors *that the crowd doesn't use* when analyzing football games.

5. *The crowd tends to like favorites.* If there is one absolutely predictable trait of the *New York Post* panelists, it is their penchant for picking favorites. It is rare to find a week when the consensus picks more underdogs than favorites. Why? Probably Error #4, above. Many unsophisticated bettors stop their analysis after they determine who should win a game; they never ponder by how many points they expect the favorite to win.

Most successful football bettors prefer to wager on the underdog. Underdogs tend to be bargains in at least three ways. One, they are often given too many points because of the crowd's tendency to bet on what it perceives to be the better team, even if laying more points than the crowd would like. Two, with underdogs you can still lose the game outright and have a chance to win. Three, and most important, when you bet on an underdog, you always know that the team has an incentive to win your bet for you, because all teams are trying to win the football game. Let's say that the 49ers are favored by 9 over the Falcons. If the 49ers are ahead by 8 points late in the fourth quarter, the team has little incentive to try to score again. They will be concerned with keeping the ball away from the Falcon offense and grinding down time, and more frightened about giving the Falcons good field position than about not scoring another field goal. This conservative but totally appropriate strategy will murder the backers of the 49ers; even though their team has dominated the game, they are likely to lose their bet. But if the 49ers, favored by 9, are leading the Falcons by 10, the Falcons have every reason to go for a point-spread victory: They are trying for an outright victory! Even if they fail in their attempt to win outright, the Falcons' efforts are more likely to give you a point-spread win than the efforts of a favored team trying to sit on a lead.

6. *The crowd doesn't place enough emphasis on the home-field advantage.* This is one "mistake" that I almost left out, because there has been so much published about the home-field advantage, and any bettor with any pretensions whatsoever can pontificate about how Denver fares at Mile High Stadium or how hard it is to beat Don Shula in Miami.

Still, my analysis of the *Post* writers indicates that they have not appreciated the importance of the home-field advantage and the hardships of a team facing several consecutive road games. Some believe that the home-field advantage is already totally factored into the point spread. It may be, but winning bettors seem to rely on its importance far more than the crowd.

7. *The crowd places too much emphasis on recently televised performances of teams, particularly on* Monday Night Football *games.* One of the best bets in football, all other things being equal, is to *favor* a team the week after it has given a bad performance on *Monday Night Football*. It is true that teams might be motivated to play particularly well on a night when they know they will have national exposure, but this does not necessarily mean that the Monday night game will better reveal their ability. Most members of the crowd are not able to analyze whether a poor performance is due to

the assets of the winning team or the deficiencies of the losing team. That winner on the nationally televised game will be facing totally new personnel next week. Do not expect the same scenario to unfold.

A national football game is like an unpaid advertisement for a team. If the message the team conveys is positive, an unwarranted glow tends to surround the team for weeks without the crowd realizing why it is so predisposed. When a team fails in this situation, it is often shunned, especially if the crowd backed it in the television game. Our hallowed principle of reversion to the mean tells us that we can often find good value by betting for a team that has blown a big game, or against a team that has won a big game.

8. *The crowd likes to bet on teams who "must win" late in the season, and overprices them.* My friend, Dan Gordon, a professional handicapper and football columnist, who knows more about the game than anyone I know, told me about this angle. As the season progresses and it starts becoming clear how many games teams will need to win to qualify for the playoffs, the crowd realizes that many teams must win certain games in order to qualify for the playoffs or to acquire home-field advantage. The crowd then backs the teams that must win, and this sentiment tends to push the line much higher than if the game were played earlier in the season, especially if the opponent is a team whose playoff status is already confirmed. The crowd assumes that the nonplayoff opponent will have no incentive to play hard and that the opponent who has already made the playoff will likely have a letdown.

Actually, in this case, the argument the crowd makes is logical, even true. But the crowd, as it always does, inflates the importance even of its insights, thus pushing the point spread to often absurd limits. One should be especially wary of backing a team, even as an underdog, that is vastly inferior athletically to its rival. Emotion counts for a lot in football, but it doesn't make up for a wide receiver being five-tenths of a second faster in the one-hundred-yard dash than the man covering him.

9. *The crowd's image of many teams is frozen in the past. The crowd is slow to react to emerging talented teams and slow to shun winners from the past.* Along with his reliance on favorites, this has been Jerry Lisker's downfall. He continues to see teams as they were a year (or more) before. By the time he realizes that a new team has emerged as excellent, the "discovery" has already been on a hot streak *and is now overpriced.* Lisker then gets punished for hopping on the hot team's bandwagon.

We all tend to retain outdated images of people and things. For example, I was heavy in high school and college, and lost quite a bit of weight after college. Obviously, when my family and friends first saw the new, smaller me, they were surprised. But I started noticing that whenever I returned home, my family and friends would continue telling me that I had lost weight since I last saw them. In many cases, I had actually gained weight. They were, of course, comparing my current appearance to the fixed image they had of me in my teen years, when they saw me every day. It is similarly difficult for longtime NFL fans to see, say, Seattle, favored over a mighty franchise with a winning tradition, like the Rams, when they still perceive Seattle as an expansion team. In baseball, similar perceptions put pressure on the Yankees every season. It is taken for granted that the Yankees will be perpetual contenders. The crowd is mired in the past but betting on the future, a major reason why the crowd doesn't win.

10. *The crowd loves to bet on teams—that they perceive to be good—who are small underdogs and who the crowd thinks should win outright.* At first glance, it would seem that the crowd is merely doing what I suggested under Error #5—picking an underdog who actually has a chance (and the

motivation) to win the game outright. The only problem is that the crowd seems to pick the wrong side of these games. Dan Gordon calls these "Lucy games." Whenever the line seems a little funny, with the seemingly better team as underdog, Gordon noticed that the "better" team never seems to win. There are obviously emotional factors that the crowd is simply not factoring into the game. Other than lopsided underdogs (more than 14 points), who have a bad record of covering, this is about the only type of game in which the crowd tends to select underdogs rather than favorites.

11. *The crowd tends to look at the scores and won-lost records of teams' past performances but not look carefully at the caliber of the competition they faced.* In horse racing, many handicappers believe there is a type of horse that always gives a game try but seems to come up short every race, finishing in the money but never winning. The horse simply fails to possess the "will to win." This theory makes some sense, *provided that all of these races are against the same class of horse.*

It is harder to make generalizations about two football teams who both have the same 3-to-5 record. If a 3-to-5 team has played its eight games against teams with a combined .625 record, it might be superior to another team that has an overall 5-to-3 record whose opponents are a combined .375.

The crowd, however, tends to put such a mystical patina on winning that it ignores *who* the wins were against and *how* those wins were achieved. A team that has incurred a series of losses against strong opposition *is* likely to win versus a team with the same record that has lost by the same margins to weaker teams. A team that has won by flukes, lucky penalty calls, and last-minute turnovers despite being dominated by the other team's defense, *is* more likely to lose than a team that has lost by flukes, unlucky penalty calls, or by last-minute turnovers despite dominating the other team's defense.

If you wish to be a "fundamental" handicapper, stressing the football factors in selecting your picks, there is no substitute for doing your homework and finding out why and how the scores of previous games ended the way they did. For the crowd, you can be assured, won't have done its homework.

12. *The crowd underemphasizes the importance of emotion in football games.* Even good fundamental handicappers are always aware of the emotional components of the football games they are handicapping. Compared to any other American professional sport, football is a game of emotions. Most of the time when an undermatched team triumphs against a juggernaut, the victory has an emotional component. Very few teams are capable of playing at a high emotional peak for an entire season. Most professional handicappers try to figure out when the emotional peaks and valleys are likely to occur. Here are some of the questions the "emotional handicapper" thinks about, but the crowd only occasionally does:

- *What happened the last few times these teams played?* If the Jets blew out the Patriots on the last meeting, the Patriots are often underpriced at the next opportunity. Two reasons to consider the Patriots, assuming that they are approximately of the same caliber as the Jets, are: 1) Reversion to the mean indicates that the blowout was one extreme; the next game is likely to flatten out the luck of the last game and 2) more important, the Patriots are likely to be highly motivated to avenge their previous embarrassing performance.
- *Is this a traditional rivalry?* Games that involve traditional rivals tend toward upsets. Both teams are usually motivated for these matches, so you would think that the emotional factors would tend to neutralize; but this isn't the case, probably because the team with a currently poor record can help save its season, emotionally, by vanquishing the favored rival.
- *What's being said in the newspapers and on television?* It is a cliché that the boasts of opposing players that get put up on locker-room bulletin boards provide the best

motivation to win. This cliché, evidently, has some basis
in fact. There is no better way for the Bears to motivate
the Vikings than to make disparaging remarks about the
Minnesota team. While cocky boasting is expected to
hype boxing matches, it is seen as bush league in football.
Beware, especially, of betting visiting favorites who are
quoted in the hometown paper bragging about their team
or belittling the home team.

Sometimes even the comments of a local television
sports announcer or newspaper columnist can motivate
a team. In this case, the poor opposing team isn't even
responsible for the comments. They are the passive victims of the other team's revenge.

- *Is there a key injury to a team leader?* As we have already
mentioned, it is often an excellent bet to favor a team
that has incurred a key injury. Injuries to vital players
tend to make teams rally emotionally, to realize that they
"are all in this together."

- *Is one of the teams coached by an emotional, Knute
Rockne type?* George Allen is probably the best-remem-
bered emotional coach. He was famous for having his
teams "up" for big games. Allen's teams also tended to
be overpriced, for at least two reasons. Under our general theory that no team can sustain a high for an entire
year, the corollary to that notion is that although Allen
could get his team up for the big games, his teams often
let down for the "little" games. Big games are big games
only because it is assumed that good teams are going to
win the little games. The other reason that Allen's teams
tended to be overpriced is that bettors were forgetting
that when they saw an emotionally high Allen team, they
were seeing the team at its very best. The teams of the
intense but less emotional Don Shula, for example, usually build in emotion and in the quality of their play as
the season progresses.

It is best not to place too much emphasis on the
importance of the emotional coach, except to remember

that such a coach will tend to do better in games that have an obvious emotional component, and worse in games that don't.

As we have just seen, these emotional factors can cut both ways, and the importance of emotion in football wagering is no longer a secret. Soon, it seems, we will have Dr. Joyce Brothers on *NFL Today*, picking against the spread. Despite plenty of publicity about emotion, which the professional handicapper might overemphasize, the crowd still underemphasizes emotion.

✓     13. *The crowd puts too much emphasis on the quality of a team's offensive backfield, especially its quarterback.* Although most casual football fans can name the starting quarterback for 90 percent of the NFL teams, few could name the starting front four for any but their home team. Quarterbacks and running backs receive the bulk of the media attention, but winning handicappers stress the importance of the offensive and defensive line.

Gerald Strine, one of the few writers who has put his picks on the line in public and consistently won, emphasizes the importance of defense, especially the defensive line, in his excellent book, written with Neil D. Isaacs, *Covering the Spread*. Although Strine and Isaacs stress analysis of offensive/defensive match-ups more than I do, it is interesting to note that when they summarize what the perfect bet would be, they mention many of the factors that the crowd ignores or misconstrues. They don't mention offense at all:

> What we would like to take to the bank as solid collateral is this: a good team (in general, one of the top ten of the league's twenty-eight) getting points at home in a game that is important for it to win, at a time when it is physically sound and not mentally tired, with defensive superiority in specific match-ups, and with values that have not been realized by the linesmakers and the public. . . .

Since *Covering the Spread* was published in 1978, many of the emotional factors that helped provide Strine with an edge have become well-known recipes for success—they are now factored into the odds. The closing line is a reflection of how knowledgeable the bettors are. If enough people read *this* book, maybe the line will not, as it does now, tend to favor teams with star quarterbacks and running backs.

One of the factors that most excites me about this system for betting football is that I have other checks to see if the *Post* panelists are still betting the same way as the crowd. When the *Post* panelists are doing well, an abnormally large number of favorites should be covering the spread and the public should be winning more than 50 percent of their picks, a statistic that should be easy to assess by observing the expression of your local legal or illegal bookmaker. My football maven, Dan Gordon, assures me that the best recent years for favorites and, thus, for the public, have been 1982, the strike-shortened season, and 1985, the two years when the *New York Post* writers have done the best and my system has performed the worst.

The biggest potential flaw in my system, of course, is that one day Jerry Lisker might wake up and see the error of his ways. "If I never win picking the teams I truly favor," he might contemplate, "perhaps I should pick my favorite teams and then print their opponents as my *Post* selections." What if Jerry Lisker realized that he could do better by going against what he believes? It could happen, just as I suspect that the program for The Computer has changed to make it more effective over the years. If The Computer's picks start betraying the thirteen principles we discussed above, it might be eliminated as a negative indicator.

I have no illusions that this system can be frozen in stone. After all, Jerry Lisker could retire! This is why, when given access to a list of experts, it is important not only to trace their success records, but to analyze *why* they have failed in their selections. When one of your negative indicators starts winning unexpectedly, you will be in a position to understand whether he has changed his handicapping methods or whether he is simply on a lucky streak. As long as your negative indicators' picks conform with the crowd's way of thinking, you have no reason to worry about betting against them.

## *Fine-Tuning the* Post *System*

There are a few other configurations of the *Post* handicappers that I have bet on in the past. None of these three approaches will outperform our five-step approach, but they are all marginally profitable and will enable you to make more bets than you would otherwise. Still, it would be more profitable in the long run to bet more money on the superior configurations (such as when all the negative indicators go with one team and all the positive indicators pick the opponent, or when the panel unanimously picks one team) and forget these. But for what they are worth, here are three other methods I use.

1. If at least two out of the three negative indicators go for one team, and at least two of the three positive indicators go for the opponent, the team favored by the majority of the positive indicators is a play *unless Jerry Lisker agrees with it*. Remember, our cardinal rule is "never bet on the same side as Jerry Lisker."

2. About twice a year, all the other seven panelists will back one team in a game and Jerry Lisker will be the lone dissenter. It is rare for Lisker to be alone on a limb like this, and at first I assumed, since five out of the six indicators favored betting Lisker's choice, this might have been the one time it was best to go along with Lisker or to pass the game. But Lisker has a losing record even in these games. Go against him. (Remember, though, that this particular configuration has not occurred often enough to be statistically valid.)

3. Sometimes when Blumenfeld is the lone dissenter among the negative indicator trio, I read his comments about the

game as an insight into how he decided on his selection. If possible, I want unanimity among my negative indicators, rather than a two-out-of-three configuration. I have found that when Blumenfeld's arguments are most logical and persuasive, starting to make me feel dubious about going the other way, Blumenfeld is usually wrong in his selection! When his analysis seems arbitrary or full of the conventional wisdom of the crowd, his pick is usually right. Yes, Blumenfeld's reasoning—not only his actual pick—is a negative indicator!

In particular, I have found that Blumenfeld's record is poor when he argues against a team's chances because of a key injury. Go the other way.

Blumenfeld's most insightful analyses go wrong, presumably, for the same reason that the *Post*'s best-bet selections do worse than their regular picks. The handicappers feel most strongly, and can argue most persuasively, when there seems to be a fundamental football explanation for their stance. They feel there is a discrepancy in the ability of the two teams that the linesmakers have not discovered. Their failure, which I think Blumenfeld shares, to be as sophisticated in their analysis of betting strategy as they are in football judgments, doesn't serve them well in assessing the *value* of a given point spread.

Before I developed the *New York Post* system, I used to pick against the spread for fun, based on the usual football fundamentals. I was awful. I never broke .500. So my point is not that I am an expert on football but that a few general principles helped me develop a winning system applicable to football and almost any other game with odds where you are competing against your fellow bettors:

1. *Your focus should not be on analyzing the athletic abilities of two football teams.* You are assuming that the opening line does a fairly good job of assessing the relative strengths of the team, the home-field advantage, and the obvious emotional factors. Your real area of concern is the attitudes of the other bettors and why their crowd mentality will make some teams underpriced and others overpriced.

2. *Conventional thinking is wrong.* If your opponents when playing football are the other bettors, you should not be afraid to run counter to the majority; in fact, it is the only way to win. By identifying the thought processes behind the crowd mentality, you can pinpoint benchmarks, as I have found in the *New York Post* handicappers, who can represent the thinking of the crowd, simplifying your job. If you can find a few friends who can simulate the crowd's thinking as well as Lisker, The Computer, and Blumenfeld, they will serve you just as well as my system.

3. *One caveat.* I am not advocating betting football illegally. In fact, I'm not even recommending betting football where it *is* legal. I don't like to play games that are rigged against me, and in football betting, you are always facing the damn 11-to-10 vigorish. If you are smart enough to make money at football betting, you are probably equipped to make much, much more in the stock market. But that's the subject of the next chapter.

**For more information:**

*Covering the Spread: How To Bet Pro Football*, Gerald Strine and Neil D. Isaacs (New York: Random House, 1978). Strine and Isaacs's classic is sadly out of print, but it is available in many libraries. Although some of the material is dated, it is worth seeking out this pioneering work.

There aren't any books on betting NFL games in print that I can recommend highly. But I can recommend two football columns:

"Playing Football" is Gerald Strine's Thursday column in the *Washington Post.* Strine handles an imaginary bankroll and has an uncanny knack for pulling out losing seasons by conquering the playoffs. He is a master of the Super Bowl spread. Yes, Strine is "guilty" of raising his bets when he has fallen behind, but he *does* win the big bets. Strine seems to stay perpetually in the black. I only wish the rationales of his selections were in greater depth. Still, Strine's chatting about football is more valuable than the "great insights" of most football touts.

Dan Gordon writes a weekly column on betting football for the New York *Daily News*, *Los Angeles Herald-Examiner*, and the *San Francisco Examiner.* "Smart Money" is the name of Dan Gordon's football column in the *San Francisco Examiner*. On Tuesday, Gordon talks about the previous week's games, and this column is especially helpful if you want to learn the story behind the scores in the newspaper.

His Friday column in all three papers is similar to Strine's. Gordon has had many winning seasons. Although Gordon's record in his maiden effort for the *Examiner* was not stupendous, his analysis of the games was trenchant, and his knowledge of gambling strategy is unsurpassed by any other football columnist in the country. I can't promise you a fortune if you read Gordon, but I will guarantee you you'll know more about betting football.

## 1986 NFL Season Update

I decided to use a simple system for 1986, one that could be verified easily by readers of this book:

1. If all three of the negative indicators (Lisker, Blumenfeld, and The Computer) picked one team, I chose the other team as a regular (one unit) bet.
2. If all three of the positive indicators (Gallo, Gola, and the Odd Couple) dissented with the three negative indicators, I wagered two units on the game.

I did not use any of the best bet variations or bet any game in which all three of the negative indicators didn't concur.

The season began disastrously for me. Jerry Lisker went 13-2-1 on his selections in the first week, and I was lucky enough to win the only two games I could that week (i.e., the two games Lisker lost). Lisker continued his winning ways for a while, but eventually reverted to form, actually dipping below his career average. Here are the final statistics for all of the panelists, excluding postseason selections:

| Panelist | Indicator | Pct. | Pct. on Best Bets |
|---|---|---|---|
| Gola | Positive | .539 | .681 |
| The Computer | Negative | .511 | .479 |
| Gallo | Positive | .498 | .532 |
| Blumenfeld | Negative | .498 | .523 |
| Finney | Neutral | .470 | .447 |
| Odd Couple | Positive | .461 | .596 |
| Lisker | Negative | .457 | .447 |
| Serby | Neutral | .443 | .426 |

Gola compiled the most impressive season ever for a *Post* handicapper, with a sizzling .681 Best Bet record. Once again, no more than one handicapper finished in the black against the spread. Our two recommended journalist/football pickers, Gerald Strine and Dan Gordon, both had fine seasons and finished solidly in the plus column.

If there was anything unusual about the results this year, it was the impressive record of the *Post*'s Best Bet selections—not only was 1986 the first time the prognosticators had more success with the games they felt more strongly about, but it was the first time their consensus Best Bet record surpassed .500. For the whole season, the panelists amassed a .485 record on their regular selections and .516 on Best Bets. Note that the Odd Couple, who had a disastrous "regular" season, were second highest in the Best Bet sweepstakes. In fact, our three positive indicators finished 1-2-3 in the Best Bet race.

And how did I do? Not bad, if I do say so myself, although the poor performance of the Odd Couple and the decent season of The Computer and Blumenfeld kept me from registering an exciting one. My simple system allowed eighty-three separate plays, eight of them two-unit picks. Although my one-unit picks were mediocre, the two-unit picks were spectacular:

| Amount Bet | Won | Lost | Net Units +/− |
|---|---|---|---|
| 1 unit | 38 | 37 | − 2.70 |
| 2 unit | 6 | 2 | + 7.60 |

The net total is + 4.9 units. If we reduce all bets to one-unit bets, my record is the equivalent of 50-41, or .550. The fine record of the few Best Bet selections made this season a highly successful one.

The system described here has proven itself over many seasons now. My original goal was to develop a system that would perform better than simply betting against Lisker. Once again, I beat that goal, but barely—simply betting against Lisker in every game would have yielded a .543 record. But think of the obstacles the system had to surmount this year. The three negative indicators combined for an unusually high .489 record; the positive indicators beat that by only .04, and yet our system's record was better than any picker's season record in the history of the *New York Post*. Is this not proof that irrespective of the won-loss records of the panelists, the negative indicators think in a different way than the positive indicators? At least when all three negative indicators agree on a game, they seem to pick the wrong team for the wrong reasons.

If I have seemed coy in describing my own betting activities, let me make it clear: Outside of friendly football pools and small side bets with friends, I have never bet on a football game in my life. I certainly don't encourage you to bet football, even if betting is legal where you live. Why wager money on a proposition that in many cases doesn't matter to the principals in a game? All teams presumably want to *win* a football game, but most don't care about beating the spread. Why wager on a game where the odds (the 11-10 vigorish) are stacked against you at the start? Although my system seems to be a winning one, I'd prefer to "gamble" in the stock market.

# Are the Stock Market and Thoroughbred Horse-Race Betting the Same Game?

TWO BROTHERS HAVE TAKEN different paths. Brother John wakes up at 6 A.M. every morning, puts on a three-piece suit, and scans the *Wall Street Journal*. He commutes to his window office and advises institutional clients on how to maximize the financial return on their pension funds. He stays in the office until late at night. He's a workaholic, respected for his commitment.

Brother Joe rises at noon. He puts on his jeans and Hawaiian shirt and lays out the *Daily Racing Form* on the coffee table while he drinks his morning coffee. He had stayed up late studying the *Form* last night but wants to check to make sure he hasn't missed any interesting angles. Joe drives to the racetrack and hangs around with other professional gamblers. Joe wins a little money at the track, buys the next day's *Racing Form*, and heads back for another night's homework. His friends and family think Joe is a borderline sociopath, a compulsive gambler, wasting his talents on a lowlife, unproductive game.

John and Joe don't think much of each other. John thinks that Joe's work has no purpose. Joe thinks John is just a glorified peddler, who has sold out his intellect in order to make it in the establishment.

What neither one of them is likely to realize is that they are both playing pretty much the same game. The few fundamental differences in the rules and strategies of the stock market versus horse betting are overwhelmed by the wealth of similarities. Horse racing and the stock market belong in the same group of games that include football betting—games of odds where you are supposedly betting against the house but are actually competing against your fellow bettors.

You may accept the similarities between football and horse betting, but how does the stock market, the very essence of our capitalistic system, fit into the same scheme? To make the argument, I will show you not only that the winning and losing strategies are the same for both games, but that the cast of characters, betting factors, and betting methods are highly analogous. As with most of the other subjects in this book, I'll show how the key to winning is learning how losers—the crowd—think and then playing the opposite side.

## The Cast of Characters in the Stock Market and Horse Racing

Certain groups of people in horse racing and the stock market not only participate in the game but are watched carefully by individual players to help determine their strategy:

1. *In horse racing, they are called "tipsters." In the stock market, they are called "tip-sheet writers" or "investment-newsletter writers."*

Plenty of people in each game will, for a price, be more than glad to tell you how to invest your money. They have one thing in common: As a group, they have performed dismally.

Horse-race tip sheets and advisory services (generally phone services) work under intolerable conditions: They predict results without knowing the weather and track conditions, without knowing the physical condition of the horse that day, and most important, without knowing at what odds the horses they are recommending will run. They don't even know whether or not a horse will be a late scratch, opening up important new betting opportunities. These are all reasons why legitimate touting operations are unlikely to pick winners, but these rationalizations are almost beside the point, because most advisory services are pure shams designed to bilk suckers.

Investment newsletters are consistently off the mark as well, not only underperforming the Standard & Poor's averages with regularity but with uncanny "accuracy" becoming most bullish when the market tops and most bearish when the market is down and about to rebound. Their record has been so poor that their consensus opinion has long been used by savvy investors as a negative indicator.

The *Hulbert Financial Digest* is a newsletter that monitors the performance of other newsletters. In 1984, a year when the Standard & Poor's five-hundred-stock index rose 12.4 percent, *Hulbert* reported that 65 percent—or seventy-nine of the one hundred twenty-two portfolios proposed by seventy-three newsletters—*underperformed* the market. Twenty-two percent actually lost money.

The hottest newsletters at any given time are usually concentrated in one (currently faddish) area of the market, or are highly leveraged, so that their portfolios will drop more than others when stocks head south. Undiversified portfolios tend to be more volatile on the upside, so newsletters specializing in one segment of the market can show spectacular results at times. Many gullible investors assume that successful newsletters today will extend their streaks indefinitely. When market conditions change, "hot" newsletters are likely to take a dive unless their creators are flexible in their approaches. Many newsletters touting precious metals picked up thousands of subscribers at the height of gold prices, but watched their subscribers flee when they didn't predict the bear market in precious metals.

2. *In horse racing, they are called the "smart money," or the "inside money."* They include trainers, horse owners,

grooms, and stable workers who know not only about the relative ability of the horses, but about which horses are being primed to run their best races today and which are just going out for exercise.

*In the stock market, they are called "institutional investors" and "corporate insiders."* They either work high up in companies that are publicly traded or else have personal access to these people. They have an advantage over the individual investor, it is assumed, because they know more about the activities and the intentions of management of publicly traded companies than ordinary folks would.

In fact, there is no evidence that any of these groups have demonstrated great perspicacity. It is not clear that smart money exists in horse racing, despite an enduring myth that it does. Smart money wages vast amounts, usually right before post times. The crowd assumes that big money is smart money, but it isn't necessarily so. Big money can bring a horse from 8-to-1 down to 2-to-1. Even if the horse wins, the smart money has guaranteed itself a smaller return by betting big.

There are no doubt some unusual circumstances when a trainer has deliberately held back a horse in order to bet the horse himself at huge odds. But if his intention was to achieve unnaturally high odds, would he be talking about his schemes to stable boys? No way. By the time *you* hear a rumor at the racetrack, even if it is from someone who insists he heard it through a trainer's stable boy's cousin's barber, you can be assured that this information will be filtered into the odds.

A similar fate befalls investors who follow the antics of corporate bigwigs and major stockholders. Even the most naive shareholder is prepared for executives to puff their companies' prospects in annual reports. But do these corporate insiders put their money where their mouth is? A whole school of investors base their strategy on buying stocks that prominent board members are also buying. Their reasoning is simple: Who should be in a better position to judge the prospects of a company than its top officials? Insiders should be in a position to know whether a downturn in business is a trough or a midpoint in a free-fall.

But followers of corporate insiders operate under two distinct handicaps. One, although board members are required to release all information about purchases and sales of stocks in that company, they are under no obligation to state their reasons. It is particularly easy to misinterpret insider sales of stock: Is the chairman of the board selling five thousand shares of XYZ Inc. because XYZ is about to lose a big contract or because his daughter's college education needs to be financed? You have no way of confirming the answers. The second disadvantage that the individual has in following the activities of corporate insiders is that there is often a delay of months between an insider sale or purchase and when it is reported to the public. Not only has the impact of the transaction been absorbed in the marketplace, but the rationale that precipitated the buy or sell order may no longer be valid.

Disciplined investors who have based their strategy on buying only stocks that have had recent insider purchases have done better than most system players; any system that relies on the greed and self-interest of corporate insiders must have some merit.

You would think that the large institutions, such as mutual funds, large pension funds, bank trusts, and brokerages would have a huge advantage over the individual investor. Yet, as David Dreman proves in *Contrarian Investment Strategy: The Psychology of Stock-Market Success*, institutions as a group have historically *under*performed the stock averages, despite their proprietary research and access to corporate executives.

There are solid reasons why institutions don't perform well. Institutional investors have immense pressure to display short-term success. Individual investors who think in terms of long-term performance have a huge advantage over institutional investors who have to show good percentage gains *every quarter* or risk losing customers. To achieve short-term gains, portfolio managers usually try to ride the crest of already developed waves. As a result, they risk buying stocks at their highest point. Some managers, who have their own interests at heart rather than their customers', "window dress" at the end of each quarter, pruning away losers (i.e., short-term losers, which could be the best long-term investments in their portfolio) and buying hot stocks that have run up in the present quarter. The purpose of this exercise is to excise stocks from their quarterly report that they can be blamed for keeping, and listing stocks that will prove that they are *au courant*.

Money managers are also influenced by a similar need to appear sensible. No one has ever been fired for investing in IBM, regardless of the computer giant's price move over a three-month period. But a large holding in a financially battered company whose shares drop in price can cause second-guessing at best, and mutinies at worst, among customers. As a result, institutional managers are victims of the same crowd mentality that afflicts football bettors.

As an individual, you can buy what for you is a large amount of stock, and it will not be noticed. The purchases and divestments of mutual funds and pension funds not only attract notice, but if the blocks are large enough, in and of themselves, can affect the price of the stock. If several institutions race to buy the same stock at the same time, they will pay dearly for the privilege.

3. *In horse racing, they are called "local track writers" or "Trackmen." In the stock market, they are called "research analysts."*

If you can't pick the brains of corporate insiders, perhaps you can do the next best thing—trust the recommendations of research analysts, the men and women hired by the major brokerage houses to study individual industry groups and the companies within them. Research analysts are often extremely knowledgeable about their niches but have proven to be dismal stock-pickers (see David Dreman's book for their sorry record). Perhaps their close scrutiny of one industry tends to insulate them from an objective appraisal of the entire market.

But there is another strong reason for avoiding analysts' recommendations: By the time you read them, institutional clients and brokers themselves will have already heard and acted upon the research. There does tend to be a short-term upward blip after a buy recommendation from a major brokerage house, but by the time the average customer receives the word, the blip has already blipped.

Trackmen (the *Daily Racing Form*'s pseudonym for their at-the-track selectors) are handicappers with the extra advantage of personal access to the track. It is certainly a theoretical advantage for a handicapper to observe workouts, examine horses for physical defects, and hobnob with owners, trainers, and jockeys, but the implicit promise of the Trackmen—that they can pinpoint which horses are primed to surpass their past performances or which ordinarily strong horses are just out for the exercise—is unfulfilled in practice. Is it not probable that in reality very little of this type of "juicy" inside information is available because most trainers and jockeys are working stiffs just trying to win most of the time?

4. *In horse racing, they are called "jockeys" and "trainers." In the stock market, they are called "chairmen" and "chief executive officers."*

In horse racing, perhaps no factor is more wrongly overemphasized by the average loser than the jockey. In the stock market, assessment of management is considered a key ingredient in selecting a stock. Yet the influence of each on a horse or a company is difficult to determine. Most winners at the racetrack feel a jockey or a trainer is much more likely to lose a race than to win one. Yes, some jockeys and trainers are particularly skilled at providing winners in certain types of races (e.g., sprint specialists, grass specialists), but most elements of a race are beyond the control of jockeys or trainers—neither is capable of making a plodding horse run fast and both are capable of preventing a horse from running its best race.

The upper management of a company has more control

over its fate than the jockey or trainer over a horse, yet it must yield ultimately to factors beyond its control. No oil-services company is going to thrive when the price of oil plummets, effectively eliminating the incentive of its customers to explore for more oil. Not even the most prescient management of a steel company can forestall the negative effects of a sudden recession upon the sales and earnings of its company.

The merits of the jockey/trainer and management are already factored into the odds of the horse or price of a stock. Yet, some losing horse players insist on always wagering on the mounts of certain riders. Stock-pickers continue to hold on to stocks because a profile of the management in *Fortune* says the management is good. The cult of personality is one way for the crowd to simplify what is a difficult process—and to forget that it is betting on animals and on companies subject to the vicissitudes of a macroeconomy.

The only major player in the stock market for whom there is no equivalent in horse racing is the stockbroker. He is a bit of a financial adviser and a bit of a research analyst (although the research he acts on won't be his). What he is, primarily, of course, is a salesperson, which is why the advice of most stockbrokers should be taken with a grain of salt.

At least you know that it is always in the best interest of the investment-newsletter tipster for you to do well (you'll cancel your subscription if you don't). The stockbroker, on the other hand, has at least two possible conflicts of interest. First, the more purchases and sales you make, the more money in commissions he and his firm will make. Because virtually anyone else savvy in the market will recommend that the vast majority of small investors buy stocks or mutual funds and keep them for the long term, the activist stockbroker hurts you by charging you commission money (and, in the past, by converting long-term gains into more heavily taxed short-term gains). Second, the broker will sometimes be encouraged to sell stocks and bonds underwritten by his brokerage house.

Such a purchase *might* make you richer. It will definitely make the brokerage house richer. Remember, also, that the stockbroker is fed the same research information that makes institutions themselves poor performers in the stock market.

All in all, then, it is best to think of a broker as someone who executes your trades, not one who recommends and initiates them. And since you won't be relying on the broker for advice, why not think about using a discount broker, who will not only charge less for each transaction but won't pretend to be an expert on the market or pressure you into buying something you don't want? If you don't know enough about the stock market to have strong opinions about which stocks to buy, you should probably be investing in mutual funds anyway. I'll have some advice along these lines in the next chapter.

### The Betting Methods in the Stock Market and Horse Racing

1. *In horse racing, they're called "odds." In the stock market, they're called "price-earnings ratios."*

Odds are simple to understand in horse racing. On a $2 bet, you simply multiply the odds by two and add your $2 wager to determine how much you will be paid if you win. For example, if you bet on a horse to win at 5-to-1 odds, you multiply five by two ($10) plus your initial investment of $2, for a total of $12 per each $2 wagered. Although the odds fluctuate up to post time, you are always aware of your approximate return if your horse wins (although the place and show pools are flashed on most totalizator boards, the payback cannot be determined until it is known what other horses will finish "in the money"). Obviously, if you are going to win at the races, you are not only going to have to win often but at odds that will pay enough to make a profit.

Price-earnings ratios are simply the current price of a stock divided by the year's earnings per share. For example, if XYZ Inc. earned $2 a share in the last four quarters and the current price of the stock is $20, the price-earnings ratio would be 10. If the price of the stock dropped to $10, the price-earnings ratio would drop in half to 5. Note that although the earnings themselves have not dropped, the stock and price-earnings ratios have plummeted. Price-earnings ratios usually drop because the market thinks that the *future* prospects of XYZ have deteriorated. If the price-earnings ratio of a stock moves higher, it means that the market has confidence that the company will have a brighter future. The equivalents of favorites in horse racing or football, then, have *high* P-E ratios. The stocks with low P-E's are ones that have been abandoned by the crowd.

The assumption is that in the long run, the prices of stocks will ultimately be tied to the earnings of the company (this is not true for a few types of stocks, notably utilities). If you can find a company with a low P-E that you think will perform well in the future, you are nabbing a bargain, just as surely as a horse handicapper who finds that his favorite horse in a race is going off at odds of 8-to-1. Although P-E ratios will not tell you how much money you will make in a year if you invest in a stock, they will give you a good indication of what odds the stock market places on a good performance.

There are essentially two ways of making money in long-term stock investments: buying companies whose earnings improve and buying companies whose price-earnings ratios improve, with or without concurrent earnings increases. The most appealing feature about buying low P-E stocks is the double-bang possibility when earnings increase—not only will the price of the stock go up when earnings go up, but the crowd will get more optimistic about the prospects of your stock and boost its price-earnings ratio. If the stock doubles its earnings from $2 to $4 and doubles its P-E from 10 to 20, the price of the stock goes up not twice but four times. Although sometimes raw earnings figures are not accurate reflections of the health of a company (the company might take one-time write-offs that hurt earnings temporarily but will make the company stronger in the long run), using P-E ratios is as important in making money in the stock market as knowing the odds of the horses you favor.

2. *In horse racing, they're called "speed ratings." In the stock market, they're called "last year's earnings."*

The most popular form of horse handicapping is speed analysis. Speed theorists maintain that since what ultimately separates one horse from another is how fast each can travel a given distance, the most important information you can know is how fast a horse has covered today's distance in the past. Let's say you are trying to handicap a six-furlong race and one horse you are interested in, Merrill's Pearl, ran her last six-furlong race at 1:11. The speed rating is calculated by taking the track record for six furlongs (in this case, the record is one minute, eight seconds) and crediting the track record as worth 100 points. For each one-fifth second that a horse finishes slower than that racetrack's record at six furlongs, one point is deducted. Thus Merrill's Pearl's speed rating for the race was 85 (she was 15 one-fifth-second increments slower than the track record). This speed rating accompanies the line performance of every horse in the *Daily Racing Form*, saving the handicapper the problem of knowing the course records for every distance at every track around the country.

Although printed speed ratings save the handicapper a great amount of time, they are also a trap to those who assume that their work is over after they compare speed ratings. Obviously, a 90 speed rating at a small-time track is nowhere as impressive as a 90 at a major track such as Hialeah. The raw speed-rating doesn't take into account the speed of the track on that given day nor the competition the horse faced. The speed rating can't indicate whether a horse ran under ideal conditions or was bumped, jostled, or boxed out in the stretch. In short, the speed rating is a gross instrument, in itself, which can't make the discriminations necessary to win against the 17 percent house odds.

If a stock investor knew the course of future earnings for

the companies he follows, he could become rich. Although other events can move the price of a stock up or down, ultimately earnings are the key determinant. But as we shall see, accurate earnings *projections* still elude even canny research analysts. Therefore, most investors rely on the last four quarters to determine the earnings' growth of a stock; if the crowd sees near-term growth in a stock, the P-E will rise.

Earnings histories are as blunt an instrument as speed ratings are in horse racing. They are like the baseball standings at the All-Star break, which *tend* to correlate to which teams will be strongest in the second half of the season but cannot be *relied* upon to predict the future.

And as with using speed ratings, too many "bettors" embrace the raw figures of earnings without determining how those earnings were achieved. Did the company have an extraordinary gain to artificially boost earnings? Did the company use conservative bookkeeping practices or will it pay for currently inflated earnings with future declines? Are there macroeconomic forces that influenced the stock's earnings this quarter that won't next quarter or next year? Numbers can disguise as well as reveal. Until an investor knows the story behind the earnings report, he can't make a bet on the future or know whether the odds he is asked to stake (i.e., the price-earnings ratio) are worth the price.

*3. In horse racing, they are called "weight assignments." In the stock market, they are called "debts."*

Handicap races, usually premier events, are those in which the horses with the best credentials are assigned higher weights than horses with less impressive past performances, in order to help even out the chances of each horse. Obviously the heavier the load a horse must carry, the greater the handicap. In the 1950s and 1960s, weight assignments were given serious attention by reputable handicappers. When a horse had a bad race with its heaviest weight assignment ever, it was assumed that the added weight caused the poor performance. Contemporary handicappers realize that weight assignments have proven to be an unpredictable variable in predicting horse races, and that their importance was overrated in the past.

A company's debt serves much the same function to a company as weight to a horse—it burdens the company, in many cases preventing it from performing at its best. Some investors refuse to bet on any company whose balance sheet is not impeccable, with minimum long-term debt and generous cash flow as mandatory prerequisites. The only problem with this conservative approach is that many times a debt burden can be a long-term advantage to the company, funding new research or product development; in times of rampant inflation, debt can be profitable in and of itself (if the cash generated by the loans can be placed in higher-return investments). When the economic climate changes, however, companies saddled with large debt loads can verge on bankruptcy. A clean financial statement doesn't ensure future growth, but it does create a climate in which earnings turn into a genuine return on investment rather than as collateral for servicing a debt.

4. *In horse racing, they're called "workouts." In the stock market, they're called "future earnings projections."*

As you have seen, the biggest intellectual challenge of bettors in both games is how to interpret past performances so as to predict future performances. Workouts and future earnings projections are the factors most often used by bettors in each game to signal that a future performance might differ from the past.

The *Daily Racing Form* lists the last three workouts of each horse. Many handicappers look to workouts as indications of the fitness of a horse and the intentions of the trainer. A sizzling workout is a harbinger to many handicappers that a horse is ready to reach his peak performance on the track. If a horse, after a long layoff, puts in a few lugubrious workouts, it is supposedly an indication that the trainer might use that horse's first race as an exercise rather than as a serious attempt to win the purse.

The problem with interpreting workout figures is that trainers not only differ in their philosophies about workouts but that the same trainer can differ in practice from horse to horse. A trainer might feel that one horse must register a fast workout to prove he is fit, while he will know that another colt will tire out if he works out long and hard. Some horses need their workouts to simulate the length of the next race (many touts believe that the longer the workout, the more serious the trainer is about the race), while others can prepare for a route by breezing at three furlongs. There simply isn't any proof that there is any way to correlate workout times with race performance.

Future earnings projections, usually made by research analysts at brokerage houses, promise even more valuable information than workouts. After all, if you knew how much a company would earn in the next year, you could make money even if the stock's P-E ratio didn't improve. Accurate earnings projections would be as good as gold.

Unfortunately, the record of research analysts is horrible. The stock market will usually react negatively to earnings growth of 5 percent in a given quarter and enthusiastically to 15 percent growth. Yet research analysts' predictions, according to the scores of studies conducted by economists, are usually 15 to 25 percent off the mark even on the most visible and stable companies. When the larger economic picture changes, such as in a recession or sudden spurt of economic activity, the predictions of the analysts are wildly inaccurate. What's more, the estimates of different analysts for any particular company, as compiled in the Standard & Poor's *Earnings Forecaster*, tend to be remarkably similar, suggesting that the bulk of their estimates are derived from information supplied by the companies themselves. No one seems to do a worse job of supplying future earnings projections than the companies themselves.

Research analysts aren't dumb. But except for sleepy industries, it is next to impossible to make accurate earnings projections even a year in advance. For example, a small toy company named Coleco made a fortune in video games in the early 1980s. As Coleco grew, it decided to invest a huge sum in the production and marketing of a new computer, the Adam. The near-term earnings and financial stability of the company would be determined by the consumer and retail reaction to this new product. How is a research analyst supposed to assess the earnings impact of a new product that could plunge Coleco into red ink or make it post record earnings? He can't. So few analysts were nimble enough to ascertain just how disastrous the Adam would be for Coleco.

All bettors look for harbingers of the future, but wise bettors don't lay too much faith in them. It is better strategy to look at what harbingers the crowd believes in. If the crowd starts getting too enthusiastic about the future of a company or horse that now looks mediocre, it is time to run the other way—you'll be paying high odds or too high a price-earnings ratio for the luxury of buying an unproven commodity.

5. *In horse racing, they're called "handicaps," "allowances," "maiden races," and "claiming races." In the stock market, they're called "blue chips," "growth stocks," "speculations," and "penny stocks."*

In each game, the "quality" performers tend to be the most predictable and the least volatile. A horse good enough to be entered into a handicap race has likely won several races against decent competition. Good horses tend to be more consistent in their performance than claiming horses (horses that can be bought from their owners before the race at a specified price) and certainly more than maidens (horses that have never won a race). Because of their consistency, and the fact that the high purses offered in better races are an incentive for owners and trainers to peak a horse to win, favorites win a slightly higher percentage of big races than claiming races. But the market is rather efficient; the odds reflect the superiority of these better horses.

The most highly capitalized and best-known companies tend to be listed on the New York Stock Exchange (NYSE), the stock market equivalent of handicap and allowance races. Many of the best-known companies are components of the Dow Jones Index of thirty industrial stocks or the Standard & Poor's five hundred. Because these stocks have some kind of track record and are heavily capitalized, it is harder for blue chips or junior growth stocks to increase earnings at the high rate that smaller (often one-product or one-service) speculative, over-the-counter companies can. And because smaller stocks do not attact as much attention from research analysts, their earnings potential are even less known and less predictable than their NYSE equivalents. Thus, smaller stocks tend to exist in a less efficient market than the companies listed on the big exchange.

It is more dangerous to invest in small companies. They may not have the financial backing to weather a bad recession or new competition. They may not even have the access to enough credit to properly market a successful product. But when they are going well, their smallness and concentration on relatively few products can send their earnings, and the price of their stock, soaring. By comparison, if sales of Ivory Shampoo rise 50 percent, it will have little effect on the bottom line of a mammoth conglomerate like Procter and Gamble. Over any substantial period of time, a portfolio of small, publicly traded companies has outpaced large-cap stocks.

6. *In horse racing, they are called "taxes" and "breakage." In the stock market, they are called "taxes" and "commissions."*

When figuring out your chances of beating a game, you must include all of the expenses of doing business. A professional gambler, I guess, can write off the expense of buying a *Racing Form* just as a financial consultant could write off a subscription to the *Wall Street Journal*. All that matters, of course, is that the bettor know that the only important bottom-line consideration is how much he has won or lost after all the expenses of doing business are deducted.

There are two hidden expenses in horse racing. One is

the 17 percent or so that is taken away from the betting pool in the form of taxes and the racetrack's profit. The odds stated on the tote board are not the true ones but rather the odds *after* the track has already deducted its 17 percent take. A second deduction, breakage, is more insidious because it is invisible. In most states, payment to the successful bettor is paid in twenty-cent increments. If the true odds would give the bettor $4.75 back, the track is allowed to round off the payoff to the next *lower* twenty-cent increment, in this case $4.60. On smaller returns, such as show bets on favorites, breakage can cost a bettor one-third or more of his profit.

The bites on stock investors are more visible but can be almost as damaging to the pocketbook. The commissions on stock transactions can run as high as 7 to 10 percent of the dollar value of the trade. Generally, the smaller the trade, the bigger the percentage bite the broker takes. Much of the damage of the commission can be alleviated by searching for a good discount broker and, maybe more important, forsaking short-term trading for long-term investing, which will cut back on your number of transactions. The commission bites can add up over the years, and often exceed the income generated by stock yields.

Also overlooked by most investors is the tax implications of their purchases and sales. As this book is being written, Congress has just eliminated the long-held distinction between higher *short*-term and lower *long*-term capital gains tax rates. The moral: All that matters is how much money you make (or lose) *after* you've settled with the IRS.

Just as there is no equivalent to the stockbroker in horse racing, there is no horse-racing equivalent to a stock's dividend—an important betting factor for stocks. Some economists believe that dividends, along with earnings, are the most important long-term determinants of a stock's price. High-yielding stocks are often associated with utilities and conservative companies, appropriate only for the portfolios of widows and orphans, but low P-E high-yielding stocks have, over most decades, outperformed low-yielding stocks. Why?

Although all companies can tout their earnings prospects to their hearts' content, dividends are concrete manifestations of the financial health of a company. The fact that a company can afford to pay out, say, 5 percent of its capitalization in cash every year is an indication that the company is financially well grounded.

Skeptics scoff at high dividends. Their position is that if a company were truly high on its prospects, it would reinvest all of its earnings into the company itself, where the money could be put to better use. Economic studies have found, however, that the return on assets of low-yielding stocks tends to be no better than the high-yielding stocks. Furthermore, for the average investor, dividends are literally and figuratively money in the bank. They are an insurance policy against the risk factors in the marketplace. Both low-yielding and high-yielding stocks can go down, but at least the high-yielding stock has already given cash back to the shareholder.

A high dividend also serves as a stabilizing force during a poor market. If a financially secure stock of XYZ Inc. that sells for $20 and gives dividends of $1 a year, or a 5 percent yield, were to drop in price to $15 a share but maintain the dividend, XYZ would now yield 7.5 percent, comparing favorably to yields from CD's and bonds in low-inflation environments.

In football and horse-racing betting, most of the betting factors hurt the bettor. In the stock market, the yield is one of the important ways in which the game is rigged *for* the player.

## The Betting Methods in the Stock Market and Horse Racing

Not only do these two games share a similar cast of characters and similar betting factors, the methods and systems used to exploit these factors bear a great resemblance to each other.

1. *In horse racing, it is called a "mechanical system." In the stock market, it is called "technical analysis."*

There are two main types of investors in either game. Believers in mechanical systems and technical analyses tend to be scientific types who believe that past performances can be interpreted accurately enough to provide definitive answers to the question: What should I bet on right now? Mechanical systems for horse racing can use many different betting factors: speed, class, breeding, and weight assignments. What all mechanical systems have in common is that the system lays out strict rules about what constitutes a good bet, which the bettor follows regardless of his personal opinions. The system either dictates a bet or it doesn't. The advantage to a mechanical system is that it rules out the type of emotional or sentimental wager that can ruin a bettor. Of course, the strength of a mechanical system is only as good as the data and assumptions underlying the system.

One of the biggest disadvantages of mechanical systems is that they are inflexible. They may work for short periods of time but cannot, by definition, adapt to changing conditions. For example, during certain weeks at certain racetracks, the inside lane of the track is lightning fast, giving a decided advantage to front-runners (especially those with inside post positions) who can get out of the starting gate fast and pull over to the rail. This type of track bias cannot be predicted in advance and can disappear, with weather changes or track-maintenance policies, as quickly as it appears. The mechanical-system player will not only be unable to profit from the track-bias information but is unlikely to notice it, because track bias will not be part of his system. Mechanical systems tend to blind their players to opportunities outside of the betting factors that constitute the system.

On Wall Street, technicians are famous for consulting charts that look to the uninitiated as complex as quantum physics calculations. Technicians believe that supply and demand drive stock prices, and nothing else—not even the intrinsic worth of a company. Purist technicians are interested only in the prices at which a stock sold for a given length of time and the volume of shares traded at each price. They don't care whether XYZ Inc. sells aircraft parts or paper towels; they'll buy XYZ if the charts tell them that now is the time. Technicians rightfully scoff at those who argue that the stock market is an efficient and logical marketplace. How, then, they ask, can you explain why a stock can double in price, or halve in price, with its underlying fundamentals remaining the same?

What pure technicians seem to have in common with horse race mechanical-systems players is a naive belief that their complex games can be reduced to a few foolproof formulae. It is reassuring to think that one can conquer such complicated games armed with a chart or a calculator and a set of rules.

Every independent study of stock charts that I have seen has concluded that pure technical analysis just doesn't work. The chart formations that technicians use to assess the major trends in the direction of stock prices have been shown to have no correlation to price movements. No mechanical system of horse-race betting that I know of has ever shown a long-term profit.

There will always be folks convinced that there is a foolproof system for predicting horse races or stock price movements, but their search is likely to remain elusive.

*2. In horse racing, it's called "handicapping." In the stock market, it's called "fundamental analysis."*

The handicapper surrounds himself with all of the betting factors I have discussed and more. He treats each race as a separate entity, focusing on why one horse might be primed to perform well under the conditions of this day's race. The best newspaper handicappers select 20 to 35 percent winners and anticipate the crowd's favorite much more often. Unfortunately, they also consistently lose money. Professional handicappers are so good at agreeing with the crowd that their selections don't come close to paying the $8 to $10 price needed to break even. Because the classic handicapper tends to focus on the same information readily available to others, especially pace and the speed information available in the *Daily Racing Form*, the handicapper is generally far more successful at ascertaining quality than at uncovering undervalued investments. He wins a lot of races, but he loses money.

The stock fundamentalist is the rationalist on Wall Street. He believes that in the long term, stock selection is a logical process. He winnows out stock selections by looking at past and projected earnings, the balance sheet, cash flow generated, and the underlying asset value of companies he researches. The fundamentalist encounters many of the same problems as the handicapper. The data he researches is the same that is available to every other fundamentalist (and technician)—and is already, most likely, factored into the price of the stock. The earnings projections he scans, as we have already seen, are wildly inaccurate. How can he evaluate the appropriate P-E of a stock when he has no sure way of assessing a company's future earnings?

Increasingly, the distinctions between fundamentalist and technician, between mechanical-systems players and handicappers, are becoming blurred and even disappearing. Technicians now use fundamental factors in a mechanical fashion, and with great success. Two technicians regularly featured on *Wall Street Week*, Martin Zweig and Robert Nurock, have shunned pure technical ideology for an eclectic approach. Each sets up a series of models, ranging from interest rates to negative sentiment indicators (e.g., when investment services are high on stocks, it's a negative indicator). Robert Nurock has created ten such models, which *Wall Street Week* host Lou Rukeyser calls "the elves." On each model, the elves are bullish, bearish, or neutral. When the elves are a net plus 5 or minus 5, it is supposed to signal the beginning of a new major trend. Plus 5 sends a buy signal; minus 5 says "sell." The elves have had a remarkably successful record, calling every major turn in the stock market in the 1980s.

Although we are confirmed handicappers/fundamental analysts, we have much to learn from technicians, namely how large market forces can be ascertained by measuring move-

88 DAVID FELDMAN

ments of much smaller forces, even ones that seem to have no relation to fundamentals. If we are serious in stating that our opponent is not "the house" but our fellow bettors, then we need to find ways of measuring the attitudes of our fellow bettors—the mechanical systems in horse racing and technical analysis offer us some valuable clues.

3. *In horse racing, they are called "underlays." In the stock market, they're called "high P-E stocks."*

In the program at every racetrack, you will see the probable odds printed beside the name of each horse, a "guesstimate" made by the track handicapper. When large enough sums of money are bet on a horse to greatly reduce the odds, say from 8-to-1 to 3-to-1, the horse is said to be an underlay. Many bettors like to play underlays, for the confidence of big and presumably smart money on their horse confirms its excellent prospects.

Similarly, many investors prefer investing in high P-E stocks, because the high multiple suggests that the market is confident about the prospects of the company and because there has usually been good news trumpeted about stocks with high P-E's. But as we have already seen, strong future growth is already factored into the price of high P-E stocks, so not only are they buying an expensive stock, they are buying one that will be hit hard if the company does not live up to its sterling expectations. At this point, the stock tends to become overbought (i.e., there are plenty of willing sellers and no buyers except at bargain-basement prices).

This same principle can be seen easily with underlays. Sure, it is nice to know that others are sagacious enough to share your enthusiasm for the horse that started out as an 8-to-1 shot. But wouldn't you rather have bet a bargain that would pay off $18 rather than, at 3-to-1, $8? Unfortunately, the *horse* doesn't know that she is an underlay; she is not more likely to win just because other bettors have responded. Betting an underlay means only that your payoff will return less if you win.

4. *In horse racing, they are called "overlays." In the stock market, they're called "low P-E stocks."*

Overlays are the opposite of underlays—horses that end up with higher odds than expected or deserved. Overlays tend to be good bets for the same reasons that underlays are bad bets. If you can find merit in a horse that the crowd doesn't appreciate, you will not only be rewarded with a win but a win at a higher payback than expected. If you are right no more often than the crowd, you will come out ahead—because you will be receiving more generous odds.

A low P-E stock also offers a double bang when the company performs well, through earnings increases *and* P-E expansion. Stocks out of favor also have another feature that assures you of limited downside risk. Publicly traded companies can be taken over when their stock price gets too low. One of your goals as an investor is to buy stocks that represent genuine value. If you buy the stock of a company that is selling for less than its asset value, eventually the market (or one company or individual) will come to its senses and scoop up the bargain. Thus, many oil companies were taken over or merged in the early 1980s despite the horrible climate for the oil business. Oil companies were attractive not because their near-term prospects were bright, but because their assets in the ground alone could be sold off for more than the stock market was assessing the value of the entire company.

5. *In horse racing, it is called "class" or "breeding history." In the stock market, it is called "financial analysis."*

Whereas some speed handicappers believe that their approach can virtually always diagnose a winner if the analysis is sufficiently sophisticated, class handicappers insist that you can't win at the races solely by assessing the relative speed ratings of horses. Class handicappers feel there are intangible factors that will make one horse consistently beat another, even if both horses have run at similar times at the same distance in the past.

The founding father of modern handicappers, Tom Ainslie,

believed strongly in the notion of class; he also noted that the horse that has run successfully against better competition tends to outrun another horse with the same times that has faced weaker fields. Some class handicappers look for other such intangibles. Some stress the breeding history of the horses in the race, looking for ancestors who might have performed well at today's distance or surface. Still other class aficionados believe that what separates horses with similar physical abilities is a "will to win," and they attempt to psychoanalyze the field: Horses who post consistent speed ratings but never seem to come in first are shunned as lacking the killer instinct; horses who hate to get passed in the stretch are prized. Most class handicappers share the conviction that purely mathematical systems focusing on speed ratings oversimplify the art.

Financial analysts believe that they can best discover the value of a stock by studying the books of the company. They pore over prospectuses and quarterly reports, exploring the ratio of assets to debt, the return on equity, and the cash flow generated. Like class- or breeding-oriented handicappers, financial analysts are obsessed with finding out whether or not their subject has the disposition, the prerequisites, for winning. They are better at screening out risky bets than in discovering must-bets.

6. *In horse racing, they are called "trifectas" or "exactas" or "daily doubles"—as a group, they are called "exotic bets." In the stock market, they are called "options" or "futures."*

As if doping out horse racing or the stock market weren't tough enough, new financial instruments are being introduced constantly. At first, serious handicappers disdained the exotic bets, focusing only on win bets. Of course, the experts were being parochial, because the track's profit margin was no higher on the exotics than on straight bets and the exotics were attracting unsophisticated gamblers who were taking a flyer and hoping to make a killing. Because the opponents on exotic bets tended to be less skilled, the exotics actually offered better odds.

As strong handicappers started to look for ways to bet the exotics, they discovered that they could use the exotics to substitute for simple win bets as well. If their favorite horse was an underlay in the win pool, smart players looked for ways to pair that horse with other contenders in exactas or trifectas. This became a way of receiving more generous odds on their favored horse, even if they were forced to pick second or third favorites as well.

Many otherwise savvy stock-pickers at first looked with disdain on the futures and options markets, seeing them as only for gamblers and hustlers. The same opportunities as with exotics in horse racing, however, presented themselves in these new markets. By going long (i.e., buying) on one market and selling on the other market, hedgers have been able to take advantage of small inefficiencies in valuations. For the average long-term investor, this kind of hedging with futures and options is impractical; commissions alone would eat up much of the profit. And it remains to be seen whether these new financial instruments have any long-term effect on the price of individual stocks or the market as a whole; but the success of many of this new breed of players suggests that the market is not as efficient as many have assumed. There are pockets of opportunity for the intrepid.

It is startling to see the close resemblance among the players, betting factors, and betting methods in these two "games." Now that we have defined our terms, in the next chapter we will see that the strategies needed to win (or lose) at each game are also remarkably similar.

# How to Lose and How to Win at Horse-Race Betting and the Stock Market

THESE TWO GAMES are the most complex I will explore in this book. Neither game lends itself to simple winning systems, so my advice will be circumspect. If you want to be a long-term winner at either game, you will need to do quite a bit of study. I'll lead you to some of the best sources available and tell you about some of their winning approaches.

If some of the pronouncements in this chapter sound familiar, they should, because my strategy to win at the horses and stocks mirrors my reasoning behind the football method. The crowd thinks along the same lines in each game, so I will continue to head in the opposite direction—away from the crowd.

HOW TO LOSE: Act as if you are betting against the house.
HOW TO WIN: Act as if you are betting against your fellow bettors. Look to see what the crowd does, and then do the opposite.

"The crowd always loses because the crowd is always wrong. It is wrong because it behaves normally." Fred C. Kelly, as quoted in Adam Smith's *The Money Game*, succinctly states our philosophy, although Smith is wise enough to add that: "The believers in this rule are numerous enough to constitute a crowd, but of course anyone speaking of the crowd believes himself to be outside of it."

The odds in the stock market and horse racing reflect which betting factors are most followed by the crowd in each game. Since both games involve a semi-efficient market, it is difficult to get an edge playing favored variables such as speed ratings in horse racing or earnings in the stock market. In order to win, you will need to study what the other bettors expect. As Adam Smith puts it, the stock market is "an exercise in mass psychology, in trying to guess better than the crowd how the crowd will behave." When you have bought a stock, someone else has risked his own money in the belief that it was the right time to sell. The final tote odds at the racetrack are determined not by a theoretician but by bettors risking their own money—at any given time, most will disagree with your opinion.

To have an edge, you must find a chink in the intellectual armor of the crowd, usually not by uncovering new information but by interpreting the same information differently. For example, the crowd thinks that earnings growth is the most important determinant in the rise of a stock, so most investors like to invest in stocks after a good earnings report. Then they are disappointed when the stock doesn't move upward. These investors neglect to note that a semi-efficient market usually *anticipates* and has already discounted the good earnings report. If price-earnings ratios already reflect anticipated future earnings, then a better strategy is not to invest in stocks with "only" good earnings, but ones whose earnings exceed the expectations of the crowd. By studying the earnings projections in *Value Line* and the Standard & Poor's *Earnings Forecaster*, and noting when actual earnings exceed the consensus expectations, *even if the actual earnings are down or nonexistent*, you could make money simply by "betting" on earnings overachievers, presuming that they met your other criteria for selection.

In horse racing, you are constantly looking for reasons why

the crowd might overestimate or underestimate the chances of a horse you favor. If you can find a reason to throw out the results of a race, particularly the last race, you are way ahead of most handicappers, who feel that virtually every race is an important signal of the worthiness of a horse. We'll soon see some of the ways to throw out a race.

HOW TO LOSE: Look for the best company and buy its stock. Look for the best horse in a race and bet on it.
HOW TO WIN: Analyze the risk and rewards of each bet. Don't merely look for the most likely winner.

As you have seen in football betting, too many bettors stop their analysis at the point of identifying the best horse in a field or the best performing company on the stock exchange. You can be assured that others have spotted the quality of your selection. You need to know, however, that if you bet on a prohibitive even-money favorite, your horse truly does have a better than fifty-fifty chance of winning, or else you are going to lose in the long run.

Likewise, the stock price of an excellent company with a high P-E will fall dramatically the first time the company stumbles. Are you sure that the potential rewards (a P-E expansion of an already highly valued stock) justify the risks (a sharply lower P-E not only if the company has a mishap but if the crowd loses confidence in the near-term future of the stock market)? How many times have you heard a *Wall Street Week* guest tout a stock by saying that the company is well managed and should experience a growth pattern for the next two years? I always feel like yelling, "Okay, you convinced me that it is a good company, but convince me that it is a good stock!" Everyone else on Wall Street knows that the company is well managed and making money. I want to know whether the price of the stock is going to advance. The prospects for the company and for the stock are not necessarily the same, even for a booming company, if the P-E valuation is too high.

How to Lose: Assume that if you have access to a wealth of information, you will become wealthy. Assume that the big shots in the market have a big advantage over you.

How to Win: Realize that you must interpret this data contrary to the crowd or risk results as mediocre as the crowd's, and that you have important advantages over the smart money.

You have already looked at the overwhelming pressures on the institutional smart-money managers in the stock market and how they tend to act just as self-destructively as the football crowd. Sure, the institutional money manager probably has access to more information than you, but it remains to be seen how much of an advantage this is. David Dreman cites a fascinating study which concludes that the more information bettors are given, the more confident they become about their ability to win. But in fact, those given forty variables to study did no better than those given only five. As a small investor, you can often outfox institutional investors by specializing in one angle, just as those college football bettors became winners by specializing in only one conference. Institutional money managers tend to be buried in a morass of hundreds of contradictory indicators and statistics. The human mind can only absorb so many things; as often as not, the final decisions of money managers are based on snap judgments rather than on a careful analysis of all of their paralyzing data.

Imagine the plight of the poor portfolio manager who knows that the low P-E stock is horribly undervalued but can't buy it because of pressures to perform in the short term. He must also keep an eye on his competition, which is more than willing to woo away his clients, brandishing their last quarter's performance. Institutional managers are also, for the most part, buying and selling the same several hundred stocks. They are too big to buy illiquid and thinly capitalized stocks. William J. Grace, in his book *The Phoenix Approach*, reports that:

> Almost every objective survey of portfolio management and institutional research analysis supports the suspicion that the industry itself has consistently underperformed

the market averages. . . . The collective result of all surveys for all time periods is startling: Professional advice has been wrong over 75 percent of the time.

Because it is safer for professionals to keep their jobs if they follow the lead of their rivals, the shrewd investor is in a position to pick up bargains. By the time a strong consensus arises on the good value of a stock, you can hear the footsteps of the thundering herd; they have already bought the stock and are looking for new stocks. As soon as bad news develops about a company and the institutions start selling (and not enough individual investors are willing to buy to match the volume of the institutions), the stock price can go into a free-fall. Our old friend—reversion to the mean—comes to the rescue again, usually deciding that the true value of a stock is somewhere in between the appraisal of the optimistic bulls and the downbeat bears.

Mood swings tend to be overdone as much in horse racing as in the stock market. As favorites get bet down and become underlays, crowd enthusiasm for the horses tends to play on itself and build momentum. You will feel that the crowd must certainly know more than you do (although unlike the stock market, you can never be sure if the horse is being favored by just the smart money or by the small bettor as well). Just as in the stock market, however, the crowd consensus will open up pockets of opportunity for you when you disagree with it. You can't win unless you are a contrarian or you choose to sit out races where the reward is too small if you win to justify the risk.

HOW TO LOSE: Avoid stocks or horses with problems. Choose only horses that did well in their last race or stocks whose last earnings report were favorable.
HOW TO WIN: Look for bad performances as an opportunity to find bargains. Remember that the odds you receive should reflect the future prospects rather than the immediate past performance of your bet.

The crowd always gives up on an investment opportunity when it has disappointed them in the recent past. The institutional stock investor tends to overreact just as much to bad news as to good news. When a stock price reacts negatively to bad earnings, for example, technical analysts discern weakness in the stock's chart and sell their holdings, further increasing the downward momentum. Most portfolio managers wouldn't even consider investing in a company in actual financial distress ("How could I explain it to my boss? To my clients?").

The stocks of troubled companies tend to become so oversold and undervalued that they often sell for less than the resale value of their underlying assets, such as the oil companies, whose oil reserves at $12 a barrel were still worth more than the total capitalization of their stocks (which were once high-flyers when oil sold at $40 a barrel).

Several institutional money managers do specialize in what are euphemistically called "special situations." These managers look for distressed companies that they think will either turn their bad fortune around, be bought out by another company, or else be sold for their underlying asset value. Usually, the stock is an excellent bargain if any one of the three scenarios comes to pass. These contrarians figure that if the assets of a company can be sold for more than the value of the stock, their downside risk is nil. It may take *longer* for them to receive their reward from the successful investment in a special situation, but they take virtually no risk and an almost sure profit in the long run. One mutual fund, Mutual Shares, has specialized in investing in these kinds of special situations, with spectacular results. While Mutual Shares tends to be average in its performance during bull markets, it does fantastically well during down markets, not only outperforming the stock averages but actually making money while the overwhelming majority of stocks are going down.

Other managers follow a slightly modified strategy. A newer mutual fund, the Legg Mason Value Trust, doesn't invest in candidates for bankruptcy like Mutual Shares will, but its manager, Ernest C. Kiehne, literally looks for trouble. He seeks out companies that have a blemish that has made the crowd bearish on the stock, such as a poor earnings report that Kiehne sees as temporary. Kiehne is actually strict in screening his stocks for financial health, moderate debt, and low price-earnings and price-asset value ratios. Still, simply by picking healthy companies that are temporarily out of favor, the Legg Mason Value Trust fund zooms during bull markets and has done well during corrections (it hasn't been around long enough to weather a long-term bear market).

All of the great fortunes on Wall Street, from Bernard Baruch's to today's Warren Buffet's and Laurence Tisch's, have been made by investors seeking untrendy or distressed companies that were worth more than the crowd thought. They were the brave few who were willing to stand alone among the thundering herd and keep it simple: They bought low and sold high.

My approach to horse-race betting has been similar to these Wall Street winners. When I first became interested in horse racing, in junior-high school, the *Racing Form* had a column every day called "Horses in Trouble." No, this was not a crime blotter, but a list of every horse in that day's racing card who experienced a troubled trip in his last race. Perhaps he broke slowly from the gate, or was bumped, or had to be steadied by the jockey, or raced so wide that he had no realistic chance to win. If the trouble was serious enough to throw out the race, I thought, perhaps the crowd would ignore the excuse and dismiss the horse because of the bad performance.

It worked. I was a pretty smart kid, although unfortunately not rich enough to make my bets anywhere but on paper. Nevertheless, I soon refined my system. I came to the realization that a lousy horse could have racing luck as poor as a good horse, so I no longer thought that trouble in the last race meant I had a surefire bet. I realized it was much more sensible simply to *throw out* the last race. If the horse did not figure to be a contender in today's race after discarding

his previous race, why should I bet on him? Is the horse any
better because it got bumped in its last race? No, it's not
automatically better, but it is automatically a better *value*, so
I bent over backward to bet a horse in trouble in his last race
if I could find any justification for thinking it would be a strong
contender. This method has worked for me over the long
term.

My other main adjustment was to realize that certain horses
are chronically in trouble, just as some companies are always
on the verge of bankruptcy. In particular, some horses have
a habit of breaking slowly or racing wide. These horses I
tended to pass up.

The biggest problem with the "Horses in Trouble" method
is that the *Racing Form* notations are far from complete and
can't sufficiently convey the extent of the trouble your prospective pick was in during his last race. For this reason,
personal observation is much more accurate in measuring
trouble. As a sporadic racegoer, however, I have found trou-
ble-searching, when combined with more traditional handicapping notions, to be profitable simply by using the *Racing
Form* comments.

Another one of my favorite horse-racing tips involves two-
year-olds. Many bettors shy away from betting on freshman
horses, because most are lightly raced and some have never
raced before. How can you evaluate a horse's form when it
has never raced? But I have found one angle that has worked
well; in fact, it is the only mechanical system I have ever
encountered that has been profitable for me: When a two-
year-old puts on blinkers for the first time, bet him.

Blinkers are placed on a horse when the horse seems to
have been distracted by other horses or by the dirt flying on
the sides of him. Most horses are raced the first time without
blinkers, but blinkers are added if the horse is obviously bothered. The blinker system is really just a corollary to my "Horses
in Trouble" method. The horse's distraction is an excuse for
its poor performance in previous outings. Donning blinkers
does not make a slow horse run faster but will make the crowd

skeptical of its chances. A two-year-old adding blinkers for the first time, particularly if it gave a poor performance in its last attempt, is sure to be underpriced. A horse that dons blinkers for the first time *and* encountered trouble along the way is an even more commanding bet.

I eventually refined my blinker angle in the same way as the "Horses in Trouble" method, throwing out the last race and determining whether any justification existed for backing the horse based on his other performances. If the horse had put in one decent performance, or was highly regarded in the odds against a similar or higher class of horse, this became reason enough to bet the horse. I found that if a horse donned blinkers in his second race ever, and he was highly regarded but failed in his first race, he was a particularly good bet. It is a little-known fact that two-year-old favorites win more than any other type of favorite. A first-time racer that was favored and was badly beaten *but had an excuse* (i.e., trouble or need for blinkers) invariably offers particularly excellent value.

Most bettors stress the importance of fast workouts with two-year-olds, but I have found betting on horses trying blinkers for the first time to be far superior. They don't win as often as favorites, or even horses in trouble, but they usually pay huge odds when they do win.

HOW TO LOSE: Bet on favorites. Bet on high P-E stocks. HOW TO WIN: Bet on the best *value*.

Almost every argument I have made has been to support this point: If you are going to make long-term profits in horse racing, football, or the stock market, you should act like the bargain-hunter at a garage sale—scrounging around wherever you can find *good value*. You have already seen that in all these games, mood swings are overdone, so that bargains become greater bargains and overpriced goods become even more expensive. But there is also a long-term tendency toward efficiency and reversion to the mean, which means that if you catch the bet right before or right after it is most underpriced, it is hard to lose.

Because good values are easiest to find when expectations for the horse, the football team, or the stock are lowest, expected performances have little price effect. The more bad news that is expected in the future, the more good things that can happen to the investor, particularly if he can find some angle, some excuse, some reason why the crowd is wrong in its pessimism. It is important to remember that if you are accurate in assessing the low valuation of your bet by the crowd, this pessimism is reflected in the odds. The underdog football team doesn't have to play *well*, necessarily, to win the bet, only better than expected. The 10-to-1 shot doesn't have to win as often as favorites, only one out of nine times. The low P-E stock doesn't need spectacular earnings reports to increase in price, only better than expected reports. And if the expected lousy earnings reports come in, the stock will likely remain at the current price, not fall. The same cannot be said of the high P-E stock, which has built-in great expectations and follows through with only good earnings. It will drop.

In *The Money Game*, Adam Smith comments: "Value is not only inherent in the stock, to do you any good, it has to be value that is appreciated by others." But by the time the crowd's consensus has agreed on the worth of a stock, it has already risen in cost. It is far better to find opportunities in little-known or seemingly unexciting stocks that the institutions are not following. By the time the stock attracts the attention of the institutions, their purchasing volume will drive the price of the stock upward.

In a survey conducted by CDA Investment Technologies, which tracked the performance of stock managers handling a total of $339 billion in equity funds since the beginning of the 1980s bull market until 1985, the top manager in every category (bank, insurance company, and investment advisers) used a value-oriented approach. Each stressed long-term profits and tried to find bargain-priced stocks. Ironically, the low-risk, low P-E approach has performed better than the more aggressive high P-E approach even during bull markets when high P-E stocks are reputed to rise fastest.

The importance of value in horse racing is even more apparent. Since the crowd is excellent at picking the correct favorite, and since betting favorites has always been a money loser, you must find a reason to run contrary to the crowd's thinking in order to win at this game. You must find the horse that offers the best value, not even necessarily the horse with the best chance to win.

## Differences Between the Two Games

From a betting standpoint, the most obvious difference between the two games is that one game is rigged for you and one is rigged against you. If a "house" did not take out its 17 percent, horse racing would be an easy game to beat. But the house *does* take its nasty cut. Just by buying the stocks in the Dow Jones or Standard & Poor's Index, you would have beaten inflation over any decade since the Depression. It's hard to lose money in the stock market over the long haul, although it is easy to underperform the popular averages (it must be, because as we have seen, professional money managers underperform the market with regularity).

The fact that your stock is backed with assets, capable of being liquidated if necessary, is another important difference between the two games. Most value-oriented investors try to find companies whose stock prices are near or below their liquidation value, assuring them that even if management does a poor job, they are unlikely to lose much of their investment. A horse or football team provides no such collateral. If you lose your bet, you lose 100 percent of it.

As I have mentioned, the other games have no equivalent to a stock's dividends. Although the cost of paying out the dividend ultimately comes out of the value of the stock's shares, high dividend stocks (usually low P-E stocks) have appreciated in value more than low-dividend, high P-E stocks, thus allowing their investors to make money in two ways.

With stocks, you can give your money to a professional organization to manage with genuine hopes of success. Most investors do not study the stock market with enough vigor and do not have enough money to properly buy a diversified portfolio of stocks. For most investors, buying a no-load (i.e., with no purchase or sales charges) mutual fund with a value orientation is a painless way to invest in the market. No equivalents exist in the horse-racing world. If there were, no one would trust them anyway.

There is one further, significant advantage to stocks over the horses. Horse racing is a zero-sum game. The racetrack serves as a money handler, taking out its cut and then redistributing a given pool of money. The winners win exactly the same amount of money as the losers lose (which is one of the reasons why one must look at your fellow bettors as your opponent). But the stock market is not a strictly zero-sum game. Money earmarked for stocks has grown faster than the supply of stocks, due to the ever-increasing wealth of our country (and of late because of the burgeoning money wielded by pension funds and IRA accounts). This surfeit of demand over supply has served to drive the prices of all stocks upward.

It is possible to beat football or horse racing, but it ain't easy. Better to make them diversions and concentrate on an easier game—the stock market. Perhaps no simple system will beat the stock market, but if you combine my advice with the wisdom recommended in the following books, you should win big.

**For more information:**

*Contrarian Investment Strategy: The Psychology of Stock-Market Success*, David Dreman (New York: Random House, 1979). This book, and everything else written by David Dreman (including his column in *Forbes* magazine), is well worth reading. Dreman, the managing director of his own investment firm and the author of two other excellent books, is the leading advocate of low P-E investments.

*Contrarian Investment Strategy* is particularly recommended for its excellent discussion of why and how the crowd always goes wrong and why the individual investor has an advantage over the big institutional players. Dreman is skeptical of anyone's ability, including his own, to forecast the market. If no one can predict the future, reasons Dreman, then why not buy stocks that offer you the least risk and the best possible odds? Irrefutable logic, and entertainingly written to boot. Don't put a dime into the stock market until you've read this book.

*Security Analysis*, Benjamin Graham, David L. Dodd, and Sidney Cottle (New York: McGraw-Hill, 1962).

*The Intelligent Investor: A Book of Practical Counsel*, Benjamin Graham (New York: Harper and Row, 1973).

These two books have been the basis for modern fundamental analysis. Graham, who died in 1975, wouldn't consider buying a stock unless it was financially strong and priced cheaply, as calculated by about ten financial criteria. And although Graham's emphasis on debt/equity and price/book value ratios is deemed old-fashioned by technicians, Graham's strict qualifications for stocks worthy of investment have continuously outpaced the market averages. *Forbes* cited a study in *Financial Analysts Journal* which revealed that from 1974 to 1981, "NYSE and Amex companies that met the Ben Graham criteria outperformed their counterparts in terms of total return by better than 2½-to-1." Graham was more than willing to pass up opportunities in stocks that didn't meet his rigid criteria  Graham was only interested in buying stocks that were cheap; this one insight enabled him and his followers to profit in good markets and bad.

*The Phoenix Approach: The Contrarian Investor's Guide to Profiting From Out-of-Favor, Distressed and Bankrupt*

*Companies,* William J. Grace, Jr. (New York: Bantam Books, 1984).

I discovered this book after I wrote the bulk of this chapter, and in a sense I am glad that I hadn't read it before, for his approach is so similar to mine and so well written that I might have given up and asked to reprint excerpts. Grace has written an easy-to-understand explanation of contrarian strategy, including a discussion of financially distressed companies, that echoes the winning approach of Mutual Shares, the mutual fund we discussed. Highly recommended.

*The Science of Winning: A Random Walk on the Road to Riches,* Burton P. Fabricand (New York: Van Nostrand Reinhold, 1979).

This is the only other book I know that includes a lengthy discussion of strategies in both horse-race betting and the stock market. Fabricand focuses on the relative efficiency of both games. The author strongly disagrees with the notion, widely held in academic circles, that the stock market is so efficient that stock-picking is really a "random walk." Much of the book is theoretical and mathematical in nature, but his stock system is rather simple in execution: He advocates betting on stocks whose actual earnings reports exceed forecasts.

*Winning On Wall Street,* Martin Zweig (New York: Warner Books, 1986).

In this book Zweig shares some, but by no means all, of the models he uses to evaluate trends in the market and individual stocks. Because he is one of the few technicians with a consistently strong winning record, his techniques are worth reading about. While fundamentalists are always looking for bargains, Zweig argues against "fighting the tape" (i.e., betting against the dominant trend of the market). This advice might grate on a die-hard fundamentalist, but Zweig's arguments are convincing and his breadth of analysis fascinating. Zweig is one technician who doesn't speak in gobbledygook and is willing to admit occasional fallibility.

*  *  *

Until the 1970s, it was hard to find a decent book on thoroughbred betting that wasn't written by Tom Ainslie. But in the last decade, information about horse racing has exploded. While a lot of charlatans still pose as experts in this field, more great books have been written on betting thoroughbreds in the last ten years than in the history of the sport. Here are some of the best:

*Picking Winners: A Horseplayer's Guide*, Andrew Beyer (Boston: Houghton Mifflin, 1985).

*The Winning Horseplayer: A Revolutionary Approach to Thoroughbred Handicapping & Betting*, Andrew Beyer (Boston: Houghton Mifflin, 1983).

Andrew Beyer is the most influential writer in the field today. His *Picking Winners*, originally released in 1975, became the bible for speed handicappers. Beyer realized that unadjusted speed ratings were too inaccurate to be profitably used, and showed how it was possible to actually compare speeds on any given day at different tracks. This book is still a valuable resource.

But in the 1970s, Beyer became disenchanted with his own methods. He saw that the edge he obtained with his adjusted speed ratings was disappearing; too many others had adopted his techniques. The market had become more efficient.

Beyer noticed a new breed of winners, trip handicappers. These bettors feel that the most important determinant in whether or not a horse wins a race is the nature of his trip— whether or not the horse races under ideal or horrible conditions. Did the horse run wide around the turns or did she save ground on the rail? Was she a beneficiary of a favorable track bias, or was she trudging through rough terrain? Was she given easy access to the head of the pack, or did she have to compete with other horses at a burning pace? Or was she able to lie back in front of three speed merchants burning each other out before they got to the stretch, merely breezing into the lead in front of the exhausted pacesetters?

DAVID FELDMAN

Beyer concluded that the nature of a trip could render speed ratings not only misleading but irrelevant. In his book on trip handicapping, *The Winning Horseplayer*, Beyer shows how two horses with identical speed ratings on the same track can be wildly different in ability. Rarely does someone who has fostered a school of thought, as Beyer did with speed handicapping, have the intellectual honesty to reverse his position, and this openness of Beyer's makes anything he writes worthy of careful reading. Beyer would rather make money than prove his old theories correct.

Beyer's trip handicapping is similar in many respects to my "Horses in Trouble" and blinker strategies, for although Beyer doesn't emphasize this fact, horses with bad trips in recent races are obviously going to be overlays, and thus offer more value. Beyer's trip analysis covers more circumstances than my limited system and is therefore more often valuable.

Beyer's approach in *The Winning Horseplayer* requires attendance at the track and intense time spent observing the various trips of the horses in each race. For this reason, only the most devoted horse bettors can fully utilize his methodology. Trip handicapping is much more subjective than the more mechanical speed handicapping, but it is also more profitable.

*Winning at the Races: Computer Discoveries in Thoroughbred Handicapping*, William L. Quirin, Ph.D. (New York: William Morrow and Co., 1979).

As the title of his book indicates, Quirin has used his computer to generate results on the efficacy of many approaches to handicapping. He seems to have no axes to grind: Quirin is the rare writer in this field who is not emotionally attached to any one method of handicapping, and his exhaustive studies cover a larger universe of actual races than any others I've seen. As Tom Ainslie says in his foreword, "Dr. Quirin is to the best of my knowledge and belief the only person who combines (a) thorough mathematical competence, (b) thorough handicapping competence, and (c) un-compromising adherence to the rules of scientific inquiry."

Dr. Quirin spends much of his book explaining the utter futility of betting only on favorites, which consistently win one-third of the time. In 4,800 races Quinn studies, a $2 bet on every favorite yields an average $1.81 return—the 17 percent take of the house, unfortunately, more than compensates for the tendency of the crowd to underbet favorites.

Among Quirin's most important findings are the correlation between speed at the beginning of a race and the finish order. If you could determine which horse will be ahead at the first call, you could easily beat the races. But pace is far from easy to predict, so much of the book is devoted to how to determine which horses are likely to lead the field early.

With the use of the computer, Quirin is able to mix and match variables in order to determine which betting factors are most important. Quirin finds that jockeys, class ratings, and speed ratings don't have much correlation to success, and, indeed, horses with positive ratings with these factors tended to be underlays, because the crowd *does* believe in their efficacy. Quirin did find three factors that, regardless of other conditions, always do enhance the chances of a horse: at least one win in the last ten starts, some early speed, and the requirement that the horse's last race be within the last ten days.

The most fun for the average bettor will be in reading Quirin's computer-generated systems, many of them long-term winners. He confirms two of our pet theories. One, that two-year-old races are more often won by favorites and that maiden two-year-olds who lost their last race but were highly regarded tend to be excellent bets (especially, we would add, if they don blinkers in this race). Two, Dr. Quirin debunks the importance of weight in dooming the chances of a horse. In fact, one of his most profitable computer-generated systems involves betting on horses in sprints who carry 120 pounds or more and who won their last race (they netted an average of $2.40 per $2 bet).

Quirin's computer-generated systems are extremely specific in their instructions, making it particularly easy for the average bettor to find Quirin's selections at the track without rereading the whole book.

*Beat the Racetrack*, William T. Ziemba and Donald B. Hausch (New York: Harcourt Brace Jovanovich, 1984).

The "Dr. Z" system is based on the same conclusion as Quirin's, that the crowd is excellent at picking winners but that the track take robs you of the chance to make a profit by simply betting favorites. The horse-race crowd is remarkably efficient at picking favorites, perhaps the most impressive proof being that the closing-line odds are far more accurate than the morning odds.

You would think that if the crowd were so good at picking winners, they would be equally skilled in place and show bets. They aren't. Favorites are consistently underbet in place and show pools. Prohibitive win favorites even pay more to place than to win, on occasion. The Dr. Z system is based on the authors' findings that in two to four races a day, the place and show bets are out of proportion enough to give a player an edge of 20 percent or more. In these instances, the Dr. Z system instructs that a bet should be made.

Handicappers have always had a macho component—many seem more concerned about their ability to pick winners than their ability to make money. This is one reason why "serious" bettors tend to shun place and show betting and why the place and show pools are less efficient than the win pool. The other main reason is that many bettors are put off by the relatively low payoffs of place and show bets. Bettors who lose their entire stake when they are wrong are not excited about a mere 50 percent return, which stock investors would die for. The Dr. Z system is designed for those who are willing to win a relatively low rate of return on each race but at relatively low risk. Properly used, however, a fairly large bankroll is necessary.

Although at times the authors are a bit vague in their

instructions, and their system requires fairly complicated computations just before post time, the Dr. Z system is most impressive, a classic example of contrarian methodology.

*High-Tech Handicapping in the Information Age*, James Quinn (New York: William Morrow and Co., 1986).

Despite its forbidding title, this book is strongly recommended for just about anyone interested in handicapping. Quinn feels strongly that it is silly to rely on one mechanical system. Not all handicapping methods work equally well in different types of races (e.g., speed ratings work much better in sprints than routes; breeding analysis is much more valuable on grass surfaces than the dirt). So Quinn stresses that the modern handicapper should be a generalist, taking advantage of the information explosion that has occurred over the last ten years, using whatever works best in a given situation. A generalist will have more chances to bet than an angle or system player. In order to make an equal amount, the system player must bet a higher percentage of his bankroll.

Quinn reviews the work of his colleagues, including all of the books we list here. His comments are generous and accurate, and he finds important potential drawbacks even to winning systems. He notes that a possible weakness of the Dr. Z system, for example, is that it is susceptible to the last-minute plunges of big bettors. One big bet on a Dr. Z play by a high-roller can nullify the inefficiency that prompted the bet; a track full of Dr. Z proponents with large bankrolls would create a nightmare.

Like all sensible handicappers (i.e., like us), Quinn prefers betting overlays to underlays, and, like us, looks for reasons why a horse might have a possible advantage in today's race that he didn't have last time.

As the title suggests, Quinn has much to say about how computers can aid you in handicapping, but even if you count on your toes, *High-Tech Handicapping* is highly recommended. It is the best consumer guide available to modern theories of handicapping.

*How Will Your Horse Run Today*, William L. Scott (Baltimore: Amicus Press, 1986). Distributed by Liberty Publishing Co., 50 Scott Adam Rd., Cockeysville, MD 21029.

When searching for strong overlays, your primary emphasis must be on why a horse that is now out of favor might perform better in his race today than in the recent past. William L. Scott has devoted a whole book to this subject of form. Although Scott, in his other work, emphasizes the importance of class more than any of the other recommended authors, here he explores what factors can lead you to eliminate from consideration horses that look like contenders to speed handicappers, and how to determine which horses are most likely to be at their peak today.

# WINNING
## AGAINST
## THE
# ESTABLISHMENT

KAS

# How to Get Good Service in a Fancy Restaurant

WHEN SURVEYED, patrons answer that poor service is their number-one complaint about restaurants—more than food quality, ambience (although excessive noise is the current number-two complaint), or high prices. Even an experience in a restaurant with outstanding food can be ruined by neglectful, haphazard, or abusive treatment by the service staff.

Almost every medium-sized or larger city has one or more fancy restaurant. Customers often don't feel comfortable in fancy restaurants, further compounding service problems. In these establishments, diners are often intimidated ("Which one's the captain and which one's the maitre d'?" "Is the menu going to be in French?"), made to feel ignorant, or made to feel lucky to have had the honor of dropping a hundred dollars or more for the upscale chow. While you are unlikely, in a fancy restaurant, to be treated as crudely as you might in a diner or fast-food store, you can encounter behavior much more trying—receiving perfunctory or condescending service while those around you are treated royally. Even the food at the winners' tables looks better than yours. It is this *uneven* treatment, the necessity to perform special tricks to attain the attention and favor of the staff, that causes some patrons to resent the fancy restaurant.

I wondered whether there was a way to be treated well in a fancy restaurant without being a VIP, without laying out hundreds of dollars in tips, and without losing dignity in the process.

I talked to restaurateurs, service staffs who work at fancy restaurants, and to patrons who win this particular game and feel comfortable doing so. What emerged was a strong consensus about the proper relationship between a diner and the service staff of a restaurant, and a set of ground rules that lead not only to better service on the part of the staff but also to a more fun dining experience for the customer.

Of all the games in this book, the dining experience is the one with the least ostensible conflict among the participants. Your "opponent" might seem to be the service staff, but for the most part, they want to make you happy (if you're happy, you'll tip more!). So let's see how the average customer can make the service staff happy and inspire them to try to make you happy.

## Before You Arrive at the Restaurant

Your relationship with a restaurant starts with your phone call to make a reservation. Be sure you make a reservation, even if you want to dine at a traditionally slow time. You want to do everything you can to build a relationship with the service staff. Every maitre d' appreciates reservations as far in advance as possible, so that he may better plan his needs for that night.

I suggest calling in the afternoon or at the beginning of the dinner shift (around 6:00 P.M.), when the maitre d' is likely to be present but unpressured. Ask him his name and introduce yourself as you would to a new acquaintance. This is your first and best opportunity to register with the maitre d' that you might be a pleasant, even special customer. Mention that the restaurant was recommended by a steady customer (by all means, name the friend). If you have special desires (you need a romantic table, want a specific location, are allergic to smoke, or are celebrating your twenty-fifth anniversary), let the restaurant know now; any decent maitre d' will not only accommodate you but work overtime to make the occasion special for you.

But you needn't have a special request to draw the attention of the maitre d' (in small, fancy restaurants, you might even be talking to the proprietor). One of the most effective ways to establish an immediate relationship with the person on the other end of the phone is to do a little homework and mention that you saw an article about the restaurant in the local newspaper or magazine. Name a dish you are looking forward to eating. Restaurateurs, like any other human beings, appreciate sincere compliments. They want to know that you are not seeing your dinner as just another meal.

This first call to the restaurant needn't be a folksy conversation. In fact, it shouldn't be. The person on the other side of the phone probably has many other tasks to perform. Be brief, but pleasant, and you will already have made a friend.

Sometimes there is a problem booking a table in a fancy restaurant. This can be a particular problem if you are on a short vacation or business trip. My advice is to be polite but persistent. Try calling several times and make sure that you identify yourself. Restaurateurs tend to admire people who care enough to make an effort to get into their restaurants. Even the fanciest restaurants do not make it a policy to turn away phone reservations arbitrarily. If it is not possible to get a table, call further in advance next time.

The easiest way to make an enemy of the restaurant is to be a no-show. If you know you must cancel, or even if you are late, let the restaurant know as soon as possible. Cancellations will allow the restaurant to make back its money, as well as to give our above persistent caller a shot at a meal.

## Before the Food Comes

François Martine, manager of the Westwood Marquis Dynasty Room and former maitre d' of Los Angeles' famed La Toque, observes that the way customers act in his restaurant generally mirrors the way they act in the outside world. If customers treated the service staff as human beings, he concludes, there would rarely be a problem. Some customers, however, are afraid to act naturally in a fancy restaurant, feeling they have to put on airs. Some are cowed by the slightest hint of formality.

Relax. When you enter the restaurant, introduce yourself to the host or maitre d'hotel; and if he or she is the person you talked to on the phone, greet him or her by name. Ask for a nice table (and if you have already been promised one, gently remind him). Every restaurateur I talked to insisted they didn't have any *bad* tables, but most establishments have less desirable ones. If you don't make your wishes known, the maitre d' might assume that you don't care or wouldn't appreciate the difference.

New customers in a fancy restaurant are often the most paranoid about being placed at a bad table. It is true that regulars and VIP's *do* tend to be accorded favoritism. Regulars form the financial base for most restaurants, and VIP's are presumed to attract patrons and to recommend the restaurant to other bigwigs. If you have asked pleasantly for a nice table and are given a poor one, I recommend asking nicely whether another table might be available (you might mention specifically what you don't like about the table—its smallness or proximity to the kitchen, for example). If you are led to a mediocre table, why not accept it with grace? If you enjoy your meal and want to return, make sure you talk to the maitre d' and tell him that you loved your meal but would prefer a different table in the future. You might even point out a specific table or area you would prefer. Your bad table problem will disappear.

Some patrons solve all of their problems with a big tip. It is true that a ten-dollar bill can motivate just about any maitre d' to change a seating assignment, but bribes are not the way to gain the respect and affection of most good service personnel, at least in the type of restaurant at which it is truly worth winning. Smiles and enthusiasm will suffice, and be easier on the pocketbook.

Service staffs tend to respond to patrons showing any kind

of effort. A nice meal is a little like dancing. Trying to dance a tango with a partner whose feet are chained to the floor is an exasperating experience. Show that you are interested. Don't be afraid to ask questions about the menu or the preparation of dishes in which you have an interest. The waiter will not think you are ignorant but will know you are interested. Ascertain the name of your waiter and make eye contact with him. You must remember, even if you are slightly intimidated by a fancy restaurant, that a waiter is likely to fear you. Your tips provide his livelihood. It is in his best interest to make sure you are pleased. In fine restaurants especially, the entire staff, from the proprietor down to the busboy, sincerely wants to provide a satisfying experience. They pride themselves on performing excellent service. The good waiter *wants* to please you even without the financial incentive.

A good dancer is sensitive to the needs of his partner. If you find that a waiter is leading you in a certain direction, consider following. If you order the sea bass and the waiter gently suggests the turbot, he may be implying that the bass is not the freshest. He is not chastising you for your choice and it is unlikely that he is trying to push the sea bass. François Martine concedes that in the days before such effective refrigeration, restaurant proprietors used to urge waiters to recommend perishable dishes past the peak of freshness. But now that proper refrigeration guarantees a longer shelf life, this practice has been abandoned.

Particularly if you are unfamiliar with the cuisine of the restaurant, it can be a wonderful experience to let the kitchen order for you. Tell the waiter that you have heard about how wonderful the chef is and would like the chef to orchestrate your meal. Karen Puro, the former chef and co-owner of New York City's famed Dodin Bouffant told us that the staff loved to compose the meals for her patrons. It allowed the chef not only to be creative in selecting the food but to utilize the ingredients that were freshest. Putting your meal in the hands of the kitchen also implies a trust and adventurousness that restaurateurs crave (obviously if you are allergic to or dislike

one or two foods, make sure the waiter knows). Ms. Puro
added that when she received such requests, she had a tendency
to give the customer more food, not wanting to let down an
intrepid diner.

Don't let all of the ritual and rigamarole surrounding wine
selection upset your dining experience. If you know little
about wine, don't fake expertise. Do not hesitate to ask advice
from the sommelier or waiter. It has been our experience that
even in fancy restaurants, they will suggest excellent, moderately priced wines. If you have a price range in mind, let
the service staff know. They won't look down on you for not
being rich (they aren't rich themselves, remember). If the
wine steward does treat you patronizingly, you are probably
in a restaurant that doesn't deserve your patronage: A fancy
restaurant is not necessarily a fine one.

Are the tables with regulars and VIP's getting better food
than you are? Probably, yes. Puro said that in her small
restaurant, the chef generally knew which plate was being
sent to every known customer. It wasn't that unknown customers received bad food, but if one piece of salmon was
clearly nicer looking than another, the regular or the bigwig
would be given the superior piece. But Puro insisted that a
customer needn't be a celebrity to attain favored status: A
regular was treated just as royally as a food critic or business
potentate.

## After the Food Arrives

If you've followed the ground rules I've laid out, chances
are that your meal will proceed beautifully by the time the
food is served. If the food is not to your satisfaction, call the
waiter or captain and inform him. Obviously, if a piece of
meat ordered rare arrives well done, any reputable restaurant
will supply a substitute, but there is a gray area when a dish
is unpleasant and the customer is unsure whether it is *supposed* to taste this way. As long as you are pleasant in manner

while complaining, the service staff is unlikely to be annoyed. In fact, several restaurateurs I talked to indicated that they felt Americans were too hesitant about complaining. Restaurateurs are not concerned about the obnoxious boors, but proprietors worry about the customer who never lets his objections to the food or service be known and then never returns or, even worse, relays his bad feelings about the restaurant to others. In a good restaurant, a complaint will become known to everyone from the waiter to the captain to the maitre d' to the chef—it is often the most useful feedback they receive. For this reason, don't be surprised if the service staff greets your comments with respect and resolve.

The service staff is most likely to grouse about customers who are arrogant or whose actions directly affect their pocketbook. Besides no-shows, poor tippers and cheap customers (such as those who want to share an entree) are most likely to raise the ire of waiters. Ironically, the better the restaurant, the more likely the insensitive diner will get away with this behavior without any overt display of displeasure by the service staff. Still, one can never become a favored regular customer by tipping 10 percent. The most delicate issue in many restaurants is how to deal with the customer who lingers interminably over coffee or after-dinner drinks. If a restaurant can turn over a table every hour and a half instead of every three hours, it can obviously double its gross income (and the waiter can double his tips). In most fancy restaurants, waiters will try to be discreet about coaxing recalcitrant diners to leave. If they do try some subtle ploys (such as asking, for the third time, if they can bring anything else), consider giving up your table. You are not only depriving the restaurant of revenue but other patrons of the chance to be seated promptly.

If you have enjoyed the food, the service, and the ambience of the restaurant, and want even better experiences in the future, you should strive to become a regular. No fancy restaurant can expect most of its customers to come in weekly, or even monthly, but they enjoy receiving patrons known to them at regular intervals (a minimum of three or four times a year). Restaurant staffs enjoy serving regulars for at least five reasons:

1. Regulars are the best advertisements for the restaurant. Nothing is more effective than word-of-mouth advertisers, and no one more quickly spreads the word than regular patrons.
2. Regulars tend to tip better than one-shot customers. There is no incentive for a customer who has no intention of returning to tip generously. Maitre d's, in particular, tend to be tipped more by regulars, who use the gratuity to display appreciation rather than to bribe for specific favors.
3. Returning often is the most sincere compliment possible to a restaurant and its staff. Even the most experienced restaurateurs are exhilarated by the enthusiasm of a regular.
4. Regulars are easier to serve. A good service staff will remember the preferences of a regular customer. It will be easy to please him or her.
5. It is pleasant to be surrounded by friendly, familiar faces. There is a lovely shorthand, an ease and grace, that develops when a patron and restaurant staff have attained true rapport. The good waiter finds pleasure in being of service to other people, as long as the recipients are worthy of the effort.

It takes so little effort to be a worthy customer. Given a chance, most fancy restaurants will try to earn your patronage. If so, you are an automatic winner. If the fancy restaurant insists on being rude, patronizing, or arrogant, you lose by even trying to win. Find a restaurant that deserves you.

# How to Win at Taking Multiple-Choice Tests

HUNDREDS OF COACHING SCHOOLS throughout the country promise to increase their students' scores on SAT's, bar exams, civil service, and other standardized tests. Much to the chagrin of the Educational Testing Service, the largest administrator of standardized tests, these "prep" schools seem to work.

Coaching schools challenge the notion that tests are objective tools. Rather than trying to increase their students' knowledge about the subject matter of the tests, coaching schools have dramatically raised their clients' test scores by focusing on improving students' test-taking skills, even on so-called aptitude tests, which purport to measure not achievement but innate ability.

There hasn't been too much help, though, for the poor schlep who is still in school, taking multiple-choice tests. While the coaching schools have learned how to master the SAT test by performing computer analyses on thousands of previously used questions, there is no money for them in analyzing the idiosyncrasies of your history teacher. Yet your history teacher is likely to be far less sophisticated in composing test questions than the Educational Testing Service and is therefore a much easier "opponent."

It's hard not to sympathize with the lot of the teacher, beset by apathetic (or worse) students, but most teachers would rather confront the blackboard jungle than return to the more numbing world of their own college education classes. With too few exceptions, your teacher was subjected to a combi-

nation of abstract theory and busywork in college, and likely has not been trained in many of the nuts and bolts techniques needed to teach a course. Ask a high-school teacher how much training he has received in preparing tests. More likely than not, the answer will be "none." Your college professor may never have even taken one education class and is even less likely to have been trained in the fine art of composing tests.

While your teacher's training may not have included how to write test questions, he is sure to have been heavily indoctrinated with the principle of "behavioral objectives." The rationale for behavioral objectives is a logical and laudatory one. Proponents of behavioral objectives believe that before a teacher starts a lesson, he should know exactly what he wants his students to learn. In many school systems these objectives are mandated and uniform, leaving individual teachers with little freedom to develop lesson plans. Chances are, the teacher has been instructed to use tests to evaluate whether or not the behavioral objectives of each class have been met.

Although the practice of behavioral objectives was once used mainly in primary education, it has now swept into higher education, particularly in university multisection introductory classes. College administrators love behavioral objectives, for they signify that all students who successfully complete a class have all learned at least *something* in common.

For your purposes, the important thing to know is that even if it seems as if your teacher is rambling on without reason, he is trying to make sure you meet certain behavioral objectives. His tests will be attempts to determine whether you have grasped the concepts that he has been ordered to teach.

Most teachers don't particularly like making up tests. Grading them is even less fun. Although there are sadists in every profession, more likely than not, your teacher wants you to perform well on the test, if only because it validates his success in achieving the behavioral objectives he set out to accomplish at the beginning of the school year.

Follow these twelve tips, and your multiple-choice IQ will

leap. Many of these principles will help you not only in school but on sophisticated exams like SAT's and civil service exams and on other, more poorly constructed tests, such as most states' driver's license exams.

## TIP #1—STUDY

Not a revolutionary tip, perhaps, but a necessary reminder —we didn't promise you a completely free lunch. Don't assume that a multiple-choice exam is a trivia test. Most teachers feel that each multiple-choice question should measure whether or not an important learning objective has been met. Most likely, you are being given a multiple-choice exam rather than an essay exam because it is easier and faster to grade, and because your teacher feels he can measure your grasp of the material as easily with a multiple-choice as an essay format. It is far more important to know why the Confederacy lost the Civil War than to remember the name of General Lee's horse. Don't bother cramming hours before the test, especially if you are stuffing trivia into what is left of your brain. It won't work. Better to follow Tip #2, and spend the hours before the test catching some much-needed sleep.

## TIP #2—WATCH THE BLACKBOARD

The best indicators of the material to be covered on a test are in-class lectures and discussion. Listen to the teacher. Does he repeat certain key words and phrases constantly? If these phrases are ideas, principles, theories—anything abstract—they will be on your test. If not on this test, they will be on your midterm or final. As I mentioned in Tip #1, your teacher's behavioral objectives are much more likely to revolve around important principles rather than trivia—so will your test questions.

A test is a compendium of questions about information your teacher thinks you should know. In class, your teacher will give you obvious clues about what you should know. If a teacher writes a word down on the blackboard, it generally means two things. Either he thinks you are too dumb to know how to spell the word or else he thinks you are too dumb to know how to spell the word *and* thinks that the word is important for you to know. If he writes the word down and underlines it or puts asterisks next to it, you should do the same on your notes. Unlike essay exams, which occasionally ask the student to speculate, evaluate, or apply principles to new fields, multiple-choice tests ask you questions about material you have already covered. If you understand all of the concepts that your teacher underlines, literally or figuratively, in class, you have nothing to worry about on test day.

## Tip #3—Try to Answer the Question Before Reading the Answers

A multiple-choice question is a fill-in question with a crib sheet. When reading a multiple-choice question, try to answer it before looking at the choices (called "alternatives" by testing experts). This is the best way not to be misled by the tempting array of incorrect possibilities (which are called "distracters") with which you will be provided. Think of a multiple-choice exam simply as a fill-in test with alternatives there to bail you out when an answer doesn't come.

## Tip #4—Do the Easy Questions First

It is often difficult to determine whether there will be a time problem on a test. The best strategy is always to complete questions that come easily to you and to skip over problem questions and come back to them. *Don't linger on any one question.* If you find a question that stumps you, cross out the distracters on the exam (if you can't write on the question sheet, make check marks with light pencil next to the alternatives that are likely possibilities). When you return to the question, you will at least be worrying about three possibilities rather than five.

Skipping over troublesome questions and finishing easy questions first accomplishes many things. First, it allows you to score points easily. Since questions that you find easy will score as much credit as hard ones, there is no reason to try for the long bomb when a one-yard plunge will do. Second, finishing easy questions will give you more confidence for tackling the harder ones. It is a lot easier to remember how to compute price-earnings ratios when you are trying to work yourself up from a B to an A rather than from an F to a D. Third, skipping over a question you have already wrestled with gives your mind extra time, consciously or unconsciously, to make connections and refresh memories. Occasionally, you will find when you return to a question that one of the alternatives stands out as correct, even though you aren't sure why you hadn't thought of the answer the first time through. Fourth, and most important, this strategy is a more efficient use of your time. Finishing easy questions first allows you to know how much time can be budgeted for the harder questions.

Be clear about whether all questions are worth the same number of points. The vast majority of teachers do not weight multiple-choice exams, but a few do. Obviously, if a difficult section is worth more points, it might be worth spending more time on these questions initially.

Nowhere is this tip more important than on the SAT test. All the questions are worth the identical amount, yet the difficulty level and time requirements of the different questions vary widely. Within each section, the difficulty of questions is supposed to get progressively higher with each question. This is the most important reason to try to solve the questions in order. In the verbal sections, the reading comprehension questions take much longer to answer than the antonym or analogy questions, yet they are worth no more points. It would be folly to even look at the reading comprehension questions until all the other verbal questions had been tried at least once.

## Tip #5—When the Alternatives Are Numbers, and You Don't Have the Slightest Idea of the Answer, Pick One of the Middle Range of Options

Think of your teacher trying to determine the distracters for a question. She knows that Sergeant Alvin York captured one hundred thirty-two Germans in the Battle of Argonne, and she is so conscious of this fact that she can't quite believe that students will be dumb enough to select an answer much different from that. She is also afraid to make the correct answer too different from the other alternatives, for fear it will stand out (if the choices were, say, 6, 15, 21, and 132). Her solution is usually to make the two extreme possibilities incorrect, so that when you have no idea which number is correct, you should choose one of the middle numbers. This is not a foolproof tip, but it works more often than not.

## Tip #6—When in Doubt, Pick Choice *B* or *C*

In multiple-choice exams with four alternatives, *A* is consistently the least-correct answer. The probable explanation for the phenomenon is that teachers feel that if the student immediately sees the correct answer, he won't even be tempted by the distracters. Choice *D* is the second-least correct answer. Again, this predilection probably reflects an unconscious desire of the teacher to hide the correct answer.

This tip does not apply to standardized tests, which usually scramble alternatives at random in order to avoid exactly this kind of bias.

## Tip #7—Do Not Get Concerned About Patterns of Answers

Myths abound that teachers like to compose tests with answers that fit in neat symmetrical patterns (such as *ABCDABCD* or *ADBDCDDD*). They don't.

## TIP #8—WHEN IN DOUBT, GUESS

Policies vary about penalties for incorrect answers. Some teachers impose no penalty for guessing and merely tally the total correct answers. It is obvious that the correct strategy, then, is always to answer every question, even if it necessitates guessing wildly.

The Educational Testing Service penalizes 25 percent for an incorrect guess on questions with five alternatives. (On questions with four alternatives, a misguess is penalized one-third of a point.) But when you consider that by eliminating only one of the five distracters, you have evened out your chances, you should probably guess anyway. Anytime you can eliminate two distracters, you should definitely guess.

One of the weirdest findings of the coaching schools is that when test-takers do not know the answer for sure but can eliminate all but two distracters, they then tend to select the wrong answer far more than 50 percent of the time. When you think about it, though, this phenomenon makes sense. If you know enough about a subject to rule out three possibilities but not enough to know the correct answer, chances are strong that you will select the alternative you are most familiar with. But if you are attracted to the alternative with which you are familiar, why don't you know the answer? Because it is the wrong answer. For this reason, if you have narrowed down the alternatives to two, it might be the best policy to select against your first instinct.

## TIP #9—ON MATH QUESTIONS, AVOID THE OBVIOUS

No one has less mathematical aptitude than I, but this one tip kept my test scores mediocre rather than pathetic. When confronted with a problem that reads like gobbledygook, avoid the obvious. Many math problems give you two numbers and ask you to find another number. A fictional example: "The base of a Pythagorean triangle, *A*, is 6 feet, and one side, *B*, is 4 feet. What is the length of side *C*?" Most test-takers won't have the slightest idea what a Pythagorean triangle is, let alone how to find the size of one of its sides. What the loser does when confronted with such a problem is to find an easy relationship between the two given numbers. He will add the 6 feet and 4 feet and look for an alternative of 10 feet. Or he will multiply 6 feet times 4 feet and guess 24 feet.

The correct answer to a math problem is seldom the result of adding, multiplying, subtracting, or dividing the two given numbers. If you have nothing else to go on, there are worse strategies than simply eliminating the result of any arithmetical combination of the two given numbers; on most multiple-choice exams, this will eliminate at least two distracters, already giving you a better-than-even chance of scoring positively on the question. Precisely because losers tend to look for the easiest possible relationships between given numbers, answers such as 10 feet and 24 feet would be the most popular distracters for this question. Once you have eliminated these out of hand, the diagram will often provide clues as to which of the remaining alternatives is correct.

### TIP #10—SELECT COMPOUND ANSWERS THAT INCLUDE THE SIMPLE OPTIONS YOU ARE MOST SURE ABOUT

Some multiple-choice exams include compound alternatives, the kind where alternative *D* might be "*A* and *C*" or "all of the above." Although at first compound alternatives seem more difficult, they actually are often easier to diagnose. Remember, the compound alternative allows you to be correct with only partial information. For example, if you know that option *C* is incorrect, then you can rule out not only *C* but also *D* ("*A* and *C*"). When you are positive that *C* is correct but are unsure about *A*, it is generally better to guess that *A* is correct as well.

Many teacher-composed tests have only a few questions with compound alternatives, most commonly "none of the above" and "all of the above." Consider this phenomenon from the teacher's point of view. Why would a teacher only include "all of the above" or "none of the above" on a few questions? Because the most difficult part of constructing a multiple-choice test is thinking up effective distracters. When a teacher runs dry of ideas, the easiest path is to tack on an "all" or "none" distracter. The average loser at tests tends to answer *D* whenever he doesn't know the answer, but generally, when there are only a few compound alternatives on the test, he'd be better off trying one of the first three alternatives.

There is one exception to this general principle. When questions are posed directly about the meaning or importance of abstract principles discussed in class, if two of the alternatives seem reasonable, "all of the above" is probably the correct answer. The teacher, perhaps too straightforwardly, is trying to test several behavioral objectives directly in one question.

## TIP #11—RECHECK ALL ANSWERS

Expecially when you have a separate answer sheet, be sure to recheck your answers, not so much to rethink the content of your decisions as to ensure that you have transcribed your selections accurately on the answer sheet. In many instances SAT-takers have carelessly left one answer blank and marked each subsequent answer for the question that preceded it.

## TIP #12—LEARN HOW TO READ MULTIPLE-CHOICE EXAMS

Whether the beginning of a test item is in the form of a question ("With what demographic group did Walter Mondale's presidential campaign have the most success?") or an incomplete statement ("Walter Mondale had the most success in his presidential campaign in attrracting . . ."), the part that presents the problem is called the "stem." If you can learn how to read the stem, as well as the distracters and alternatives, from the teacher's point of view, you have a running start toward performing as well as someone who knows the subject matter better than you do. Although most grizzled students have probably absorbed many of the tips above, few have consciously analyzed the diction in test questions. The Educational Testing Service has gone to great pains to neutralize the biases of the wording in their tests, and to a large extent, they have succeeded, but even they are not immune, and your teacher or employer is almost certain to fall prey to the weaknesses discussed below.

1. *In multiple-choice tests, the longest alternative tends to be true.* What is the teacher's biggest fear when composing a test? She is afraid that because of sloppy word choice, she will have to throw out a question for being unclear, unfair, or worst of all, inaccurate. A winning test-taker looks for signs of uneasiness in the teacher as surely as a poker player looks for twitches in other players that might indicate a big hand or a big bluff. One of the ways in which many teachers betray the correct alternative is by making the correct choice longer than the distracters. Usually, this is because the teacher is trying to be fair in describing the correct alternative and doesn't care as much about portraying distracters as vividly.

On true-false tests, however, short statements tend to be true, since it usually takes more words to successfully lull students into taking the bait.

2. *Absolute statements tend to be false.* Many sentences contain implied absolute statements. The phrase, "dogs are mammals" really means "*All* dogs are mammals." Test-makers try to avoid absolute statements of any kind, for if a test-taker can come up with one possible exception to an absolute statement, an otherwise true statement is invalidated. When you encounter a word that clearly makes a statement absolute, it is usually a warning flag telling you the statement is not true. Below are the most common words that are used to denote absolutism. When they are contained in an alternative, the choice is usually incorrect; when they are contained in a true-false question, the question is usually false:

| all | necessarily | none |
| always | necessary | only |
| every | never | without exception |
| must | no | |

3. A corollary to the above rule: *Statements with qualifiers tend to be true.* Because teachers are aware of the problem with using words that signify absolute statements, most teachers will couch their correct answers with qualifiers to ensure that a snotty kid won't find one exception to render a statement untrue. Qualifiers allow for exceptions—that is their purpose —so they are usually an indication that a statement is true. You wouldn't say "*Most* dogs are mammals." Probably not. But most teachers (note how I've qualified my statement) try to play fair by qualifying true statements. They realize that there may be exceptions to principles you have learned, and will reflect this recognition on the test, even if these exceptions weren't talked about in class.

The following fudge expressions all tend to make the statement that they accompany true, both on multiple-choice alternatives and on true-false questions:

| about | hardly ever | rarely |
| almost | (un)likely | seldom |
| approximately | many | several |
| around | most | some |
| commonly | occasionally | sometimes |
| few | often | usually |
| (in)frequently | probably | |

4. *Positively loaded alternatives tend to be correct.* Although they know that the primary purpose of a test is to measure a student's comprehension of material, many teachers also want their tests to be a learning experience for the student. This is one of the reasons correct alternatives tend to be longer and more carefully detailed than distracters. If you have a teacher who wants tests to be a learning experi-

ence, he is likely to want you to learn what is important and uplifting, rather than what is depressing and downbeat. Suppose you encounter the following question:

What was the major contribution of the Lincoln-Roosevelt League?
A) Financed Abraham Lincoln's presidential campaign
B) Planted cherry blossoms in Washington, D.C.
C) Worked for social justice after the Great Depression
D) Lobbied for gun control in the U.S. Senate
E) None of the above

You have no idea what the Lincoln-Roosevelt League was. By simply adding the principles you have already learned, you can solve this question. First of all, *E* is most unlikely to be right. The teacher seems to have resorted to the "none of the above" option, as previously discussed, because he is running out of even marginally good alternatives (*A* is patently ridiculous because neither Roosevelt was likely to have a League named after him before he was born). This leaves *B*, *C*, and *D* as possibilities. When you have narrowed down the field of alternatives and are stuck, it is often helpful to reread the question. Note that you are asked about the League's "major contribution."

*Major* is a qualifier, suggesting that the organization had other accomplishments. The word *contribution* strongly hints that your teacher feels that the League's undertakings were positive and important. With these inferences in mind, could the correct answer be anything but *C*? Would lobbyists for gun control be described as "contributors?" Would your teacher really care if you knew who planted the cherry blossoms in Washington, D.C.? If one alternative seems to be more positively worded than the others, it is usually the correct choice.

5. *Fancy words or technical phraseology tend to be correct.* Your teacher feels safe in the jargon of his field and tends to forget that to the student it sounds like a foreign language.

What is osmosis?
A) Diffusion through a semipermeable membrane
B) An ape in the gorilla family
C) A plant
D) A measuring device

Again, the teacher lacks imagination in constructing distracters. He figures that if you can't understand a distracter, you won't guess it; but would any student faced with the long, jargon-filled option of A not realize it has to be the answer?

6. *Check to make sure that the stem and the alternatives of each question are parallel in construction, and that they make sense grammatically.* Some teachers are so lazy that they don't bother to make all the distracters parallel in construction with the stem. In the above question, for example, you can eliminate B for this reason alone. If the answer were "an ape in the gorilla family," the question would be "What is *an* osmosis?" If you see a stem such as "The fruit Adam ate was an . . .", the correct answer had better start with a vowel.

7. *If two alternatives are very close in meaning, both are probably* not *the correct answer.* Most teachers want to avoid confusion and complaints that they are nit-picking in their answers.

8. *If two or more of the alternatives are all-inclusive, eliminate the other choices as possibilities.* If one group can be subsumed by a larger group, forget the smaller group. Here is an illustration:

Which group provided Walter Mondale with the most popular votes in the 1984 election?
A) Women
B) Men
C) Liberals
D) Minnesotans

A careful reading of the question will indicate that although a disproportionately high percentage of liberals and Minnesotans voted for Mondale, there is no way that either could account for as many popular votes as the much larger pools of men and women. If you happen to know that Mondale was more popular with women than men, you will answer the question correctly. At least you have been able to eliminate two distracters immediately and have a much better chance of guessing correctly.

It is as much your teacher's responsibility to construct fair and unbiased exam questions as it is your responsibility to prepare for the test. If you happen to encounter a teacher savvy enough to have learned these rules, you must rely more on good old Tip #1: Study. Tests would be less obnoxious to take if we felt that they actually measured skills and knowledge that was important. Too often, they merely measure trivia recall.

If you seem to have little aptitude for taking tests, and even reading this chapter doesn't improve your scores, take heart. We all find out, after we leave school, that in real life, our tests are all open book.

**For more information:**

*None of the Above: Behind the Myth of Scholastic Aptitude*, David Owen (Boston: Houghton Mifflin, 1985), a fascinating account of the Educational Testing Service, and an eye-opening report on the secrets of the coaching schools that have taken on ETS.

*Constructing Achievement Tests*, Norman Gronlund (Englewood Cliffs, NJ: Prentice-Hall, 1983). Learn how to take tests by learning how teachers and institutions are taught to construct them.

# How to Win at a Tax Audit

MOST TAXPAYERS ARE so frightened at the prospect of an Internal Revenue Service audit that they are quite content to get out of the audit alive without a detour to Sing Sing. "Winning" an audit, to them, is a foolish fantasy.

If winning an audit can be defined as the taxpayer not having to pay additional taxes, rest assured that you absolutely *can* win your tax audit, and it need not even be a traumatic experience. There are so many misconceptions about tax audits that it is no wonder the average American feels he doesn't have a chance.

## Six Misconceptions About Tax Audits

1. *They are going to throw me in jail.* First of all, the IRS itself is not going to send you to jail. They don't have the power to do so. In most cases, the IRS would rather get your money in the treasury than your body in the slammer. If the criminal justice system prosecuted every taxpayer who was suspected of padding his deductions, we would need more judges than civil service workers.

The main purpose of auditing most personal returns is to deter dishonesty. Our tax system depends upon voluntary compliance. Every time someone regales his friends with the gruesome details of his audit, scores of people are, the IRS hopes, scared into being truthful in their tax returns. For the

IRS to receive the maximum amount of revenue, the IRS must instill fear of the auditing process.

It just isn't cost effective for the IRS to prosecute the average expense-account chiseler. The IRS is practical enough to realize that its main aim must be to make that would-be chiseler honest on his return. The audit is its only effective weapon.

2. *Nobody ever wins a tax audit.* Not true. About 75 to 80 percent of audits result in more tax. About 5 percent result in a refund. There is no change in the taxes of 15 to 20 percent of the taxpayers who are audited.

As you will see, the IRS chooses to audit returns that are most suspicious, and yet about one-quarter of those audited do not pay any additional tax. Some cynics believe that auditors are on a quota system and are under pressure to collect some money on every audit. This simply isn't true. Revenue agents are subjected to certain pressures that can actually help you during your audit. We'll talk about these later (see "Know Your Opponent").

3. *The IRS loves to dig up old returns and audit them.* Except in cases of suspected fraud, there is a three-year statute of limitations on returns. In most cases, audits are performed six months to one year after filing, and if later than that, usually only because the local IRS office has fallen behind in its paper work. As an ex-IRS employee so eloquently phrased it, "The Examination Division is no more fond of 'old' returns [filed more than twenty months ago] than it is of dead fish." One of the reasons the IRS is reluctant to drag out two-year-old returns is that it puts pressure on it to settle the case before the statute of limitations runs out.

4. *If the IRS is auditing me this year, it will reopen all of my old tax returns and dig for more dirt.* Your auditor does have easy computer access to your returns for the two previous years and has the right to challenge any of your deductions

for those years. In many cases, your tax history might resolve some of the agent's doubts and questions about suspicious deductions. More likely, however, your old returns will raise more problems (e.g., "How can this person who has made $15,000 a year for the last three years have $18,000 in business expenses every year?").

In practice, however, old returns are not consulted that often for one simple reason: It's too much work and extra time for the revenue agent. Usually, only when a tax return arouses deep suspicion about the veracity of the taxpayer are the old returns pulled.

5. *An audit takes forever, will delve into my private life, and will be very unpleasant.* Most likely, an audit of your personal return will take approximately one to two hours, will not delve deeply into your private life, and will be more boring than traumatic. In most cases, audits of personal returns are confined to just a few specific questioned items. Unless new suspicions are aroused at the time of the audit, it is most unlikely that the examiner will train a flashlight in your eyes and bellow, "Where were you the night of April 14!?" With few exceptions, audits are conducted at an antiseptic local IRS office. They rarely will want to invade your home.

6. *Once you are audited by the IRS, you are put on a "hit list," and are likely to be monitored indefinitely.* Untrue. In fact, sometimes an audit can work to your future advantage. If you have successfully passed an audit of any particular issue (for example, your medical expenses for 1986), you would not be subject to an audit *on that issue* for the next two years. This policy of the IRS is particularly helpful to those who annually have one deduction that seems, at first glance, to be particularly large to the IRS.

The important point to remember is that it is highly unlikely that the IRS will stage a vendetta against any individual taxpayer. Tax returns are chosen for auditing by a computer program called DIF, or Discriminate Information Function. DIF selects returns that display a good chance of exhibiting "tax errors" and most important, show potential for additional revenue owed. DIF automatically weights the different deductions and compares them to the returns of others in the same profession, marital status, and income range in your geographical area. If one of your deductions is a little high, and others are average, it is unlikely that a human will ever even consider your return for auditing. The DIF program reduces your entire return to one number. A score of 300, unlike bowling, isn't a perfect score. It is the DIF score that will start to arouse the interest of the IRS. A 400 DIF score will almost certainly be audited.

The computer doesn't differentiate between a high DIF score realized by one extremely high deduction and one that features several moderately high deductions. If your DIF score is high enough to reach the "semifinals," it means that a human being will scour your return to see what interested the computer in the first place. Perhaps you earn $25,000 a year and yet claim you have contributed $10,000 to charity. Not many people donate 40 percent of their gross income to charitable causes. If you include documentation from a museum that it has received this original oil painting from you, along with the appraisal of a reputable art dealer who informs the IRS that your dear departed grandmother bought it from him thirty years ago for $10,000, and that it is now worth $100,000 (art, unfortunately, for tax purposes is only worth the purchase price), you are likely never to hear from the IRS. The computer has flagged your return because your deduction is unusual. The IRS wants proof that you have made the contribution and that the art is indeed worth $10,000. They aren't interested in knowing, and are unlikely to question, why you were willing to unload a $100,000 painting for free.

Although the charitable contribution might have been the element that alerted the DIF program to your return, the IRS agent may examine any issue in your return if he wishes. He is not privy to the details of the DIF formula, and the computer does not tell him why your return was selected for examination.

Are there certain types of people most likely to be audited? Absolutely. The IRS is funded by the federal government and must constantly justify its existence by proving that its auditing process is a cost-effective mechanism. It is not difficult to figure out, then, that people with large incomes are much more likely to be audited than the average wage-earner. Anyone with an income over $200,000 is likely to have his return examined by a human, not necessarily because wealthy people are more likely to abuse the tax system, but because the amount of money the IRS can collect when they do abuse the tax system is much more substantial.

You have a much greater chance of being audited if you live in a big city than if you live in a rural area. Residents of New York and Los Angeles are the two most audited in the country.

Anyone who conducts an unconventional business, particularly a cash business, is more likely to be audited. The IRS is also interested in mail-order and barter businesses, which have abused the tax system in the past.

The IRS compiles what it calls a "problem preparers" list, a compendium of incompetent and unethical tax preparers. This list is not made public, yet if your accountant is on that list, it can automatically trigger an audit. It is crucial that the person who helps you with your return is not on that list. We'll talk about how to hire the right tax preparer a little later.

Some masochistic souls still file their own returns. If you use the short form or do not have many outlandish deductions or take the standard deduction, you are unlikely to have problems. However, if you fill out a complicated return without the help of a preparer, it may arouse the interest of the IRS. The IRS doesn't necessarily feel you are more dishonest than an accountant but may feel you are less likely to be accurate in your computations than a professional. Most important, the IRS will, rightly or wrongly, assume that a competent preparer will insist on you supplying some documentation before taking large deductions. If the IRS examiner is familiar with your preparer and respects his work, you may be given the benefit of the doubt. Although the DIF program won't give you a free ride simply because you have a good accountant, the human examiner is free to use his best judgment in weighing the ethics and competency of your preparer. It could make the difference in whether or not you are audited.

Some people are afraid to make claims for tax refunds, fearing that it may open an old can of worms and trigger an audit. They're right. The IRS examiner will not necessarily mistrust your claim, but he will have to look over your return before processing it. If your return is honest, you have absolutely nothing to fear and no reason not to try for the refund.

Before I discuss the specific deductions that tend to trigger audits, it might be wise to add one word of warning to those who see deduction items on their tax return as a chance to try their hand at creative writing. If you are going to lie about a deduction, which we do not advise for practical as well as moral reasons, don't be so stupid as to list your total deductions in round numbers. The IRS examiner is unlikely to believe that your business entertainment cost you exactly $500 and your medical expenses exactly $1,500. At worst, the examiner will think you are committing fraud. At best, he will think you made a nice estimate the day before you filed the return. In either case, you will be audited, because the examiner will assume that you do not have the receipts to defend your claim.

There are certain types of deductions that the IRS has found most likely to be abused. These vary from year to year. The tightening of restrictions on tax shelters has led to less abuse in this area, but the IRS still takes a hard look at "legal" tax shelters. Here are ten deductions that can serve as red flags. There is no reason not to claim a legitimate deduction in any of these areas. If you have the proper documentation to back your claim, you have nothing to worry about, but large deductions are likely to arouse the interest of all red-blooded IRS examiners. In no particular order:

1. *Medical deductions.* This should be one of the easiest of all deductions to document, but the IRS has found that many taxpayers have a hazy idea of exactly what medical expenses are deductible.
2. *Casualty losses.* This is probably the number one red flag to the IRS, because it combines all of the elements that make the IRS salivate. Casualty losses usually combine large dollar amounts, an estimate and a loss that is hard to prove in the first place. (The IRS tends to be suspicious about the veracity of those making the estimate and about the dollar amount of most estimates; any deduction that requires an estimate, including charitable contributions, will be carefully examined once flagged.) It is absolutely essential to keep original receipts of all big-ticket items that you buy for your home or office. The value of many items must be determined by the original purchase price. Although you may be insuring a diamond ring for its replacement cost, the IRS will be interested in how much you paid for it.
3. *Tax shelters.* Because the IRS has totally eliminated the deductibility of so many tax shelters, they are concentrating now on the legitimacy of currently allowable ones. In particular, they look at how much money you have to put up versus what you will get back in return. Any time you claim more than a 2-to-1 ratio, the IRS is likely to be suspicious.
4. *Depreciation.* Particularly if you filed without the help of a preparer, the IRS is likely to look carefully at depreciation claims, not because it is an area of heavy fraud but because so many taxpayers simply don't understand how to depreciate items properly.
5. *Bad debts and interest-free loans to relatives.* Very strict laws govern what constitutes an enforceable bad

debt or a deductible interest-free loan. You may have been genuinely stiffed by your ex-best-friend, but unless you have fulfilled all of the obligations under the law, you can't claim a deduction. Rightly or wrongly, the IRS is likely to cast a jaundiced eye, or at least a doubting eye, at business transactions conducted among family members.

6. *Hobby losses, vacation rentals, and second homes.* A minefield of abuses. You had better back up all your claims.

7. *Home office.* Same as above. Even if you have a legitimate office in your home, and it is clearly necessary for your work, make sure that you don't take an unrealistic fraction of your total housing payment for the office. Not many two-story homes consist of one-third office space.

8. *Auto expenses, entertainment, and gift expenses.* This is an area that is often padded at the last minute. Taxpayers assume they can get away with a little undocumented expense here, and they probably can. Just remember, though, that if these expenses tally higher than normal for others in your profession, the DIF program will flag your return and you will have to prove all of these claims.

9. *Educational travel.* This deduction is often abused and audited because the definition of what is "educational" is open to many interpretations.

10. *Financial losses.* The IRS examiner is a wage-earner. He may wonder how you have been able to eat when you have earned $15,000 in the year, have nothing in the way of interest earnings, and yet have spent $40,000 on "legitimate" deductions, when he has barely been able to scrape along on a $25,000 income and virtually no deductions. Perhaps you have been the lucky recipient of an interest-free loan from your Uncle Harry. Perhaps you have stashed $200,000 in cash under your mattress and decided to blow some money. All things

are possible, but the IRS are curious folks and will want to hear your side of the story.

With the IRS alert to so many red flags, our strategy will be to win at the audit by not being audited in the first place. If you should be audited, you will be able to enter the fray confident that you will win. Your strategy will consist of a three-pronged attack:

1. *Be extremely aggressive about taking deductions, but scrupulously honest.* Do not let the IRS' skepticisms about various deductions deter you from claiming them. Claim any deductions that you think have a good chance of being allowed. But don't cheat. Always report *100 percent* of your income. Just because you have not received a W–2 form for some freelance work does not mean that the IRS is incapable of tracking down your income source. Unreported income is the item most likely to interest the IRS in prosecuting you for tax fraud. Almost any other disagreement on a tax form can be viewed as a difference in interpretation; unreported income is seen by the IRS as a fraud, unless the amount is piddling.

Generally speaking, if a deduction is disallowed, the worst that can happen to you is that you will pay interest on the money owed. You have had use of that money in the meantime, which is one of the reasons it pays to be aggressive in claiming deductions as long as you know you have been honest and that an audit will not reveal new sources of income or a lack of evidence to support your deduction claims.

2. *Hire the right preparer.* For most individuals who itemize, it is probably best to get help in preparing your return. A competent accountant who has mastered the yearly tinkering with the arcane tax codes can save you hundreds or even thousands of dollars.

Unfortunately, there are many incompetent and dishonest preparers. No one can stop an unemployed aluminum siding salesman from setting up shop as a tax preparer. Although a CPA degree is no guarantee of excellence, if you cannot obtain recommendations from friends, hiring a CPA might not be a bad idea. At the very least, customers have recourse when they have a problem with their preparer, and the prospect of peer-group review of the preparer's ethics tend to make CPA's a safer bet. Of course, a lofty degree will not help you at an audit if your return isn't solid. IRS agents will not be cowed by a CPA from a blue-chip firm.

You are going to want a preparer who works on taxes all year long. There are at least three reasons for this. First, a good tax preparer will want to talk to you in the fall to find out whether it is advantageous to take certain deductions in this year or the next. A good preparer will want to help you *plan* your taxes and not merely serve as a walking calculator. Second, if you do get audited, it won't be helpful if your preparer is now selling waterbeds in Marin County. Unless you know the intricacies of your return as well as the preparer, it is important to be able to return to the person, not just the firm, that completed your return, to justify all of your deductions. Third, most of the big chains of tax preparers are extremely conservative in their approach. Too conservative. The main reason they can offer to accompany you to your audit for free and/or pay additional penalties is because they are so unaggressive in their claims that their returns rarely get audited. Although these storefront operations tend to be considerably cheaper than full-time preparers, they are not a good value unless they can save you as much money on your tax return as an accountant.

If you use the short form, take the standard deduction, and are unlikely to be chosen for a segment of "Lifestyles of the Rich and Famous," chances are you can fill out your return yourself or take it to any of the inexpensive tax-preparation operations. The DIF computer will not penalize you for preparing your own return, or for choosing H&R Block instead of a big accounting firm. But if DIF has singled you out, an examiner will probably assume that a competent tax preparer has seen receipts before claiming a sizable casualty loss. When you have prepared your own, the examiner can't make that assumption.

3. *Document every deduction carefully.* One accountant we talked to has a simple policy before each audit. He writes down the total dollar amount of every deduction he has claimed for his client on one side of a page of paper. On the other side, he lists the total dollar amount of documentation (in the form of canceled checks, receipts, diary notations, etc.) for each deduction. If the two sides match, he expects not to drop one additional cent in the lap of the IRS. If you follow the advice of anything in this chapter, let it be this: Keep all of your receipts, note what the receipt is for, make sure it is dated, and file it away in an accordion box separated by categories.

The onus of documentation for claimed deductions is totally on the taxpayer. The IRS examiner may believe that you donated $200 to the United Fund, but if you have no proof that you did, you are unlikely to receive your deduction. Some wrangling between the IRS and taxpayers is about interpretation of law, but the vast majority of discrepancies are caused by inadequate documentation of claims that would be granted easily if the taxpayer could prove his or her case.

The more specific and comprehensive your documentation is, the more likely an examiner will be to let a little lapse go. When an examiner sees a diary of business expenses with the explanation, "Larry, $33" she has no idea whether Larry is a client of yours. Diaries should state not only who you saw and how much you spent, but where you ate, when you ate, and what the specific business purpose of the dinner was. And because your dinner cost more than $25, you should have a receipt for that dinner anyway. The IRS isn't interested in nickel and diming you for business meals, but they do want to feel confident that your diary was filled out contemporaneously during the year and not after you found out that you were going to be audited. If most of your documentation is excellent, the IRS will be more likely to let you get away with a few "Larry, $33"s. The IRS is under no obligation to allow you an undocumented deduction just because you have a verbal explanation for it.

In her excellent book, *How to Survive a Tax Audit*, Mary L. Sprouse recommends bringing your documentation for each questioned deduction in a separate envelope, using an adding machine to total the amount of receipts you had for each category, and stapling the adding-machine tape to the outside of the envelope. "The auditor will check the receipts against your tape and write down your total. If she finds your totals are trustworthy, she will begin to accept them without checking."

Be careful not to bring in too much documentation. Specifically, don't bring in receipts for deductions for which the IRS has not expressed interest. Your strategy will be to confine the audit only to the areas which the IRS has told you they wish to examine.

At times, you may wish to append to your return a letter explaining the circumstances surrounding a deduction on your return that you know is abnormal and may trigger the DIF program. If you earn $25,000 and have claimed you donated $10,000 to charity, DIF might red-flag your return. If you attach the proper documentation, photocopies of both sides of your check, and perhaps a short explanation, you can often preempt an audit before it begins. Your explanation will *not* trigger an audit in the first place, since the DIF program will evaluate your return before a human being ever reads your explanation.

One other tactic might decrease your odds of being audited: filing as close to the April 15 deadline as possible. As you might expect, very few taxpayers file their returns in January, some because they do not yet have their W–2 forms in hand, many more because they are procrastinating or want to avoid paying additional tax until the last minute. Most taxpayers wait until within the last month to file.

Some experts, such as ex-IRS official Paul Strassels, believe that by filing late, when the IRS is swamped with returns, a marginal return that might be audited in February might be passed up when there are more obvious targets to pursue. The IRS denies that this is true.

## When You Are Audited

Even if you follow the splendid advice in this book, you may still be audited. Nobody is safe from the prospect of an IRS audit, because the IRS carries out a program called the Taxpayer Compliance Measurement Program (TCMP) in which randomly selected Americans are chosen and given a comprehensive examination—a dreaded line-by-line audit. There are two purposes for this type of audit. One is to scare the heebie-jeebies out of us. It is assumed that anyone receiving a TCMP audit will complain about it to several hundred other people over the course of his lifetime and that these hearsay tales of horror act as an effective deterrent to potential wrong-doers.

The second and most important purpose of the TCMP audit is to compile information to provide the IRS with data regarding the average level of deductions for citizens in various professions, income levels, and demographic groups. The information compiled in the TCMP program helps set the trigger levels for the DIF program. The level of proof needed to claim deductions is extremely high on TCMP audits, not so much because the IRS wants to collect the extra money, but because the IRS wants assurance that their DIF targets are statistically valid.

Do not worry about a TCMP audit, for now. Chances are, with normal luck, you will never undergo one. Let's assume that you get a note, like most folks, from your friendly IRS examiner informing you that they would like to discuss three items on last year's return. The letter will ask you to bring documentation relevant to those areas and inform you that if

you wish, you may bring along a representative or send a
representative in your place.

## Who Should Go to an Audit?

This is one area where there is little agreement, but there
are three distinct schools of thought, and here are their valid
arguments.

1. *The taxpayer should not go to the audit.* If the taxpayer
does not trust his preparer, he should hire another preparer.
If he does trust his preparer the taxpayer should stay home
the day of the audit. All the taxpayer can do at an audit is to
screw up, usually by volunteering information that will open
up a new can of worms:

"I see that you attended a business convention in Aca-
pulco, Mr. Taxpayer," says Ms. Examiner. "What day did the
convention end?"

"Friday afternoon," Mr. Taxpayer replies.

"I see that you took off your expenses through Sunday
night."

"Well, uh. I stayed over the weekend to talk to a few
potential clients. And my wife wanted a longer visit with her
family."

"But you wrote your wife's trip off as a business expense?"

"Umm. Well, you see, she was at the convention most of
the time. Of course, she did a little shopping and some visiting
with the relatives, but she was a real, ummm, asset to me,
and umm . . ."

Mr. Taxpayer has dug himself into a hole from which he
will not recover.

2. *The taxpayer should go to the audit alone.* It usually
costs you money to hire your preparer to accompany you or
to represent you at the audit. He may well save you some
money but not enough to cover the costs of his services.

If you have been honest, what do you have to fear? The IRS agent wants to size you up, so that he will be able to see whether to forgive slight lapses in documentation.

Even if your examination does not produce the intended result, you now understand the issues of your case and can hire your preparer to represent you during the appeals process. At worst, you have lost a little time by flying solo first.

3. *The taxpayer should go along with his preparer to the audit.* The auditor wants you there not only so that he can assess your honesty but because if there is a simple question he wants clarified that the preparer cannot answer he will be able to process your examination more quickly.

Even the most honest preparer might do a better job with his client present. He might settle a little less easily with you there. On the other hand, a less-than-honest preparer might run up his time during the audit (most accountants charge by the hour) if you were absent.

This approach combines the best features of both of the above schools. The preparer can do most of the talking, can deflect potential problems because of a greater knowledge of tax law, and can handle unforeseen technical questions that may arise at the audit. He can also supervise his client and keep the client from putting foot into mouth. But the client also has the opportunity to assure himself that the preparer is doing a good job and to assuage any fears that the IRS examiner may have that he is anything less than honest.

Clearly, all three arguments have merit. If the success of your audit is likely to hinge on questions of interpretation of tax provisions rather than on matters of proof or documentation, it is essential to have representation. If you feel confident that you have absolutely no skeletons in your closet and can prove the validity of all of your questioned deductions, you probably will not be hurt representing yourself, especially since you can bring in representation to help you with appeals.

Most of all, you should analyze your own personality frankly.

Can you really stay cool through an adversarial proceeding in which your honesty may be implicitly questioned? Can you shut up when there is nothing to be gained by talking? If you were an accountant would *you* want you there?

If you think that you might want to go to your audit, you will need to know a little bit about your adversary before you determine how you should act on the day of the examination. He will carry the title, "office auditor," and examines individual returns and small to medium-size businesses. (Auditors who examine partnership and corporation returns often make field trips to examine books and are called "revenue agents.")

Although your office auditor is on the lowest rung of the IRS ladder, he has complete authority to resolve your audit without any second-guessing from above. He has no dollar quota to meet, but he does have one strong pressure—to close cases as soon as possible. The IRS is understaffed, and your auditor will want to resolve your case as quickly as you do. This actually enhances your negotiating position if you are found to have some liability. Since he wants to wrap up your examination at one sitting if at all possible, you may find him receptive to a little bargaining.

IRS employees are not ogres. In fact, they are remarkably similar to other human beings. As a group, auditors tend not to be overly ambitious types. They have chosen a job with great security and benefits but only so-so pay and advancement opportunities. They are not auditing you because they are jealous that you make more money than they do, and it is highly unlikely they will resent you for deducting more money for expenses than they make for salary.

Auditors are trained to be dispassionate, since they must confront some taxpayers who are rabidly angry and others who are morbidly frightened. They have seen it all. You are not going to intimidate an auditor and you are not going to become his best friend. A good receipt will work much better than a winning smile.

The auditor is just as wary about you as you are about him. You should assuage his two biggest fears: that your records will be horribly disorganized, which will mean an endless audit, and that you will be unpleasant.

You are going to be highly organized, preparing for the audit by following my recommendation of having some form of documentation for every deduction you have claimed. You are going to be friendly and pleasant but businesslike.

Remember when you were in school and the teacher asked a question and your sole desire in life was that he would not single you out to answer? If you were good at eluding his grasp, use those skills again. Your goal is to meld into the crowd. Do not be Miss Congeniality or Big Man on Campus. Be a bore.

It is just as important in an audit as in the Army, to never, *never*, volunteer information. Don't try to be "helpful." If the auditor asks you a yes-or-no question, answer "yes" or "no." Allow the auditor to take control of the audit. If you try to steer the auditor away from a particularly vulnerable area in your return, he is likely to head straight for the jugular. Letting the auditor take control of the audit makes him feel more comfortable and confident, and he will probably feel that you are relaxed and not defensive, which is how innocent people usually act. At the very least, following the auditor's lead is certain to make your audit go more quickly.

If it is clear that you are going to owe additional tax and you do not agree with the amount of the assessment, it is important not to tell the auditor about your intention to file an appeal until the end of the audit. He will have no motive to bargain on other points if he knows you are going to appeal one of his earlier decisions.

Similarly, if in the course of your preparation for the audit, you find an expense or deduction that you failed to declare on your return, wait until the very end of the audit to bring it to the attention of the auditor. Some ill-informed taxpayers think that by coming in with a new bargaining chip, they can trade their old unlawful deduction for a new one. It doesn't work like that. If you walk into your audit and proceed to slap receipts for rediscovered expense items, you are more likely to raise the suspicion of the auditor and be subject to a review of your entire return. Wait until the end of the audit, when you have presumably built up some trust with the auditor, to raise the subject of a new deduction. If it is valid, you will get your refund.

If you are unhappy with the results of your audit, you still have several paths to pursue. Before a formal appeal, you can attend an informal conference with a second auditor or the group manager above your first auditor. Your tax preparer (or any representative) can plead your case before this informal appeal if you wish, but it should be the same person who filled out your return. If you lose the initial argument, the appeal process becomes much more formalized and positions tend to harden, since the IRS considers time lost on arguing cases money lost. This is why the IRS likes to settle cases and tends to prosecute criminally only flagrant offenders who have bilked the government out of lots of money.

When we visit a loved one in the hospital, we might find the high jinks of the staff in questionable taste. How can they be joking around when our loved one is sick? How can they laugh when they are around such misery? They joke around, of course, because they are human beings who have the same psychological needs and quirks that everyone else has. Because their work involves so much stress, they may need to be "insensitive" more than most people.

You may find your auditor lacks empathy. Your audit may seem like a momentous, precipitous event in your life. Chances are, your audit is a crashing bore to your auditor. Whereas the revenue agent has a chance to snare millions in a corporate field audit, your auditor is reduced to haggling over hundreds or a few thousands of dollars about documentation on business expenses. You simply can't expect someone who has processed thousands of returns, who has listened to almost as many excuses, to become emotionally involved in your case. Your auditor isn't your friend and isn't your enemy. He is essentially a fact-checker.

Let's face it. If you are willing to be honest and willing to exert a little bit of effort to document your expenses, by keeping all of your receipts and dumping them in an accordian file, noting unreceipted expenses in a diary, and then, once a year, compiling the information, you are going to have no trouble whatsoever in your audit. Although the audit may be the scariest subject in this book, it is one of the easiest to win.

**For more information:**

There are plenty of tax-return guides filled with useful strategies for reducing your tax liability. The most famous, a perennial best-seller, is *J.K. Lasser's Your Income Tax*, which is thorough and accurate but daunting in its comprehensiveness and textbooklike layout. If you can master all of this book, you either didn't need it in the first place or should consider a career move into accounting.

Most people could probably settle for a free publication, *Your Federal Income Tax* (also known as Publication 17), published by your friends at the Internal Revenue Service. The only problem with Publication 17 is that you are learning about tax strategy from a source that has its own bias. The manual doesn't attempt to withhold information about deductions, but it does not recommend an aggressive posture in claiming deductions for gray areas in the tax laws.

An alternative to Publication 17 is *The Arthur Young Tax Guide*, which is a profusely annotated version of the IRS manual. Although the Young guide is actually longer than the Lasser guide, it is much more easily comprehensible to nonexperts, and its excellent design reduces the chance that you will skim past the tip that will save you hundreds of dollars.

There aren't too many books devoted solely to audit strategy. Lasser publishes one (*How to Avoid a Tax Audit of Your Return*, J. K. Lasser, New York: Simon and Schuster, 1984), but I would recommend more strongly two of the sources mentioned in this chapter: Mary L. Sprouse's *How to Survive a Tax: Audit What to Do Before & After You Hear from the IRS* (New York: Doubleday, 1981), and Paul N. Strassels and

Robert Wool's *All You Need to Know About the IRS: A Tax-payer's Guide* (New York: Random House, 1981).

Both Strassels and Sprouse were ex-IRS employees who have found the light and gone to work for the other side. Each book is strongly recommended, although you probably need to buy only one, because their strategies are virtually identical. Strassels and Wool are particularly good at suggesting how to avoid being audited in the first place, and they try to capture the frame of mind of the IRS agent who you will have to face. Strassels is clearly a convert, and is feisty and combative in his attitude toward the IRS.

Sprouse is as moderate and measured in her words as the Lasser tax guide, but she writes more engagingly. You don't get the feeling that any of her advice will land you in the slammer. Best of all, she gives you a real, unjaundiced, feel for what it is like to work at the IRS. She will make you feel that the person sitting on the other side of the desk from you at your audit is another human being who is just trying to do his job. Not an unworthy opponent. And not an unbeatable opponent.

# How to Win at a Job Interview

IN AN IDEAL WORLD, a job interview wouldn't be the crucial element in winning a job. The efficient worker without facile verbal skills would not be handicapped, as he surely is, by the necessity to perform in the strained and artificial environment of a job interview.

But we do not live in an ideal world, and in many careers, the interview is the most crucial determinant in getting a job offer. Theoretically, your résumé should be of paramount importance, for what better predictor of work performance could there be than the applicant's track record laid out in black and white? Prospective employers, however, distrust résumés. They expect to read bloated job descriptions and exaggerated academic achievements, and yet they are usually too lazy to check the résumés for accuracy. Employers, as a rule, also distrust references. And for good reason. References are always good. Every Tom, Dick, and Sally is "enterprising," "ambitious," "industrious," "a self-starter," and "a real catch." For the most part, references on résumés are treated like a steady pulse rate: They are a necessity, but having them isn't enough to help you get a job.

Most job interviews are conducted not by trained personnel specialists but by the prospective managers of the applicants. Personnel specialists tend to focus more on the qualifications of the applicant. Managers are much more likely to want to put a personal stamp on hiring, to find employees who match their own conception of the "right man for the job." For the dirty secret of job interviewing is that the most

important qualification the manager is looking for is likely whether or not she thinks you will fit in with her and other members of her department. The manager is wise enough to realize that an impressive résumé won't tell her whether or not you are a jerk, a nuisance, a threat to her job, a slob, or an inarticulate oaf. A good résumé combined with a so-so interview can lead to a job offer, but a superb résumé combined with a disastrous interview will never lead to a job offer. Whether the interviewer is conscious of it, the biggest item on your interviewer's agenda is to answer one question: Do I want to work with this applicant or not?

If the answer is "yes," you may be able to overcome a lack of experience or academic background. But you might not be able to. No interview can refute your life experience. If you have been self-employed for ten years and yet claim that your strength is your ability to work with others, the interviewer is justified in asking whether or not the decade of self-employment doesn't constitute a predilection toward solitary work. The more job experience you have, the more the interviewer is going to look to your work record, rather than your interview, as the evidence on which to base his assessment. If you have not shown any leadership ability in twenty years of work and are applying for a management position, it will be hard to convince an interviewer not to believe your résumé rather than your spiel. Most managers believe that history repeats itself. If you haven't distinguished yourself in your last position, why should she believe you will become a star now?

Applicants without significant work experience have even tougher problems. Many women are entering or re-entering the job force after years or decades working as a housewife. Recent high school and college graduates, in many cases, haven't even been able to prove their maturity, let alone their work expertise.

Employers see school and housewife recruits as a potentially valuable source of workers, primarily because they cannot expect to find people already in the workplace who are as intelligent and mature *who are willing to work as cheaply.*

Employers have to pay more for those with considerable work experience, so although your pay might not be wonderful at an entry-level job, inexperience can actually enhance your chances of being hired (when employers complain that someone is "overqualified" for a job, it usually means they don't want to pay someone what he is worth).

Applicants without much work experience often think that résumés are a joke. Will the employer laugh when the work experience line on the application is filled with "camp counselor" or "babysitter" or "PTA vice president." Absolutely not. Besides the interview, your résumé is about the only evidence an employer has on which to base his decision. The fact that you were head cheerleader of your high school or citizens' watch coordinator on your block might not be the most pertinent qualifications for a bank-management internship program, but these activities indicate enterprise and commitment and an ability to work with others. Employers in most fields aren't so much interested in the training you have received in school as they are in the personality traits you demonstrated during those years. After-school jobs, academic excellence, and sports prowess are valuable indications that the student has demonstrated maturity, stability, and ambition. One of the best ways to win a good entry-level job is to contribute to your school or your community as much as you hope to contribute to your job.

## Preparing for the Interview

You may be stuck with your background, but that doesn't mean you can't learn how to highlight your achievements and downplay your weaknesses on your résumé and during your job interview. Plenty of books and courses will teach you how to prepare for your job interview. Most of their suggestions are common sense, ones that anyone mentally acute enough to buy this book would carry out unconsciously. Some of the most common tips include:

1. Get to your interview early. A lack of punctuality can kill your chances immediately.
2. Dress conservatively and appropriately for the job you are pursuing.
3. Learn about the company. Give the impression that you are seeking not any job but a position at this particular company. If you are being interviewed by your prospective manager, try to learn something about him or her. Let your studied observations about the company drop casually throughout your interview.
4. Throughout the interview, refer to your interviewer by name. Folks are supposedly sent into paroxysms of delight when they hear their own name.
5. Send résumés that highlight your achievements in each of your jobs and activities, not just a list of jobs and activities.
6. Try to take over the interview and manipulate the interviewer into asking the questions you want to answer (more about this later).
7. Be prepared to discuss a salary range, but force the interviewer to name numbers first.
8. Make consistent eye contact with the interviewer.

Your only problem in executing these suggestions is that experienced interviewers have already faced scores of applicants who have been trained in the same techniques. Only a fool is likely to be seduced by the sound of his own name endlessly repeated. Only an incompetent can be bulldozed by an applicant "taking over" the interview. Only a buffoon will be entranced by a stream of compliments directed toward the company. There are plenty of foolish, incompetent, buffoonish interviewers out there, and these techniques might help you get a job offer from them, but you can't rely on these superficial guidelines. Don't they strike you as patronizing and cynical? If you were an interviewer, wouldn't you resent these attempts to snow you?

I think so. Nothing is inherently wrong with these eight

suggestions, but they are too calculated. If you are interested in the person you are talking to, you automatically make eye contact, you instinctively learn about him or her.

Perhaps the most important preparation you can make for your interview is to answer one question: Am I positive I want this job that I am interviewing for? If you are certain that you do, then you might need to model your behavior in the interview according to how you perceive the interviewer wants you to act.

Most of the time, however, you are *not* certain you want the job for which you are interviewing. Most applicants act as if the purpose of an interview is merely to garner a job offer, when an interview is actually an opportunity for you to see whether the company is right for you, and not just if you are right for the company. Especially if your prospective manager is directing it, the interview is an invaluable opportunity to preview your boss, to cut off a potentially horrendous relationship before it begins.

So here is my radical suggestion: Why not be yourself at your job interview? If you display your genuine personality and the manager hates you, perhaps this is God's way of informing you that the two of you were not destined to work together. If you exhibit yourself at your best and the manager or company doesn't want you, you might have saved yourself years of suffering and job stagnation. If you put on an act in the interview, and your future boss loves you, will you be stuck with your new personality on the job? Like an actor identified with one role, you will wonder if your boss hired you because he liked you or merely was entranced by the character you played. Learning the ropes of a new job carries enough pressure without having the added burden of creating a new personality at the same time.

A personal story. The only nine-to-five jobs I have ever had were in television programming, and I had only three formal interviews, all with my prospective bosses. Résumés and academic background were of little importance to all three. All three wanted me to criticize the slate of shows for which they were responsible. Each of them put me in a vulnerable position, forcing me to possibly attack shows that were their favorites and, even worse, in some cases, which they had created, developed, and supported. Since the interview was my first meeting with each of them, I had no idea which shows were their pets and which were their least favorites.

It briefly raced through my mind to soft-pedal the many problems I saw in most of the shows, but good sense drove me to tell the brutal truth instead, for the following reasons:

1. How can I prove to them that I could be valuable on the job unless I can demonstrate that I have suggestions to improve the shows they already have on the air?
2. I am opinionated in real life. If my future boss can't take criticism about projects she is involved in, she won't like me once I am on the job.
3. I didn't want to work for a boss with whom I couldn't be free with my opinions.
4. They asked me a simple question in good faith. Don't I owe them the truth, as I see it?
5. I was genuinely interested in their reaction to my comments. I love talking about television, and I wanted my hour to be lively whether or not I got a job offer.
6. Most important, if they did like what I had to say, I was getting off on the best possible foot, with my employer perceiving me as bright and daring for going out on a limb.

In two out of the three cases, my interviews led to job offers. Both women who gave me offers were most gracious in hearing my criticisms and rightfully interpreted my various misgivings about their shows as genuine interest in improving the programming. I was rewarded for my negative comments more than I would have been for the vague compliments that some manuals suggest you drop intermittently throughout your interview. Best of all, the reaction of these two women to my honesty immediately made me excited about working for them. What could be more fulfilling for a new employee than the knowledge that a future boss will take your suggestions seriously, and not be threatened by a criticism or a disagreement?

After I accepted the offer of one of the two women, I later interviewed for another job at the same network. The interview format was much the same (no talk about my past, a lot of talk about his current and future problems), but his reactions to my criticisms were immediate and definitive. He didn't want his shows criticized, or at least he didn't want *me* to do the criticizing. I knew within five minutes that I was not going to get an offer. The gentleman was polite enough to hear me out and give me about a half hour of his time. Perhaps he thought my criticisms were hogwash (and they might well have been), but his defensiveness made me leery of working for him. We both benefited from the exchange. Sure, my ego was hurt that I didn't get an offer for a job I thought I was qualified to do, but by the time I walked out of his room, I was convinced I would have turned an offer down anyway.

A job is at a specific location and involves interacting with specific people. One of the best things an interview can provide you with is an opportunity to see whether or not you would enjoy working for this particular company, for this particular boss. If I were a little less stubborn, I could have modulated my behavior when I noticed immediately that my interviewer wasn't responding well to my criticisms. If I were absolutely sure that I wanted the job he had to offer, I would have stopped my criticisms.

A job interview is a little like a first date. If you stay on best behavior, you might win a second date, but you are never going to find out if there is a chance for a long-term relationship until you let down your guard. There is no reason not to put your best foot forward on a first date and every reason to be polite and considerate of your date's sensitivities. I would argue that most interviewees would be better served if they went into an interview *not* thinking that their sole purpose is to garner a job offer but rather assuming that the purpose of the interview is to see whether a marriage is in order between you and the company, between you and your boss.

Before going to your interview, be aware that interviews differ. In many cases, your first encounter with a company will be a screening interview, in which the interviewer (usually someone from the personnel department) does not have the power to hire you. You need not plumb the depths of your soul in such a situation, any more than you would with the parents of a first date. The screening interviewer is primarily interested in providing the manager who is empowered to hire you with candidates who are qualified for the job. In a screening interview, stick to the facts as much as possible, and avoid areas that might create controversy. The screening interviewer receives flak only when he sends an obviously unqualified candidate; he is more likely to be criticized for sending a verbally gifted but inexperienced candidate than a boring qualified one.

College recruiters visiting campus are conducting screening interviews. Recruiters rarely, if ever, have the power to hire a student. The best that you can hope for is an invitation to visit the home office of the company that the recruiter represents.

The limitations on the recruiter are obvious. He must see tens of students in a matter of hours, and he must concentrate on selling his company at least as much as on weeding out unqualified duds, because he is aware that many seniors will sign up to see any recruiter in their desired field. College recruiting can be a numbing and exhausting job, for the procession of young hopefuls can easily become a blur to the recruiter. If you can display some humor along with the ambition, if you can stand out in a dignified way, you are likely to make a friend of the college recruiter. College interviews tend to be low-key affairs. Remember that because few college seniors have impressive work records, a winning personality will be crucial in receiving a second interview.

## Types of Interviews

Until the past few decades, job interviews tended to be
tension-filled confrontations: Interviewers posed questions;
interviewees answered questions. The best way to evaluate
how a prospect would perform on the job was to introduce
extra pressure into the interview itself. This style, known as
the "stress interview," is still popular with many interviewers,
particularly with older interviewers trained in this school and
with managers who have no formal background in interviewing techniques.

For the most part, stress interviewing is in disrepute among
personnel professionals. For one thing, it is impossible to
duplicate the stresses of the workplace in an interview. Some
people are (rightfully) nervous in an interview situation; it
doesn't necessarily follow that a nervous interviewee cannot
stand up to the stresses of the workplace. Perhaps our candidate would not make a good game-show host, but does a
trace of nervousness make him unqualified to be an engineer?
By placing the emphasis on stress management, the scope of
the interview is immediately limited to only one personality
trait, for if the artificial stress induced in the interview hurts
the performance of the applicant, he will never be seen at his
best. Most experienced interviewers would prefer to see candidates at their absolute best. If the candidate in a relatively
comfortable state is not impressive, he can be eliminated from
consideration without any qualms.

Most important, studies have shown that stress interviews
are not as statistically reliable as those taken in a low-stress
environment. Doesn't it make sense that an interviewer can
best evaluate the potential of a candidate in the workplace
when both the interviewer and the prospect treat each other
like human beings rather than strategic objects?

"Open-ended" interviews have been shown to be much
more effective in finding candidates who will be successful on
the job. Stressful question-and-answer interviews give the

applicant a chance to censor his replies, because it is obvious that every statement out of his mouth *counts* in the evaluation. It also leads to the interviewer talking too much. An interviewer can learn much more in an environment where the applicant feels safe to admit weaknesses and point out what *he* thinks is important. An open-ended question such as, "What would you think about a job that required constant travel?" is much less threatening but also harder to answer automatically than "Can you take constant travel?" which leads to the inevitable positive response.

Ideally, unqualified applicants have already been weeded out before the first interview. The interviewer can then spend his time trying to understand what makes the applicant tick: What motivates the applicant? How has the prospect applied his training in the past? What are his or her values? How is he or she likely to work with other staff members?

Too many candidates try to tailor their presentation to a conception of what they think the interviewer wants to hear, when in reality, modern interviewers are trained not to fix on an image of what qualities they are seeking in advance. In his excellent book, *Interviewing for Managers*, John Drake emphasizes this point:

> During interviews, emphasis should be placed upon understanding the uniqueness of the individual being assessed rather than evaluating his sameness to others. . . . The interviewer [should] initiate the interview without a preconceived set of sought-after characteristics (with the exception of job knowledge); that is, the interviewer must not begin the interview with the intention of determining if the candidate possesses specific traits, qualities, aptitudes or abilities. . . . When the interviewer has developed a mental portrait of how the applicant behaves and functions, then, and only then, the interviewer can relate the emerging qualities to the requirements of the job.

## What Are Interviewers Looking For?

Not all, perhaps not even most interviewers, use Drake's emergence approach, but you may be surprised how untrivial the traits are that professionals look for in applicants. In his book, *Professional Interviewing*, Cal W. Downs reported the results of a poll of college recruiters ranking how important they thought each of twenty-two criteria were in their evaluations of prospective employees. In order they were:

1. Enthusiasm
2. Oral communication ability
3. Leadership potential
4. Confidence in self
5. Aggressiveness and initiative
6. Emotional stability
7. Writing skills
8. Scholastic record
9. Pleasing personality
10. Personal appearance
11. Moral standards
12. Poise in interview
13. Efficiency
14. Interest in people
15. Extracurricular activities

The following are a few of the factors that received low ratings for importance:

16. Loyalty
17. Preparation for interview
19. Formulated long-range goals and objectives
20. Realistic salary objectives
22. Work experience of a particular type

Note the realism inherent in the low ranking of some of these factors. Certainly loyalty and long-range goals would be highly cherished, because these traits could lead to long and valuable service to the company. Experienced personnel professionals, however, are practical enough to realize that it is impossible to assess loyalty in a short interview and that very few youngsters, even mature ones, have really formulated long-range goals and objectives.

This poll should also assuage some of the most common fears of applicants. You may be surprised that poise in interview, personal appearance, and work experience are not crucial determinants in getting job offers. Interviewers are trying to find basic rather than polished skills, personality traits rather than "perfect" experience. From this poll, it becomes evident that the interviewer's assessment of your personality is by far the most decisive factor in determining your fate (especially because the interviewer will assume he can assess your skills and experience by reading your application or résumé). The subjective impression left on the interviewer, your demeanor and attitude are more important than the content of the words you say.

As you progress in your career, interviewers will not be looking for the same qualities that they seek in entry-level applicants. The last-place finisher in the college recruiters' wish-list, "Work experience of a particular type," is likely to zoom to the top of the list, along with other factors not even mentioned—recommendations by former employers, and because much recruiting is done covertly and thus without access to such recommendations, your reputation in your field. The higher the position you seek, the more likely you will be interviewed by your prospective boss rather than a personnel official. The bottom-line question for the boss will likely be: Will this applicant make my life easier? Along with sterling qualifications, the interviewer is most likely going to focus on whether he likes you. Does he *want* to work with you?

You can't do too much to change the impression you leave on people, so consider not trying to change your personality during the interview. In particular, don't worry inordinately about nervousness. Even aggressive and ambitious people get nervous in interviews, and your interviewer is sure to have seen worse cases than you. Again, view the interview as if it were a first date. Don't look on each interview as an exercise in life and death but rather as an honest exchange that you hope will lead to a long-lasting relationship.

If you are perceived as a wimp, you are as unlikely to succeed in a job interview as on a first date. Everyone is insecure, but self-confidence is one trait that interviewers invariably seek. As H. Anthony Medley says in *Sweaty Palms: The Neglected Art of Being Interviewed*:

> Believe in yourself. Even if you don't believe in yourself, if you make the interviewer think that you do, you'll be on the right track. . . . Everyone has doubts. We all have them. But keep them hidden.

You must do some selling of yourself in order to succeed at your interview. If you don't sell yourself, the interviewer is likely to believe that you either can't or don't know how to sell yourself or, worse, that you have nothing worthwhile to sell. If you are a naturally aggressive and gregarious person, touting yourself will come naturally. If you are a naturally modest and shy type, keep in mind that the interviewer can't be expected to know something about you that you won't reveal. He is not Perry Mason, poised to plumb the inner recesses of your being. You needn't be a carnival barker to let the interviewer know where you think your strengths lie. If this seems difficult to you, it is worth working on your self-confidence, for you will need it every day of your life in the business world.

A recent poll of personnel professionals asked them what their most frequent complaints were about interviewees. Obviously, this is valuable information. If you don't fall into any of these categories, you'll go a long way toward winning with interviewers:

1. *Poor communication skills.* A disconcertingly high number of interviewees lack basic oral skills. Vagueness, lack of clarity, evasiveness, and lack of conciseness

drive interviewers up the wall, as do folks who will never start talking or never stop talking.

2. *Badly prepared applicants.* Being totally passive about the interview will often be interpreted as poor preparation. Interviewers expect applicants to know a little about the company they represent and possibly about the position for which they are interviewing. Interviewers can learn about you from the questions you ask about the company, yet many applicants see it as the duty of the interviewer to be a game-show host, reeling off endless streams of questions.

3. *Vague interests.* Nothing infuriates interviewers, especially with candidates already in the workplace, than confronting those who are interested in "everything," who would find every position in the company "challenging," and still have no idea what they want to do when they grow up. At best, the interviewer will assume you are trying to manipulate him by not saying anything that might offend. At worst, he will assume you are an airhead, without goals or direction.

4. *Lack of motivation.* As we saw, enthusiasm is the number-one factor for interviewers. Interviewers dislike lethargic, agreeable types who will assent to anything proposed to them.

5. *Unrealistic expectations.* Never go into an interview with the attitude of "what's in it for me?" Many applicants believe that they will become the center of attention of the company the moment they enter it, and expect to be treated as stars rather than as aspirants. This type of bravado won't win points with interviewers, especially if it is accompanied by an obsession with starting salary and benefits.

## COUNTERING PLOYS BY INTERVIEWERS

If I have been pollyannaish in my expectation about the quality of your interviewer, this is the time to warn you that he could well be an incompetent, a boor, or worse. If your bum interviewer is your potential boss, even an unpleasant interview may be a blessing in disguise, warning you not to covet the job.

Many bad interviewers, however, are merely poorly trained and are winging the interview or doing to you what they were subjected to in their job interviews. Several ploys that interviewers might try with you are easy to spot. You instinctively know when you are being tested rather than being drawn out to reveal your true self. Because the interviewer does not mean to offend or hurt you, but sincerely thinks these ploys are a means to find out what makes you tick, the best tactic is to be aware of the ploys and parry them subtly without letting the interviewer know you are aware of the game he is playing. Here are seven of the most common interview ploys, with suggested defenses.

1. *The stress interview.* Some interviewers genuinely believe that their role should be that of a Marine boot-camp drill sergeant, constantly confronting the applicant. Always maintain your composure when faced with such an interviewer. He is likely to be the type of single-minded man (few women are inclined to give stress interviews) who will admire you simply for weathering the interview, without regard to anything else he learned about you. The problem with the stress interview is that he is unlikely to learn much else about you besides whether you can tolerate the stress, and thankfully this type of interviewer is on the endangered-species list.

2. *The meaningful pause or the silent treatment.* A far more stressful ploy than the confrontational approach, used by more than a few interviewers, is the meaningful and calculated pause. Some interviewers will, during every interview, refuse to respond verbally to one or more answers of the interviewee. Usually, they will choose to remain silent after they have asked a multifaceted question which they feel has not been answered sufficiently. If you feel you have an-

swered the question to the best of your knowledge, you should remain silent and maintain nonthreatening eye contact with the interviewer. He thinks he is testing your self-confidence and poise, and he is waiting for you to fall into the trap of dissembling about your answer. When a lull occurs in a conversation, there is a tendency to want to fill the vacuum. If the interviewer does not help you fill in the conversational slack, he is almost certainly testing you with this ploy.

3. *Ambiguous questions.* Many interviewers love to ask ambiguous questions because they feel that they can learn more about the applicant's priorities and thinking processes than if they asked specific questions. For example, if you are asked "What is most important to you?" it is unclear whether you are being asked this question in a business context alone. An answer of "my family and my religion" is just as appropriate as "a challenging, lucrative job." Although ambiguous questions usually do lead to more revealing answers than directed questions, they also provide opportunities to reveal assets about yourself that aren't easily stated in a résumé, application, or a more direct question. If you want the interviewer to know that you donate hundreds of hours a year to community service, the chance to let him know is when he asks an open-ended question such as "What is most important to you?" Your tangible service becomes proof of the lofty values you espouse.

4. *Questions about other places of employment.* Your interviewer will ask you questions about your former jobs and may start zeroing in on an unpleasant job experience. He might goad you to bad-mouth a former company or a former boss. Even if your ex-boss had an IQ lower than Archie Bunker's, don't ever engage in character assassination. The interviewer doesn't want to know about your ex-boss, and he is not expecting you to admit that you botched up your work. He is testing you to see whether you are discreet, mature, and most of all, loyal.

5. *Salary questions.* The interviewer may or may not bring up the subject of salary. The higher the position you are interviewing for, the less rigid the pay scales tend to be, so the more uncomfortable the discussion becomes. I wish there were an easy answer to how to handle this problem, but there isn't. It is to your advantage if the question of salary is never discussed. You want the interviewer to choose you for the job before the question of salary arises, for you are more likely to receive higher pay if their commitment to you precedes any numbers being thrown about. At all costs, try to force the interviewer to mention a salary (or at least a salary range) before you name a figure. After all, he is the one offering you the job.

More than likely, the interviewer will ask you about how much you have been making at your last job. Again, it is preferable to hear about the salary range for the prospective job before you tell him about your salary. Many books will recommend inflating your salary when confronted with this question, but it is our policy never to lie in the interview— and only partly for ethical reasons. Lies have a way of catching up with you; it is a burden to have to start a job trying to remember what you told whom. Also, your interviewer might know more about you than you think. Especially if your last job was in the same industry as the position you are applying for presently, your interviewer might be able to find out exactly how much you earned at your last job. Getting caught in one lie usually results in your application landing in the wastebasket.

6. *Questions about your failures.* If an otherwise sensitive interviewer starts asking tough questions, particularly about your shortcomings, do not become alarmed. There is actually reason to believe your interview is going well. Professional interviewers are trained to be impassive. They are trained to downplay your mistakes, and for good reason. If they let you know that your answers were displeasing, it would serve to

clam you up. They want you to keep your defenses down and blather on and reveal your shortcomings.

Don't ever assume that you can read an interviewer's reactions. Most good ones will praise your accomplishments (whether they are impressed with them or not) and downplay your failures. Just because an interviewer does not confront you about an admitted weakness does not mean that he has not noted it or thinks it is unimportant. There is no reason for an interviewer to become confrontational when you start talking about problems, for your openness confirms that some rapport has been established. Often, when an otherwise sympathetic interviewer seems to be grilling you about an admitted problem, he is trying to clear up what seems to him to be contradictory or unclear information. It does not mean he is feeling negatively about you.

Most applicants don't know how to answer the question "What do you think is your biggest shortcoming in business?" Some books will recommend that you stonewall, refusing to concede weakness. Others recommend naming a weakness that isn't really a weakness but a strength that will impress the interviewer even more, like the old chestnut, "My problem is that I have a tendency to work too hard. Work becomes everything to me."

I have just finished reading scores of books used to train professional interviewers, and all I can say, again, is why not try to be honest? Interviewers are told in these manuals to watch out for the applicant who sees no weakness in himself. If you admit, honestly, that you get nervous during public presentations, it is unlikely to hurt your chances unless the job requires constant public speaking (and would you want such a job in these circumstances?). The interviewer will admire your honesty and self-confidence in clearly and directly admitting a weakness.

7. *Self-appraisal questions.* Closely related to the above ploy, many interviewers love to ask you open-ended self-

appraisal questions such as, "Where do you see yourself in ten years?" or "What is your biggest strength and biggest weakness?" Again, consider being honest in your response to these types of questions. One training manual for interviewers that I read went so far as to state that one of the best ways to measure the truthfulness of an applicant is to see whether he will acknowledge his weaknesses, in temperament and background.

Especially in a screening interview in a large company, where there may be several positions available, honest replies to these types of questions can help you find the right job. For example, most prospective bosses might shy away from an applicant who says that his main weakness is a huge ego. Who needs an engineer who thinks he is Muhammad Ali? But a big ego could be a huge plus for a salesperson. A strength such as thoughtfulness or meticulousness might be deemed a weakness in certain action-oriented jobs, for example, sales and some entrepreneurial positions.

It is amazing how often the best defense against a tough question is the truth.


## You and Your Interviewer


Most of the time, your interviews will be with people not formally trained in interviewing techniques. Although you are likely to be focused on your own performance, try to empathize with your interviewer. While you are wondering whether your answer made any sense, he might well be musing about whether or not he has just asked the right question. See it as your responsibility, as well as his, to make sure the interview proceeds smoothly. Demonstrate interest in him and his company. Try to get him to tell you as much about the job as soon as possible so you can better edit what you want to divulge about yourself.

Many manuals for job interviewees recommend taking over the interview, but in my experience this isn't the best strategy.

A good interviewee should be as sensitive as the expert dance partner and equally willing to follow the lead of his partner. If the interviewer wants to cha-cha, you should be willing to cha-cha, and to show your individuality and flair within the confines of what the interviewer seems most interested.

While you are sweating bullets at your interview, it might be hard for you to maintain perspective, but try. Your prospective employer is as eager to find an exciting candidate as you are to find a fulfilling job. Large corporations spend millions of dollars to recruit. Most interviewers are therefore looking forward to finding someone they will like and can wholeheartedly recommend. The best way to win at an interview is to work hard at school and work, to have a pleasant personality, and then to be yourself at your interview. It may be impossible to believe, but the ideal person your interviewer might be seeking is the real you.

**For more information:**

*What Color Is Your Parachute? A Practical Manual for Job Hunters and Career Changes*, Richard Nelson Bolles (Berkeley, CA: Ten Speed Press, 1986). Scores of books tell you how to behave on an interview. Most of them insult the intelligence of the interviewer and the interviewee alike, and are filled with key words that the interviewee must repeat, as well as obvious comments about proper clothing and body gestures. *What Color Is Your Parachute?* has been a paperback best-seller for the better part of a decade and rightly so. Bolles's book is about much more than getting a job. His focus isn't on tricking the interviewer or deciding what persona to adopt for which interview. Bolles wants you to concentrate on deciding what *you* want in a job, and finding the right places to channel your talents and personality. You can follow all of the advice in the book, keep your dignity, and maybe even nab that dream job.

*Sweaty Palms: The Neglected Art of Being Interviewed*, H. Anthony Medley (Berkeley, CA: Ten Speed Press, 1984).

Medley's tactics are a little more manipulative than his fellow Ten Speed Press friend, Richard Bolles, because Medley sees the interview in a more confrontational context, but the advice in *Sweaty Palms* is always sensible and more specific than Bolles's.

*Interviewing for Managers*, John Drake (New York: Amacom, 1982). *Professional Interviewing*, Cal W. Downs, Paul Smeyak, and Ernest Martin (New York: Harper and Row, 1980). It might be enlightening for you to read how managers are trained to interview job prospects. You might even be disappointed to read how earnest and nonconfrontational they are advised to be. Both of these books do not encourage stress interviewing, not only for humanitarian reasons but because they feel that stress interviewing does not give a chance for the interviewer to see the real applicant. Although neither of these two books is as lively as the Ten Speed Press books designed for the job-seeker, the Drake book, in particular, is as sensitive in its own way as *What Color is Your Parachute?*

# WINNING
## AGAINST
# AGGRESSIVE
# OPPONENTS

# How to Avoid a Salesperson

IT'S HAPPENED TO ALL OF US. We get a phone call from a stranger whom we suspect is a salesperson. He asks us an innocuous question. We mumble "yes." And the next thing we know, we are engaged in a ten-minute conversation about insurance that we know we are not going to buy. We realize that his sales pitch is totally programmed, that it no longer matters whether we respond "yes" or "no" to his questions because he is ready for either. We can choose to hang up abruptly or sit it out passively. How can we get out of the conversation gracefully (the salesperson has our name and phone number; he could call back if we hang up, thinking our phone was accidentally disconnected)? Best of all, how can we avoid the ten-minute spiel in the first place?

On a crisp winter day, you decide to go out with your wife to look at new sports cars. You can't afford to buy a new sports car. In fact, you can't afford even a ski trip this weekend, which is why you're out looking at cars instead. Your only qualms about undertaking your car-gazing trip is your fear of encountering persistent salespeople. Sure enough. You are on the lot drooling over a Mazda RX-7 when a salesperson in a plaid sportscoat saunters over:

"It's a beauty, huh!"

"Yes, but we're just looking."

"Uh-huh. So what's your line of work, Mr. . . . ?"

And before you know it, your fantasy quest has metamorphized into an encounter with your new would-be best friend, Mr. Salesperson.

\* \* \*

Is there any way to train salespeople to handle you the way you want? To help you find the most suitable product when you are actually in the market to buy? But to leave you alone when you are browsing or merely loitering in their establishment?

I could never believe that salespeople like these games any more than we do. After all, if I *know* I am not going to buy something, no salesperson is going to convince me. If the salesperson really knew in advance that I wasn't going to buy his product, he probably wouldn't want to waste his time with me. A long-acknowledged axiom of sales, the 20-to-80 rule, states that 20 percent of a salesperson's customers buy 80 percent of his goods. A corollary is that 20 percent of a sales force sells 80 percent of the company's goods. These surprising ratios indicate how silly it is for the average salesperson to bother trying to coax a reluctant browser into buying. A far more economic use of the salesperson's time would be to try to find a potential prime customer who will become one of the cherished 20 percent, or even to call up one of his best customers and make sure that he is happy, since the loss of a big, steady customer is a calamity for a salesperson.

There is another reason why that salesperson is wasting his time bullying or cajoling you into buying an item you have no intention of purchasing. Salespeople rarely truly sell their products. Rather, a customer with a need comes to the salesperson, and the salesperson fills that need with a product or service. Although a salesperson may have a wonderful pitch extolling the virtues of his vacuum cleaner, if you don't have a need for cleaner rugs or a need for an easier way to clean your rugs, his pitch will be worthless. Most salespeople are trained to find out what the customer's needs are. This isn't an easy task, because the customer often doesn't know himself what his underlying need is. He may think he is interested in a sports car because of its greater performance, when he really wants to feel more masculine. One of the reasons automobile salespeople probe with personal questions is because they are trying to identify the psychological needs you are trying to fulfill with the purchase of a new car.

But very few salespeople are capable of creating a need in the customer's mind that doesn't exist before they met. If you want to repel a salesperson, you must convince him that you don't *want* anything, or at least that you don't have the same want that he is selling.

Salespeople are taught by sales managers that customers hate to be sold but that they love to buy. The purpose of the salesperson is not at all to convince someone to buy something he doesn't want, but to direct an already strong buying impulse toward his particular product.

After reading almost fifty books about sales, including manuals designed for training salespersons and sales managers, I was impressed with their agreement on all of these concepts. Without exception, they stressed what Hank Trisler stated succinctly in his book, *No Bull Selling:* "People buy on emotion and justify with facts. People buy for their reasons, not ours." These insights explain why salesmanship, in general, is much lower-key than it was thirty years ago. Salespeople are now trained to become minipsychologists, relying less on memorizing the specifications of their products and more on being able to analyze the customer's subconscious needs. The salesperson isn't trying to change the customer's mind but to learn how it works.

The effective salesperson is the empathetic one, constantly trying to feel what his customers feel, if only so that he can better manipulate the customer into buying the product and satisfying his unmet psychological needs. As *The One Minute $ales Person* puts it, "My purpose is to help other people feel good about what they bought and about themselves for buying." Now that salespeople no longer think of themselves as selling products but rather fulfilling the emotional needs of their customers, they are harder to get rid of, because your rejection of their product might not *really* mean rejection of their product but merely rejection of the particular emotional appeal upon which they've based their sales pitch.

Getting rid of an unwanted salesperson is a favor to both parties. Most salespeople work on a commission basis and would gladly leave you alone if they knew they had no chance to make a sale. The goal of every salesperson is to "make a close," to extract a customer promise to buy. The salesperson is not rewarded for a near-sale. Our goal is to convince the salesperson that we don't want his product long before he tries to make a close. We'll outline the seven steps that most sales pitches contain and explain the best tactics for trying to cut off the salesperson before you are lulled, by sheer momentum, into buying that vacuum cleaner that you didn't want for conscious or subconscious reasons.

## STEP #1: PROSPECTING

Chances are, when you were a kid, you sold Girl Scout cookies or Christmas cards. You peddled your wares to your parents, the parents of friends, and your next-door neighbors. If you were really ambitious, you started banging on the doors of strangers. But a funny thing started happening. These strangers didn't automatically say "yes." You had no idea, when you banged on a new door, what the reaction would be.

Professional salespeople are not in much better shape than the erstwhile door-to-door peddler. The only way for the salesperson to make his job easier is by prescreening his potential customers, so he doesn't have to waste his time approaching people who have no money or no intention of buying his product.

If a salesperson's job is not to convince someone to buy his product but to find someone who already knows he has a need for it, and if the salesperson knows that 20 percent of his customers will supply him with 80 percent of his commissions, then the most important determinant in a successful selling career will be the ability to find the right prospects and to keep them happy after the sale (another popular selling axiom is that eventually 80 percent of your commissions should come from old customers and referrals from old customers). A prospect is anyone who needs a given product and can afford to buy it.

A good salesperson simply won't waste his time trying to sell to a person or company who isn't a genuine prospect, but he will do almost anything to obtain the name of a good prospect: buy mailing lists, beseech existing customers for referrals, or if desperate, call blind leads on the phone. Many naive customers think that the soft-sell techniques that salespeople start with will continue throughout the selling process. In reality, the effective salesperson during an initial contact is trying to ascertain whether the customer is a genuine prospect. When trying to sell a big-ticket item, the salesperson will ask a series of probing but nonthreatening questions about your lifestyle, financial state, and seriousness about buying. If this contact is over the phone, he is probably not going to try to close over the phone. His only goal is to obtain your agreement to meet with him in person. Do not accept a face-to-face appointment with a salesperson unless you are seriously interested in buying. He has already screened you, and he thinks you are a prospect. Once he has you in person, he will be trying to close as soon as possible.

Do not worry about offending a salesperson by turning down an invitation to meet with him in person. You are doing him a favor by disabusing him of the belief that you are a genuine prospect. With the possible exception of closing, prospecting is the most important step in selling. If you gently inform a salesperson that you do not want his product or that you do not need his product, or best of all, can't afford to pay for his product, you are likely to get rid of the salesperson easily. If a salesperson still persists in hassling you, insisting that you can afford the mink coat, he is either an imbecile or a trainee who is giving you a canned presentation. All you can do is repeat more forcefully that you have no interest in his product, and walk through the door (or hang up the phone). If you allow a salesperson to get through this phase thinking you are a prospect, you risk a long "relationship" with him.

## STEP #2: THE PRE-APPROACH

After a salesperson elicits some interest on your part, he next attempts to "qualify" you. With increasing overhead costs, salespeople usually only want to contact prospects who are ready to buy. He wants to know not only that you are a good prospect but that you have the authority to make the purchase yourself. If you don't, he wants to speak to the member of your family or the person in your company who can make that decision. He doesn't want to repeat his spiel over and over again to the wrong person.

If the salesperson mistakenly thought you were a hot prospect, this is the perfect time to let him know he has made a mistake, by informing him that you cannot make the decision yourself. Tell him that you must consult your wife before making a decision. Tell him that the product is excellent but that you cannot afford the payments until after you have paid off your student loan. This is your last chance to get the salesperson off your back before he launches into his pitch, which starts with . . .

## STEP #3: THE APPROACH

After the salesperson has qualified you, he will try to elicit an expression of interest from you. Salespeople in department stores, for example, are usually trained to take a low-key approach to customers—not to hover before they recognize a visual cue that you are interested in a product or have a question—for fear of driving away timid customers. So, many customers purposely avert the glances of the salesperson, knowing that anyone who actually makes eye contact with a salesperson is deemed a legitimate prospect. Picking up a product or lingering at one display is an automatic tipoff that you are interested.

Retail salespeople do not have the luxury of prospecting and the pre-approach. You have walked through their doors unannounced. A real-estate broker would kill to get an unsolicited customer walking through the door. As soon as you walk into a store, you have in a sense qualified yourself—you have signaled your willingness and ability to buy. If you have no interest in buying the merchandise and want to avoid the salespeople, you must immediately upon contact inform them that you have no intention of buying anything that day. Don't say, "just browsing, thanks," the three words that salespeople hate most. *Everybody*, genuine prospects and utter lowlifes, repeats those words when first confronted with salespeople. Inform the salesperson that you have no intention of buying anything that day. The important point is to say something that will avoid the salesperson launching into a canned or spontaneous sales presentation. You must convince the salesperson you are not a prospect, or else you will be subject to . . .

## STEP #4: THE PRESENTATION

In the good old days before the advent of motivational research, this was the point in the sales process at which the salesperson launched into the wonders of his product, regaling the customer with specifications, price points, and product advantages. In a few industries, this type of sales presentation still rules.

For the most part, however, canned sales pitches have been abandoned. In the first three steps, the salesperson has tried to learn about you in order to tailor his presentation specifically for you. The salesperson desperately does not want to offend you. Even if he can't sell you his product, he does not want anyone bad-mouthing him. (Did you know that the average person has approximately two hundred and fifty friends and relatives within his sphere that he can influence with recommendations or warnings?) If you won't buy from him today, perhaps you will in the future.

The best salespeople have discovered that the most effective way to make a presentation is to let the customer sell himself. This approach is codified in another 20-80 rule. In an effective sales presentation, the customer talks 80 percent of the time and the salesperson talks 20 percent of the time.

In the ideal presentation, the salesperson asks a series of questions. Ideally, the questions are framed, as in *What's My Line*, to elicit "yes" answers. If a customer is answering affirmatively and agreeing with the sentiments of the salesperson, it is difficult for the customer to cut the conversation.

Your best strategy *is* to disagree with the salesperson, but a skillful salesperson will make this difficult to do. For example, a water-filter salesperson might start his presentation with, "Don't you want to save on your water costs by 15 percent?" or "Don't you want your drinking water free of contaminants?" How can anyone disagree with these goals? How could a business person responsibly say "no" to either question? Believe me, at some point, the salesperson will likely make a logical step that isn't there, or try to put a different face on a problem with his product. It isn't easy to say "no" to this swell guy who has shown so much interest in you, which is why you were supposed to get the unwanted salesperson off your back *before* he got around to his presentation.

Salespeople are trained to support those statements you make that ease the salesperson toward making a close, and to withhold any support (but not to disagree openly) with those statements made by the customer which might hinder the sale. When you start disagreeing with the premises or conclusions of the salesperson, he might seemingly ignore you. Most likely, he will change subjects quickly and imperceptibly. If you let your emotional need to be a nice person get in your way, you are highly vulnerable to his presentation. If your dissents do not deter the salesperson from thrusting forward with his spiel, don't even try to stop him. Better to head him off at the next step . . .

### STEP #5: THE TRIAL CLOSE

In *No Bull Selling*, Hank Trisler states emphatically: "Here's the real key to selling: *You ask, you get.*" At some point during the salesperson's presentation, he will flirt with closing the sale. He might use the direct approach, "Are you going to charge this or pay cash?" or might be less threatening and ask "What color would match your linoleum?" In either case, the salesperson is trying to secure a commitment to buy.

Trisler claims that 60 percent of all eventual buyers say "no" the first *four* times they are asked for a purchase and that the effective salesperson must not look on a "no" as a NO. He says that 44 percent of all salespeople quit asking after one negative response; 22 percent after two rejections; 14 percent after three; and 12 percent after the fourth "no." Trisler concludes that "if 92 percent of our competition is out of the running after four no's, this must mean that 8 percent of the salespeople get 60 percent of the business *just by asking*."

The intensity of the closing pressure will probably depend upon whether the salesperson is likely to see you again if he fails to hook you with his trial close. If you have walked into a camera store out of the blue, the salesperson has no motivation *not* to pull out all the stops and close you. If he fails, he probably will never see you again. If he is a wholesale salesperson on a regular route to your place of business, it isn't in his self-interest to risk alienating you by using high-pressure tactics.

On a good day, the customer can be closed the first time the subject is broached. But most of the time, the salesperson expects an initial rebuff, because he is waiting for you to force him into . . .

### STEP #6: MEETING OBJECTIONS

You might think that this is the stage when it would be easiest to deflect a cunning salesperson. The salesperson tries to close you and you start making objections, good reasons for rejecting the product.

But your objections will not stop the aggressive salesperson. Indeed, he is trained to believe that your objections, far from a barrier to a close, are an indication that you are interested in buying.

When you start pointing out the negative features of the salesperson's product, he will now believe that you are confirming your need for the product. These objections, to the salesperson, are merely nuisances to be swatted away before he can fill that need that he is sure you have. It is very important, if you are sure you do not want to buy a product, not to get into an argument with a salesperson about the merit of his goods. You are unlikely to win an argument about the specifications and cost-efficiencies of different brands. You must convince the salesperson that you do not have the economic or psychological need for his product.

While you are bashing the quality of his product, the good salesperson will not try to argue with you. More likely, he will react like a Rogerian psychotherapist. If you say that the price is too high, the salesperson will nod his head and say, "I see" or "Yes, it isn't cheap." You are not going to deter most salespeople by claiming their product is too expensive. As soon as you bring up price as the main reason for not buying a product, the salesperson will assume that money is the *only* impediment to a close. Salespeople are trained to accept the notion that money is rarely the issue in a rejection but is raised by the purchaser when he or she has doubts about the importance of the need for the product, or some fear whether or not he is making the right choice. Rather than to lower the price of the item, which he is probably unable to do, or to argue with you about whether or not it is too expensive, the salesperson will probably try to make you feel good about spending what he will concede is a significant amount of money on his product. He will make sure that you feel that you "deserve" the highest quality. He will say, "Besides this problem, is there any other barrier to your buying?" which will make you feel like scum for rejecting a purchase for such a piddling reason as the price.

When a customer recites a litany of objections, the salesperson treats them merely as rationalizations for not buying and will meet them with silence or murmured sympathy. Only when an objection is raised several times is a salesperson trained to treat it seriously.

It is far better to act bored during the sales presentation than to raise innumerable objections. People who don't buy tend to be indifferent to the sales pitch, and your goal is to convince the salesperson that you have no intention of buying and that you are not emotionally engaged in the selling process. You are likely to get into a shorter argument if you deny your need for a product than if you reject the product on its merits.

## STEP #7: THE CLOSE

With any luck, you will never reach this stage. The goal of all salespeople, of course, is to make the close successfully. More books and training manuals have been written about how to make a close than any other subject in selling. In fact, whole books consist solely of effective closing lines.

A surprising number of otherwise effective salespeople are strangely shy about coming out and asking the customer to buy their product. If you have been dragged this far along the selling process, you are simply going to have to reject the salesperson and say "no." If you have followed faithfully the advice in this chapter, you shouldn't have gotten this far.

Of course, there are simpler ways to get rid of salespeople than were outlined in this chapter. You can hang up the phone. Run out of the store. Threaten with bodily harm.

But I've always felt that most of the callous or insensitive salespeople we encounter, like stand-up comedians, have gotten that way out of constant rejection or fear of rejection. Salespeople are vulnerable. They ask us for something. When we answer "no," they cannot always tell whether they or the product was rejected. The manipulations they utilize to lean on us to buy are calculated not only to close a sale but to protect their fragile egos.

Salespeople assume, most of the time, that we are not aware of how they are manipulating us and that we do not know how easy it is for them to read our feelings. We are not taught in school, after all, how to fend off salespeople, whereas salespeople are taught in detail how to manipulate us. If the parties on both sides of the transaction were aware of each other's tricks, there would be less need for hurt feelings, and products, not salespeople, could be rejected with unspoken rituals known to both parties. Much of the time we do want to buy things. Shouldn't we look forward to the prospect of finding someone who can sell us what we want?

**For more information:**
Almost any book on sales or sales management provides a fascinating insight into how to be an effective customer. Your library is full of such books. Here are some of the most interesting:

*How to Sell Anything to Anybody*, Joe Girard with Stanley H. Brown (New York: Simon and Schuster, 1977). The world's greatest car salesperson is unrepentant. He's also a zealot. Who else would, in the midst of a post-home-run frenzy at a baseball stadium, throw a stack of his business cards in the air? Girard now runs motivational seminars.

*No Bull Selling*, Hank Trisler (New York: Bantam, 1985). Trisler does not couch his selling advice in psychobabble. He is an aggressive seller, and because this was the most sensible manual on selling that I read, it is probably the most useful for the defensive buyer.

*The Best Seller*, D. Forbes Ley (Newport Beach: Sales Success Press, 1984). This is a perfect example of a book infected with the psychological jargon that has overtaken sales literature. Will this help you sell an encyclopedia?

8

Behind every logical Need there lurks an emotional Want. If there is no emotional Want, there will be no sale. If there is an emotional Want, but it can't be justified with a logical Need, there will be no sale. Both the emotional Want and the justified Need must exist to consummate a sale. The Salesperson of today must sell both the logical Prospect and the emotional Prospect.

*The One Minute $ales Person*, Spencer Johnson, M.D., and Larry Wilson (New York: William Morrow, 1984). Less pretentiously than the Ley book, this specimen of the *One Minute* series is fascinating. It uses the same tricks and manipulations that can be found in the Trisler or Girard books but characterizes them as soul-satisfying and constructive for both buyer and seller, rather than as easy ways to turn a buck.

# How to Win at Poker

THIS CHAPTER will not teach you how to beat Amarillo Slim at poker but if you are an average home player, it should help you beat the pants off of your friends and turn you into a winner in the low-limit games in casinos. I am not going to go into full details of the nuts and bolts of a winning poker system in this chapter (although I'll recommend some books that do), because there are so many different poker games to cover and so many variations in rules (wild cards, requirements to open, etc.) that can alter radically the proper strategy. Be mindful of the fact that I have simplified my suggestions, eliminating many exceptions that occasionally occur in order to streamline my guidelines. What I will try to do is to put you in the frame of mind of a winning poker player, to think as he thinks. If you master "The Twelve Commandments of Poker," you will turn into a winner. I'll apply these principles to one game, seven-card stud, to demonstrate how these commandments work at the table.

### The Twelve Commandments of Poker

1. *Your goal is to win the maximum amount of money, not the maximum number of pots.* Most home games are played for small stakes (and start out, at least) in a friendly atmosphere. There is usually pressure, spoken or unspoken, for players to stay in pots. If you stay in pots when you don't have the cards to justify it, you will be a nice guy but a nice loser. What separates poker from casino games such as blackjack or craps is that you are allowed to see the cards you are

going to play with *before* you make the bulk of your bet. Imagine how much you could win at blackjack if you could fold bad hands for a token ante. In poker you are given this opportunity every hand.

Except at the highest levels of poker, it pays to be conservative. If you find you are bored when you do not participate in every pot, I suggest playing for matchsticks. Poker is not your game. If you are a consistent loser at poker, you are almost certainly playing far too many hands.

2. *Remember that any money you have put into the pot is no longer your money.* Every bet that you make at poker is a separate entity. If you made a bad decision to stay in a pot to "take a look" at one more card, it should not affect your decision about whether to pay to see another card. At any given time, your decision is simple: Compute the odds against your winning; if the pot offers odds higher than your chances, bet. If the odds are poor, drop out.

At all times, play the optimum strategy. Think of yourself as trying to win for a year, rather than a day. Trying to chase lost pots is the surest way to lose at poker.

3. *The most important decision you will make on most hands is whether or not to bet on the first round.* You must consider three factors when deciding whether to bet: the strength of your hand, the up-cards of the opponents in stud games, and your position at the table. Most losers don't think enough about the importance of position. If you have ever sat directly to the right of a strong, aggressive player, you can testify to the queasy feeling of committing your intentions before the strong player. But if you are seated to the left of the aggressive player, you feel more comfortable opening a marginal hand, knowing that the strong player would be in the pot already if he had a halfway decent hand.

If you are to the left of the dealer and open with a marginal hand, you are subject to raises and reraises by the players to the left of you. If you are the last to speak, and everyone has checked to you, you can open with a hand you wouldn't have thought of betting at first position. So the disadvantages of being in the first few seats to the left of the dealer are obvious: You must commit first on marginal hands, so requirements for opening must be stronger; in draw games, you must choose how many cards you are going to throw away before the others; and you must speak first on the next round of betting. About the only advantage of sitting to the left of the dealer is that it offers the safest seat to "sandbag" (to check with a good hand, trying to fool others into thinking you have a marginal hand).

Most experts insist that if you are sitting in the first three seats to the left of the dealer in draw poker, you must have at least a pair of aces to open the betting, whereas a pair of queens (some would say jacks) is sufficient to open as dealer or in the two seats to the right of dealer. A pair of kings are required to open halfway around the table.

4. *If you don't think you have the best hand at the table, drop out.* The best hand going into the draw or the best hand going into the last down-card at seven-card stud usually wins. If your hole cards and up-cards combined can't beat the best holdings you see on the board, you should drop out automatically (because you can't see the hole cards that may be improving your opponents' hands). If there is enough money in the pot to justify drawing for a flush or straight, you may stay in as long as there is no evidence another player has a higher holding.

5. *Do not sandbag.* One of the characteristics of low-stakes games is that most players stay in too long. Check-raising is unlikely to work in this kind of atmosphere, because weak players are unlikely to fold marginal hands when you have made a normal bet but are like jellyfish when raised. You are more likely to accumulate money in the pot by a simple bet. Raise when you want to steal a pot.

6. *Do not bluff.* In movies, a bluff may separate the men from the boys. But in low-stakes games, a bluff is more likely to separate the bluffer from his money. The only time a bluff is likely to work is when your opponent is losing badly. If you see your opponent hoarding his few remaining chips, he is likely to want to make his last stand with an excellent hand. You might get away with a bluff.

The usual argument advanced for bluffing is that it "pays to advertise." If you win the pot, you've "stolen" it. If you've lost the pot and show your hand, you will be called more often in the future because the other players will think that you are "loose." These tactics are useless in a home or low-stakes game where players are all too loose to begin with.

In certain situations it is downright foolhardy to bluff:

- Never bluff against a weak player (you are losing the skill advantage you possess).
- Never bluff against a big winner, especially a weak player who is winning (unskilled winners believe in "riding" their good luck and won't fold on any hand until they've lost several hands in a row).
- Never bluff when you have been caught bluffing without winning an intervening pot (even dim-witted players remember a flagrant bluff; once you have bluffed, you will be seen as a bluffer until you've won a few pots).
- Never bluff if you are losing badly.
- Never bluff against macho types. (Often one player in every group sees it as his or her mission in life to keep bluffers honest. Although they will lose their shirts in the long run, these players will win individual pots against bluffers).
- Never bluff if you haven't played the entire hand as if you had a winner. (Many players will check or call until the last bet, and then bet the maximum or raise, trying to convince the opponents that they have caught their straight or flush. This kind of tactic will not work in small-

stakes games, in which very few players drop out after committing themselves to the first bet.

- Never bluff until you've assessed the styles of your opponents. Many players will join a game and bluff wildly at their first opportunity. Yes, this advertising will spread the message that you are a wild player, but it will also color how the other players react to you in the future. If you play conservatively for a while and see that the game is a loose one, there is no reason to sacrifice any money by bluffing once. You run a risk by advertising conspicuously. Good, aggressive players will tend to call known bluffers more often. This will work when you have the great hand, but will hurt you on the more frequent better than average hands which you will need to win in order to make your poker game profitable.

7. *Most players who wager more than the minimum opening bet, or who raise or reraise on the opening bet, are likely to stay in the pot until the bitter end.* Particularly in home games, most players are willing to stay in the pot for the token minimum bet (one unit), but few are willing to stick around for the draw with an ace-high holding when the bet is four units. This is the major reason bluffing is usually a futile exercise: If you chase out the opponents on the opening round, all you have won is the ante; if you bluff in later rounds, they are unlikely to fold. In no-limit games, where a player can be forced to bet an entire bankroll on one hand, bluffing can be a devastating strategic maneuver. In low-stakes games, players are psychologically attuned to staying in pots ("the worst that can happen is it will cost me a few bucks"). When players know that they can't make a fortune even if they win, they somehow decide to stay in pots for the action, even when their cards don't justify it.

8. *Losing players call with weak hands when they should drop out and they don't push strong hands enough. Winning*

*players drop out of more hands than losing players, but bet
more and raise more with strong hands.* The biggest mistake
that most players make is staying in the pot during the opening
round when they should fold. If you have a pair of tens in
draw poker, you should fold. Sure, you may pair your ace
kicker, but the odds are overwhelming that most, if not all,
of the other players who opened have better hands than you
do. The best hand going into the second round of bidding is
usually the best hand at the end. Would you want to stay in
the pot if you could see that your three potmates had a pair
of aces, jacks-up, and four to an ace-high flush? Of course not.
Commandment #1 tells us that our edge in poker is the very
fact that we have the right *not* to bet when the odds are against
it. When we rate to have the fourth best hand at the table,
the odds are greatly against us. And we should run in the
other direction from the pot.

But the reverse is also true. When we have a good hand,
we should take advantage of the fact that we are playing in a
low-stakes game and try to press our advantage to the fullest.
Don't be afraid to raise. Yes, you may drive out players from
the pot, but those people might draw hands that could beat
you. Meanwhile, you have increased the value of the pot when
you win. You may want to lay low on the first round of betting
by not raising or betting the maximum amount in order to
entice other players, but after the first round, be as aggressive
as possible. When you have three of a kind, you want to make
that player who is wistfully dreaming about the flush drop out.

9. *Bet with confidence even if you are not sure you have
the best hand.* If you have a hand that is good enough to stick
with to the bitter end, bet aggressively, for the reasons stated
in Commandment #8. You are trying to drive out other players even if you aren't sure you have the best hand. If you are
going to call another player's bet and you are first to speak,
it is almost always correct to bet yourself. This tactic does
leave you susceptible to a raise, but it can also win for you in
two ways. It gives you a chance to win the pot yourself right

away if your opponent drops out, and perhaps more important, it shows more strength to the opponent than your hand might really merit. After all, you are acting just as a player with a lock-cinch hand would act. You can often chase out a bluffer or a player with a marginal hand simply by opening the betting every round in a confident manner.

10. *Before deciding on whether to fold on the opening round, consider your prospects for improving your hand.* The value of a poker hand is measured not only by its current value but by its potential for improvement. Seasoned draw poker players are likely to fold with a low two-pair and stay in with a pair of kings. Why? The average winning hand at an eight-player draw poker game is jacks-up. Although it is true that a low two-pair can be converted into a full house, the odds are strongly against it (10.8 to 1), while the odds against getting another pair with a three-card draw are only 2.5 to 1. Improving a low three-of-a-kind is tough, too (8.7 to 1 against getting a full house, and there is obviously only one card in the deck that can give you four of a kind), so many seven-card stud players are wary of low three-of-a-kinds when the average winner in this game is three eights.

One way of diagnosing your chances of improving your hand is by looking at other cards on the table at stud games. If you are looking to buy a heart flush and you see three other hearts exposed on the table, your odds have slipped drastically. In draw poker, your chance of catching four to a flush is 4.2 to 1. Your chances of catching an open-ended straight (e.g., 3–4–5–6) is 5 to 1. Your odds of catching an inside-straight is . . . DON'T EVEN THINK ABOUT IT. Before drawing to a straight or flush, the odds that the pot provides you must exceed the 5-to-1 or the 4.2-to-1 odds, respectively, of catching your card.

11. *Keep track of how much money is in the pot, and calibrate your tactics accordingly.* Many weak players instinctively drop out more often when many others are in the pot,

mistakenly assuming that the odds have gone against their entering the fray with a marginal hand. In fact, the odds may have now swung in their favor. Obviously, if your chances of drawing to a straight are 5 to 1, you need many players in the pot to justify entering. The high numbers of players in the pot have not lessened your chances of drawing your straight (although they might diminish your chances of *winning* with that straight). In a low-stakes games, if you play according to the proper odds, you will rarely lose.

12. *Watch the other players as well as their cards.* Most mediocre poker players are too preoccupied with their own problems to analyze the problems their opponents are facing. Actions by players that reveal their hands are called "tells." At the highest levels, especially in table stakes games, players work assiduously at not broadcasting their emotions to their opponents, but few can succeed totally. After a while, we can start discerning patterns of behavior of our opponents. Some of these patterns are simply their style of play, whether they are aware or not that they are using a system. We might find, for example, that one player will always open with a pair of jacks in draw poker, regardless of position. This is valuable information if we are sure that he will always follow this system.

We may pick up pieces of body language that tell us when an opponent is nervous. We may have a gut feeling that an opponent is bluffing, without knowing why. In a brilliant book, *Mike Caro's Book of Tells*, the author classifies the various kinds of tells, supplies sequential still photographs of players' actions, and rates each tell in terms of how confident you can be that it will reveal a certain type of hand. Most of the material on tells discussed here is adapted from this book.

Interpreting a tell is mostly a matter of common sense. For example, it doesn't take a genius to figure out that the type of person who compulsively stacks his chips neatly is probably a conservative player, whereas sloppy stackers are usually loose and sometimes careless bettors. Neat freaks also tend to count their chips conscientiously. Many of them, when winning, tend to separate their profit from their original stake. When their gravy is dwindling, many neat stackers are extremely reluctant to part with their profit. This makes them an easy target to bluff; if they dip back into their original stake, you can fold secure in the fact that they have you beat.

Most players wouldn't even think that the way they stack their chips might influence how someone would play against them. Many tells are similarly unintentional, unwittingly revealing the dilemma of the "teller." Common sense should prevail. If you see that a player consistently acts in direct contradiction to one of these tells, trust your instinct rather than these generalities. Here are some of the most common tells and their interpretations:

THE TELL: A player shuffles a one-card draw or the last down-card in a stud game, prolonging the moment before he sees it.

WHAT THE TELL MEANS: He is building the suspense for himself. Chances are he is trying for a straight or a flush rather than to improve a two-pair.

THE TELL: A player makes a trembling bet (one that you suspect is not a performance).

WHAT THE TELL MEANS: Watch out. Unintentional shaking is almost always a release of tension rather than a manifestation of fear. He's got a big hand.

THE TELL: A player doublechecks his hole cards in stud.

WHAT THE TELL MEANS: Usually, it means the player is looking for flush possibilities. He had to check his hole cards because he remembered the rank of his cards but not the suits.

THE TELL: A player checks his hole cards in a seven-card stud game after he receives an ace and then a three up.

WHAT THE TELL MEANS: There is a good chance that the player paired his ace and was so excited he forgot what his other card was in the hole (he only remembers that it was a little card).

THE TELL: A player glances furtively at his chips.

WHAT THE TELL MEANS: This is why it is important to watch the opponents, rather than their cards as they are dealt, in seven-card stud games. A player almost always looks at his chips secretly and fleetingly because he has helped his hand with the last card and is considering how much to bet. Because he is responding favorably to the last up-card, you can often diagnose one of his hole cards.

THE TELL: After a draw or an up-card in a stud game, a player checks instantly. Or the player bets instantly.

WHAT THE TELL MEANS: He is not bluffing in either case (a bluffer is more likely to act in tempo), but chances are his draw or last card did not improve his hand or he would need a little more time to evaluate his action. The instant checker has a bad hand; the instant bettor has a terrific one.

THE TELL: A player seems unusually careful about protecting his hand from being seen.

WHAT THE TELL MEANS: Watch out! He's got a great hand.

Just as common as unintentional tells are intentional tells, conscious attempts to deceive opponents. Once diagnosed, intentional tells can be even more valuable to you, since, if correctly interpreted, they will tell you positively whether or not your opponent is bluffing (let's face it, a player may recheck his hole cards simply because he's tired; unintentional tells can't always be diagnosed properly).

One rule of thumb will explain almost all intentional tells: The actor is trying to get you to believe he has a hand opposite to what he really has. If a player is next in line to bet and looks away from the action, seemingly uninterested or dis-

Interested, he has a good hand (or else you are playing for *extremely* low stakes). On the other hand, if a player makes an aggressive, exaggerated motion in betting, it usually signifies weakness. A gentle, hesitant bet shows strength.

When you are dealt a great hand, you want to fade into the woodwork so the other players won't catch on. You will do nothing to call attention to yourself, for your biggest fear is driving everyone else out of the pot.

When you are bluffing with a bad hand, you are very unlikely to let out an involuntary sigh of resignation. You are self-conscious about whether others are picking up tells, so you may overcompensate by acting boisterously or aggressively.

Here are a few of the most common intentional attempts to deceive.

THE TELL: A player stares at you directly.

WHAT THE TELL MEANS: The opponent is displaying weakness. If he had a great hand, would he want to intimidate you into folding?

THE TELL: A player reaches for his chips to bet before it is his turn.

WHAT THE TELL MEANS: A player with a great hand is afraid of being perceived as overanxious. This is an intentional attempt to appear stronger than he is.

THE TELL: A player bets first and then looks back at his hand as you reach for your chips.

WHAT THE TELL MEANS: A definite bluffer. Again, why would someone with a good hand want to intimidate you into declining to offer your money to the pot?

Ironically, many players unconsciously provide tells while trying to deceive. For example, a player with a good hand might turn his head away from the action to feign disinterest, but his eyes gravitate toward the pot. Beware. His eye movement is probably unconscious. Your opponent has a very good hand.

Decent players will always remember the rank of their hole cards at stud. They may not remember the suit of the cards, but they will be sure to note when both hole cards are the same suit. So when a good player has hit a third spade up-card and then takes a peek at his hole cards, he is almost certainly bluffing. He may have one other spade in the hole, but he doesn't have his flush yet, even if he bets vigorously this round.

The most important thing to remember about tells is that players tend to repeat themselves in mannerisms and in strategy. When they depart from the usual, it is commonly because their hand is extraordinarily strong or their hand is weak and they are contemplating bluffing. When a player's manner becomes forced or exaggerated, he is probably trying to deceive. If so, weakness means strength; strength means weakness.

You may have noticed that our Twelve Commandments, not unlike the Ten Commandments, are a tad simplistic and general. Any of the books we recommend at the end of the chapter will provide you with more specific advice and the exceptions to these rules. Our job has been to get you thinking like a winning poker player. But to give you a little better idea how you can apply these commandments to the two most popular poker games, we'll supply some tips for how to negotiate seven-card stud and draw poker.

## SEVEN-CARD STUD

Seven-card stud is probably the easiest game for a tight player to win. If you lose consistently at seven-card stud, you are almost certainly participating in too many pots. Since draw poker has only two rounds of betting, it is clearer that one must drop out of marginal hands. A tremendous temptation in seven-card stud is to stay in the pot after the first up-card in order to see another card. This is financial suicide. *The only reason to stay in any pot is because you think you have a good chance of winning it.*

Somehow, stud players feel, because there are five betting rounds, that it can't cost them much to indulge in one wager. Since the high up-card usually bets on the first round, players do not assume that the opener must have a good hand (as is the tacit assumption in draw poker). A high percentage of players stick in the pot during the first round, so the pot odds at seven-card stud appear to be high. But the ante is low, and the pot is rich only because many players are still active. Obviously, the more active players in the pot, the harder it is to win. Yes, the opener may have started the betting only because he has an ace up, but he would act exactly the same way if he has paired his ace in the hole. Why compete with five or six other players when your own hand is mediocre?

STAY OUT OF THE BETTING WHEN:

1. You don't beat the board with your hole card and up-card unless you have a *high* three-flush or straight.
2. You have a small pair (tens or less) unless it is concealed and you have a high up-card.
3. You have no pair and no ace or king.
4. You are going for a flush or a straight and you see more than one card that would fill your flush or straight in the up-cards of the opponents.

Even if you take one up-card, you should normally fold if the fourth card doesn't improve your hand unless you originally had an excellent hand (pair of kings or aces, for example). It might strike you as crazy to fold with a pair of queens when someone makes a bet with a probable pair of kings. At least you *know* you have a high pair. Couldn't a player always bluff you out if you fold so easily? Conceivably. Remember, though, that the odds are 2 to 1 that the opponent's pair matches his up-card.

One of the hallmarks of Mike Caro's strategy in seven-card stud is to be aggressive about raising on "third street" (after the first up-card—the first round of betting). He suggests that if you have a superb hand, such as high trips (three of a kind), or an ace-high three-flush, you should call and try to attract other players. But if you have small trips or the best probable pair, you should raise immediately and chase players out of the pot before they catch their straights or flushes. "When you have a pair, try to raise players out—you don't want three-way action!" Caro emphatically insists that you should never slow-play *any* pair in seven-card stud.

If you are unsure whether your pair is the highest on the board, it is better to throw your hand away than to slow-play. You must always consider what the opponents' hole cards are. If a player stays in the pot with a four exposed, you can assume, unless he is a horrendous player, that he isn't merely pressing on a pair of fours.

In large-stakes games, it can sometimes pay off to nurse potential straights and flushes. In home games and small Vegas-style games, it is better to fold them. The average winning hand is actually much higher in home games, because too many players stay in the pot. In general, you should fold straight and flush possibilities unless the cards offer excellent opportunities if paired. And as I mentioned above, forget about flushes if you see two of the suit you need already on the board.

The main reason the requirements for staying in the pot at third street are so stringent is that after the initial betting commitment is made, you will often stay in the pot until the bitter end, with less chance of dropping out in each succeeding round. Usually, you will fold when you are convinced that someone else has the superior hand, which can often be easily deduced not only by studying the up-cards but by watching how the player acted on third street. In a low-limit game, you should never plan on driving out an opponent with a bluff once he has committed himself with a bet on third street. This is why I have slow-played on third street with excellent hands: It is my intention to bet the maximum amount on every succeeding round as long as I think I retain the best hand.

Don't overlook the obvious, however. If a player has three clubs exposed and starts betting enthusiastically at fifth street, you can assume she has at least a four-flush and should drop pairs and two-pairs. If a player on fifth street pairs her first up-card, you know she has more than one pair, or else why had she bothered to stick around until fifth street?

I recommend you follow the general strategy of not bluffing. Bluffing only works when players have genuine fear about losing the amount of money they are placing in the pot. An accountant is as likely to do better at this kind of game than Evel Knievel would. You do not need the flamboyance of an Amarillo Slim to win at low-stakes seven-card stud. If you play the odds, you don't need *any* personality trait to win. My strategy may not be the most glamorous or even the most fun way to win, but it is the surest.

## DRAW POKER

In some ways, draw poker is easier to analyze than stud, because there are only two betting rounds. It is, however, a highly technical game and its strategy is not as easily summarized as stud poker, because the requirements for opening and calling change in each betting position. Although the general tactics I have discussed apply to draw poker as well as stud, I'll refer you to more exhaustive texts for hard-line advice. But here are a few tips to whet your appetite about what is a slow-moving but intricate and fascinating game.

1. Again, in a low-stakes game you will be most successful when you play conservatively. When you are directly to the left of the dealer, you need at least a pair of aces to open in an eight-person game, because in the first seat you are subject to reraises by players who have yet to speak. If you are in one of the seats just to the right of the dealer, you can open with a pair of jacks. But no less.

2. If someone else opens the betting, you need a considerably better hand to call, normally queens-up if you are just to the right of opener, a pair of aces if you have a good position. It is rarely right to call with less than a pair of aces before the draw.

3. In draw poker you can bluff not only on your bets but on the number of cards you draw. If you have three of a kind, for example, you might want to consider drawing one card instead of two. Your opponents will assume you are trying to fill a straight or flush or to improve a two-pair (or, ironically, that you are bluffing with a bad hand). Drawing only one card doesn't significantly lower your chances of improving your hand (it doesn't hurt your chances of getting a full house at all).

4. Keep in mind that players seldom bluff on the betting round before the draw. Most bluffing occurs during the draw itself and especially on the betting round after the draw. In particular, always assume that a caller has full values for her bet. After all, who does a caller chase out of the pot? The initial bet has already been placed. Bluffers raise; they rarely call.

5. Before the draw, the odds are about 2 to 1 that a two-pair will be the best hand. But as in most other forms of poker, be wary of two-pairs: The odds are 11 to 1 against improving with your draw. You can assume that players with pairs who remain in the fray have high pairs. When you realize that players with pairs have about a 1-in-3 chance of improving, and that the least they can improve to is a *high* two-pair, you will understand the vulnerable position in which you place yourself if you play low two-pairs with several players in the pot. If you have less than queens-up, the odds are very much against you beating three other players. For this reason, you want to be aggressive about driving out those with pairs before the draw when you have marginal two-pair hands. When there are fewer players in the pot, you can be somewhat more secure. If only two opponents are in the pot, and they each drew three cards, the odds are better than fifty-fifty that neither of them improved.

6. Never, ever, draw to a bust hand, unless everyone has checked.

7. Never draw to *any* straight unless the pot odds justify it.

8. If you have three-of-a-kind after the draw and you are playing against one opponent who has drawn one card, unless you have noticed an absolutely certain tell, call your opponent. Yes, she may have drawn her straight, but if you fold in these circumstances, you will be constantly subjected to a bluff in the future.

9. After the draw, if you think you are likely to have the best hand (three tens, for example) but are facing an opponent who has drawn one card and will speak after you, it is probably prudent to check rather than bet, because you are subject to raises. You fully intend to call your opponent's bet.

**For more information:**

Read just about any poker book that you can find; there are many fine ones on the market. Most poker problems can be solved by simple mathematical analysis. As a result, there is too much good information on the market for charlatans to survive, in contrast to some of the bizarre offerings about casino games or horse racing. Although many books emphasize the importance of psychological factors in making a winning poker player, you are better off with a book that stresses poker odds; you can learn how to put on your best poker face after you learn the basics. The following books are highly recommended.

*The Complete Guide to Winning Poker*, Albert H. Morehead (New York: Simon & Schuster/A Fireside Book, 1967).

*Win at Poker*, Jeff Rubens (New York: Galahad Books, 1968).

Two authors, more famous for their exploits in the bridge world, have written excellent books suited for the intelligent beginner or home player who wants to advance in skills.

For the more advanced player, I recommend anything written by Mike Caro, who is perhaps the liveliest writer on gambling today. In particular, I recommend the chapters on poker in *Caro on Gambling* (Seacacus, NJ: Gambling Times, 1984), and the entire *Mike Caro's Book of Tells* (Seacacus, NJ: Gambling Times, 1984), which has already been discussed in detail. (Gambling Times books are distributed by Lyle Stuart of New York.) Caro's books are so much fun that you never realize how much technical knowledge you have absorbed. Caro's writing is much more technical than the two books recommended above and assumes that you have a working knowledge of basic poker strategy and terminology.

# How to Win at Buying a New Car

A GOOD NEW-CAR SALESMAN is more than someone with a large collection of loud sportscoats. He—and increasingly, she—is a person who loves to make deals. His skill is not so much in selling you a car that you don't want (the smell of a new interior and the sheen of glossy, pristine paint stimulates far more sales than any assemblage of words) as in extracting every possible dollar from you for a car on which you've already sold yourself.

Usually, by the time you enter the office of the salesman to close the deal, it is too late. You are dead meat. The salesman has become one of your new best friends, truly concerned about that expensive orthodontic work your teenage daughter requires. "Don't worry," he assures you, "I'll make you a good deal."

Do you really have to put up with this bull in order to buy a new car? If you enjoy negotiating as much as the salesman, you may want to slug it out, but most of us don't have the desire, the information, the tenacity, or the ability to win a confrontation with a specialist in selling. It is not impossible, as a book I will recommend later suggests, to "Beat the Salesman at His Own Game," but it probably isn't necessary.

You are going to do an end run around the salesman. You are not going to negotiate at all. You are going to make one offer and ask the dealership to take it or leave it. If you have done your considerable homework right, it will be an offer that the dealership can't refuse. But first things first.

## STEP #1: RESEARCH

Before you even begin to think about price, determine which make and model you desire and can afford, and which options you will need. Talk to friends and reliable mechanics about the performance and service problems they have encountered with your prospective cars. Read *Consumer Reports* (especially their annual April auto issue or their year-end *Buying Guide* issue that lists the service records and cost of maintenance for virtually every car sold in the United States) and *Motor Trend*, which is especially useful in evaluating high-performance cars.

For reasons I will explain later, it is crucial that you know exactly what you want on the day you buy your car. Your test drive, then, should not be the clincher of your deal but rather a part of your research. If at all possible, do not use a demo car for your test drive. Dealers have been known to fine-tune demos for high performance. Ask to drive the actual car you are interested in (or an identical lot car) with the performance options you need to examine. Only an extended test drive can confirm whether or not you require power steering or brakes, automatic or manual transmission, or a V–6 or V–8 engine. When you complete your test drive, do *not* attempt to negotiate. Thank the salesperson, take his or her card, and remain noncommittal—you have much more research to do before you can begin to negotiate, even if you love to death the car you have just test driven.

If all of your research confirms that the car you test drove is indeed the auto of your dreams, it is time for the subject of money to rear its ugly head.

## STEP #2: DETERMINE THE DEALER'S COST

With a minimum of legwork, it is possible to find out exactly how much your dealer has paid for "your" car. The loan officer at your bank or credit union has access to this information and usually will provide it. Be sure you add the wholesale price of options such as air conditioning, power steering, and leather upholstery.

*Consumer Reports* provides an Auto Price Service that will, for a reasonable fee, send you a computer printout indicating the retail list price and dealer's cost for your car and for every available option. The *Consumer Reports* printout includes recommendations for which options are desirable, as well as a sensible report on how to negotiate a low price on any car (for further information on the Auto Price Service only, write: *Consumer Reports*, P.O. Box 570, Lathrop Village, Michigan 48076).

### STEP #3: LINE UP FINANCING

You are in a much better position to win at buying a new car if you pay in cash. Dealerships absorb enormous interest costs for their inventory; it is difficult for them to pass up a cash profit, even if it is a small one.

With the price of most new cars in five figures, the prospect of a cash purchase is an impossible dream for many. If you are unable to pay cash for your car, you must arrange financing for your purchase *before* you begin bargaining with the dealership. If you expect to receive a significant amount of money for the trade-in of your old car, it is particularly important not to mention to the salesperson that you are planning to sell your old car. If you tip off your intentions, the salesperson is likely to offer you a generous price on the trade-in, only to get back his profit margin on an inflated price for your new car. You want to be able to bargain on both ends —on the price of your new car and on the financing of the new car—to maximize your chances of reaching your best deal.

Just as you researched the dealer's cost of your new car, you need to know how much your old car is worth. Go to several used-car lots and ask how much they are willing to pay. Consult the *Kelley* or *National Automobile Dealers Association Used Car Price Guide* or any of the publications found on newsstands that list used-car prices. Scan the classified listings in your local newspapers. Chances are, the used-car dealers will offer you prices approximating the Kelley listings, assuming the condition and mileage of your car is average.

There are many ways to sell the car for more money than the used-car dealer is likely to offer. The easiest way is to sell your car privately by placing an ad in the local paper (Sunday is usually the day when most buyers scan the auto ads). Unless your car is in especially good shape, you can probably sell your used car for somewhere between retail price (the used-car dealers' selling price) and wholesale. Don't expect a consumer to pay you full retail price, because, from his point of view, he is taking a chance buying from an unknown source.

If you order a new car rather than buying one already on the lot, you will probably have about two months to sell the old car before delivery on the new one. If you try to sell the car privately without success, you can always trade it in at the last minute. At the very least, you can go back to the used-car lot if that offer was higher than the one your new-car dealership is willing to make. Just remember that your new purchase and your trade-in are two separate transactions. If you don't negotiate each end individually, you won't get your optimum deal.

About 70 percent of all car purchases are financed. Try, if at all possible, to be among the 30 percent minority. In most cases, it is preferable to run your old car into the ground and save the money necessary to pay for the new car with cash. Not only will you save thousands of dollars in interest payments, but you will also increase your chances of getting a great deal on your purchase price when you use our system (see Step #6).

If you must finance your car, shop around for the loan on your car just as avidly as for the price of your car. Banks used to offer loans at a lower rate than most car dealerships, but this is no longer necessarily the case. As this is being written, the Big Three American auto companies are offering interest rates (in lieu of rebates or other sales incentives) that are lower than bank or credit-union rates.

If you do choose to finance your car and find a loan with tolerable rates, you should give your new-car dealer a chance to beat the terms. Once again, your strategy should be to negotiate a price for the car *before* you indicate that you will need a loan. Dealerships have many tricks to lower the purchase price of a car and make up their profit margin by offering loans at exorbitant rates. If you already have a loan offer in hand, you are in a position to negotiate the loan separately and to walk away from the loan offered by the dealership if it doesn't match your bank or credit-union offer.

### STEP #4: KNOW WHEN TO BUY

Timing your purchase is a key to winning at buying a new car. The automobile market is a classic supply and demand scenario, in which the price of a car can swing hundreds of dollars depending upon the vagaries of the marketplace. If you buy your car in the fall, right after the new models are introduced, you can expect to pay much more than if you are willing to wait until the selling pace slows.

Salespeople are human beings. When customers are clamoring for their cars, they will be reluctant to lower their commissions. For this reason, it is downright silly to buy your car on a weekend, unless it is the only time you can do it (on the other hand, the weekend is a good time to browse for cars, because salespeople will have their hands full with serious customers). During the middle of the week, customers are few, and the salespeople's compulsion to sell is at its highest.

All other things being equal, it is always preferable to buy at the end of the month. Most dealerships focus on monthly sales totals: Some have incentives (contests in which the top salespeople for the month get bonuses in cash or prizes) or less subtle disincentives (salespeople who don't meet their quotas get fired). In either case, you are likely to get a better price when the dealership as a whole is more focused on selling as many cars as possible rather than on making the biggest profit margin possible.

Consider buying your car at dinnertime. Traditionally, sales managers, who often are trained to be the killers in closing automobile sales, eat lunch in the showroom but take off around dinner. The skeleton crew of salespeople might have more leeway to make a deal without the interference of the closer (although some representative of management usually must okay any deal).

The end of the year, around Christmas, in midweek, at dinnertime, is possibly the best time to buy a new car. It meets all of the criteria: It is at the end of the month and it is a time when demand is extremely low. Christmas shopping doesn't seem to extend to automobiles, and in fact this lean time for car sales extends until potential customers start receiving their income-tax refunds in March and April.

There is only one other better time to buy a new car and that is after the models for the next year have just hit the showroom floor. In his book, *The Car Buyers Art: How to Beat the Salesman At His Own Game*, Darrell Parrish and Raymond Diazzo explain the advantages of buying the "leftover," an old new car:

> Once the year in which a car is manufactured elapses, several things happen to make a car very costly for the dealership to keep around. First, as far as the banks, credit unions and other lenders are concerned, it becomes not a new but a *used* car even if it has zero miles on it. This means they will lend smaller amounts of money for its purchase, which . . . makes it harder for the dealership to sell. Also the car depreciates and the dealership must either sell it fast or absorb the loss themselves.

The absolutely best way to find a cheap car is to locate an orphan leftover, one of the last cars on the lot of the old model year. If it meets your requirements, you can expect to buy it for at least 5 percent less than you would have a week before the new cars were introduced (see Step #5), but because the leftover automatically depreciates a year after it leaves the lot, the purchase of a leftover is advisable only if you plan to hold on to the car for several years. This is one time when advertising come-ons are true: The car dealer really does want to close out his old stock to make way for new, more profitable cars.

### STEP #5: DETERMINE HOW MUCH YOU ARE WILLING TO PAY

Because you have faithfully executed the first two steps, you already know the exact cost to your dealer of the car of your choice, including the wholesale cost of the options you desire and the mandatory tax and license fees. You are aware that the average retail markup includes about 20 percent profit for the dealership.

It is now time to set your target price. If at all possible, you should buy a car that is already on the lot. There is no reason to buy a car on the lot if it is loaded with options you don't want or is a color that repels you, but you can always buy a lot car cheaper than its equivalent ordered from the factory.

To retain its alliance with the auto company, a dealership must accept a certain number of cars every month from the factory, regardless of how well the cars have been moving. The dealer must pay interest on these cars. Obviously, a dealer is anxious to sell cars he must finance himself. Also, fixed costs are associated with a dealership obtaining any new car (these are called the "dealer's card"). For a car on the lot, you must add $75 for the dealer's card, which includes the so-called dealer's prep. For a factory order, you must add an additional $75, which reflects the true additional costs to the dealership. You should pay for no other extras.

If you are buying a leftover, deduct a further 5 percent from your calculations. This saving reflects the advanced depreciation on your car. Don't worry about this depreciation.

If you plan to keep your car for at least three years, you are still buying a new car at a bargain price.

But what should you offer? If you are in a feisty mood and are buying a car when demand is low, we'd recommend offering the price of the wholesale base car plus wholesale price of options plus tax plus license plus $75 or $150 dealer's card plus $100 in profit for the dealership. This would constitute only a 1 percent margin on a $10,000 car, which might seem minuscule, but the dealer has other ways of making a profit. For one, he'll get a 2 percent profit back at the end of the model year, when the manufacturer returns his "hold back." Also, the chances are good that your dealer might have been able to stock your car for less than the stated wholesale cost. Also, if you are trading in your car, you can only expect to get the wholesale price from your new-car dealer. Your dealer can either sell your trade-in for a small markup to a reseller or try to sell the car on his lot at a retail price. He may make more money from your used car than from selling you your new car.

Depending upon the supply and demand situation for your particular new car and market, you may need to go considerably higher than $100 of profit, but if you follow all of the steps listed here, your chances of making a deal for between $100 and $400 above wholesale are excellent. The important point is that once you set your price, you must remain firm. Remember, the goal was not only to obtain a good price for the car but to avoid the hassles of wrangling over a price with a salesperson. To maximize your chances of buying your car for $100 more than wholesale, you'll need not only all of the information you have compiled, but the right approach.

## STEP #6: BUYING THE DAMN CAR

The conventional wisdom about how to buy a car cheap advises taking advantage of the salesperson's desperate desire to sell to you. Salespeople who don't sell get fired. Quickly.

Furthermore, most salespeople are geared more toward making a sale rather than exacting the highest possible profit. Conventional wisdom suggests, then, to string along the salesperson, to vacillate about your interest in the car you've test-driven even if you are sure it is the car of your dreams. If the salesperson knows you love the car, says conventional wisdom, you'll never get the best price possible. When it becomes time to talk price, you are supposed to offer a few hundred dollars less than you are willing to spend and to demand a couple of hundred dollars more for your trade-in than you know the dealer can pay.

The premise behind all of the high jinks is a sound one: Once a salesperson has committed a significant amount of time to you, he doesn't want to waste it by not closing a sale.

There is only one problem with the conventional wisdom: It wastes your time as much as the salesperson's. This chapter was written for those of us who hate to haggle, who know the upper limit on what we are willing to spend, and who most of all want to get out of that awful showroom as quickly as possible and enjoy our new car in peace. I present the perfect scenario for making a deal:

You have decided that you want to buy a 1986 Starlet, a sporty sedan. You have waited the entire model year before making the purchase. You have spotted a Starlet that meets all of your specifications at Berkman's Cars and Trucks. You've gambled and not bought the car until it has become a leftover. You know exactly what Berkman paid for your car and decided that you will offer $12,200 for the Starlet, exactly $100 more than dealer's wholesale after you have deducted 5 percent from the wholesale cost to compensate for your being "stuck" with a leftover.

Right after the new 1987 Starlet models have arrived, you make your move. Your tactics will be the exact opposite of the conventional wisdom. Rather than stringing along the salesperson, you are going to make it as easy as possible for the salesperson to make his sale. You are not going to be coy. You are going to march into the office and convince the salesperson you encounter that you have every intention of buying that Starlet today. Remember that the dealership is eager to get rid of that 1986 Starlet, which is now technically a used car.

Your tone with the salesperson is going to be polite, businesslike, and impersonal. "I would like to buy the silver 1986 Starlet sedan," you will announce, "and I have a check for $12,200 to pay for it." At this point, the salesperson will try to slow you down. He will repeat the list price of the car, and tell you that it is clearly impossible to sell a 1986 Starlet, even a leftover, at such a ridiculous figure.

You will not argue with the fellow but merely repeat that $12,200 is all you are authorized to spend. A check already made out to his company has a way of attracting any salesperson. Your offer *is* going to be much lower than he would like to sell the car for, but you are also offering him something valuable—a trouble-free sale in which he has to devote literally no time to closing. Rather, he has become an order taker. In essence, you are offering him a small but tangible hunk of found money. Although his managers might not be willing to part with the car at that price, the salesperson almost certainly will take your offer seriously. Depending upon competitive pressures, the cash flow of the dealership at that particular time, and the demand for leftover Starlets, you may or may not get your car. Chances are, you will.

The best part about this strategy is that you have made all of your decisions without having to deal with a salesperson who obviously has his own vested interest in raising the price of your car and selling you options you don't need. If they do not accept your offer, you have to be prepared to leave and find your Starlet elsewhere (this whole style of buying will not work in small towns where there is no competition between dealerships and gross sales are lower but profit margins are much higher).

My brother, Phil, used this system to buy his company

car, a Toyota Supra, a car so high in consumer demand that dealers were known to sell it for above list price. When the sales manager swore up and down that his offer was obscenely low, Phil politely but firmly informed him that he was not authorized (luckily, no one asked him who was "authorizing" him in the first place) to pay more for the car. When the crunch came, the salespeople simply couldn't pass up a check made out in their name that would give them a profit, even a small profit.

You can't possibly exact this kind of leverage unless you pay in full in cash, but the principles remain the same. You make an ironclad offer *before* you let the sales force know that you are going to need to finance your car. If you already have an offer of financing elsewhere, and the dealership has accepted your offer, you can now demand that the dealership beat these terms if it wants to finance your car. If they don't meet or beat the offer from your bank, savings and loan, or credit union, don't take out the loan from the car dealership.

### STEP #7: DON'T GET SCREWED AFTER THE DEAL HAS BEEN MADE

A word of warning that shouldn't be needed: Read your contract very carefully, especially if you are financing your car. All promises that are made to you verbally should be *in writing*, explicitly laid out in the contract.

When you take delivery of your new car, examine it carefully. The odds are greatly in favor of there being minor damage to your car, usually caused en route from the factory to your dealer. The dealer will correct body damage if you point it out *before* you pay for the car. Likewise, it is probably wise to test drive your car (or, at least, run the engine on the lot) *before* you pay for the car. Although mechanical problems will be handled by your warranty, it is better to know early if you might have bought a total lemon.

## A Word About Imports

As this is being written, it will be much tougher using this strategy at a Honda or Toyota dealership than at a Chrysler or Chevrolet lot. In fact, you are as likely to be put on a waiting list for the "honor" of buying a Toyota as you are to make a killer deal. The profit margins on imported cars tend to be more variable than on domestic cars and because of import quotas and the generally limited supplies, a surge of demand can propel the usual profit margins on imports beyond the customary 20 percent markup of list price that domestic dealers would kill to achieve. Your best shot at getting a high-demand car at a small markup is to try to buy a leftover during the new model season. Most imports come in a limited number of inoffensive colors and have standard options, so that the imported leftover is much more likely to meet your specifications than the domestic leftover.

**For more information:**

*Consumer Reports* is particularly valuable for its surveys on the maintenance records of virtually all late-model cars. Only the experiences of other car owners can demonstrate, for example, the extraordinary reliability of Toyotas; they are perennially among the least repaired and cheapest to repair cars on the road. Examining the maintenance records of many of the most prestigious cars on the road—including Mercedes Benz and Cadillac—will make you think twice about whether that deep plunge into your pocket is an investment in the future or in your overactive ego.

*Motor Trend* and *Car and Driver*. The auto magazines are recommended for those interested in performance cars or those who can interpret arcane specifications. Just remember that a reliable car with mediocre performance will satisfy more buyers than a high-performance car that breaks down constantly or takes a fortune to maintain. After all, it doesn't

matter so much how long it takes a car to get from 0 to 60
mph when the speed limit is 55 mph.

*The Car Buyer's Art: How to Beat the Salesman at His
Own Game*, Darrell Parrish and Raymond DiZazzo (Bell-
flower, CA: Book Express, 1981). This is the best statement
of the conventional wisdom in buying a car that I have read.
The authors delve into the psychology of the salesman, and
although their advice is sound, they assume that the reader
wants to counterattack rather than to avoid getting into mind
games with the salespeople.

*Choosing the Right Car for the 1980s*, Moss Miller (Blue
Ridge Summit, PA: TAB Books, 1984). This straightforward
manual is not as much fun to read as Parrish and DiZazzo,
but it is a no-nonsense, objective guide to every step in selecting and buying a new car.

# WINNING

## FOR

## YOURSELF

# How to Solve Just About Any Mystery

*But wasn't the secretary bowling at the time of the murder? What if her twin sister substituted in the bowling league and the secretary committed the murder? What a perfect cover! Except the forensic test shows the lethal blow was struck by a right-handed person, and the secretary is left-handed. Her twin would have had to bowl left-handed to carry off the ruse, but she bowled a 198 game that night. It doesn't make any sense. Why would she want to kill her boss anyway? He had just proposed marriage.*

*It couldn't have been the security guard, could it? He was the only suspect who had easy access to the office that night. Why would kindly Lazlo be mixed up with the highfalutin lawyer? Poor Lazlo was a refugee from Hungary and was never less than respectful to the dead man. Lazlo did him special favors. Could Lazlo have been the one to make the threatening phone calls on the deceased's private line? And why did the lawyer give Lazlo $500 as a Christmas "tip"?*

One can go nuts trying to sort out the clues and the suspects in a mystery story. Juggling facts, figures, motives, forensic evidence, and psychopathology is enough to send many amateur sleuths into premature burnout. In self-defense, many readers (or viewers of television or movie mysteries) bull through a story, consciously shunning the attempt to crack the mystery, hoping to avoid permanent brain damage. Others resort to the ploy: "I am not, of course, perusing this work of art in order to arrive at something so trivial as the identity of the murderer. I am reading this mystery in order to soak up the English atmosphere and to learn more about goatherding." Oh, I suppose, there are other legitimate reasons for reading a mystery, but beats there a heart so cold or an ego so solid that it doesn't rejoice at besting Sherlock Holmes at his own game?

Stop feeling sorry for yourself. Sure, it is difficult to unscramble hundreds of clues and arrive at the one nugget of truth that will unlock the secret. But consider the plight of the poor mystery writer. He *knows* the identity of the murderer. He *knows* that the explanation of the mystery can usually be expressed in one declarative sentence. The writer's primary job, then, is to build an elaborate camouflage—a structure whose purpose is to obscure the identity of the murderer. The writer realizes that if he makes one mistake —if he is too obvious—the reader will pounce upon the culprit.

A mystery writer, then, tends to be a justifiably paranoid person. He exerts so much effort in covering up his murderer that, like the belligerent witness trying to withhold evidence from Perry Mason, the writer will leave more clues to the reader than the fictional murderer ever will.

To become a super-sleuth, you must get inside the head of the writer. In most cases, the author couldn't care less about the ostensible milieu of the book, any more than a magician cares about scarves or top hats, except insofar as it yields a rich and interesting arena for disguising his secret. What the writer *does* care about is how he is going to disguise a simple story. How is he going to make the identity of his murderer a secret for most of the book but then make that choice seem not only right but inevitable? It's a tough job.

If you are going to get into this super-sleuth business, you'll have to change your reading habits. Super-sleuths cannot be passive readers. You ordinarily read unselfconsciously. Most books you read—certainly this one—are designed to simplify and clarify information. The author is your friend, gently tugging you toward "the truth." You can read most prose on automatic pilot—the way you drive or touch-type —because efficient reading depends upon ignoring detail and retaining only obviously significant points. Just as you learn to shift to uppercase on a typewriter without being consciously aware of it, so do you read most books, assuming that your ally, the writer, will stop and underline important points.

The mystery writer won't be so cooperative. The mystery writer, like the magician, will fool you if you let him misdirect you. The magician may utilize marked cards, false-bottomed cylinders, and attractive assistants in his arsenal of tricks but the writer has only words. By looking at writing devices themselves for the solution to fictional murders, rather than petty diversions (e.g., characters' motivations or opportunities to commit murder), you are well on the way to crime-busting.

A group of Russian literary critics, the Formalists, developed several concepts in the 1920s that may provide you with tools to solve mysteries. Their research concluded that the actual subject matter and imagery of writers differed very little from culture to culture, from century to century. What did change, and drastically so, was the arrangement of these familiar elements. Formalists differentiated what they called the *story* from the *plot*. The story is the logical, chronological sequence of events in a narrative ("because Archie found his wife Lola in bed with Harry, Archie kills Harry and tries to frame his wife for the murder"). The plot is the story as distorted by the author. In a mystery, we are unlikely to see Archie actually killing Lola or framing Harry. Thus, the purpose of most mystery plots is to disguise the actual story. As the critic Victor Shlovsky commented: "The place in the work in which the reader learns of an event, whether the information is given by the author, or by a character, or by a series of indirect hints—all this is irrelevant to the story." But these devices are the essence of plotting and the key to solving any whodunit.

Your strongest weapon in unraveling the plot is another

Formalist concept. They called the story elements that were essential to making sense of the narrative *bound motifs*. If Archie never discovered that his wife was sleeping with another man, he would have no motive for killing Harry, and the story would make no sense. Archie's discovery of his wife's infidelity, clearly, is a bound motif. *Free motifs* are story elements that may be omitted without disturbing the causal/ logical/chronological order of events. In mystery stories, free motifs are those nasty details that may or may not pertain to the murder. The fact that Archie is an alcoholic could be irrelevant—but then it might be the key to solving the case.

The process of solving a mystery involves turning free, seemingly decorative motifs into bound motifs, inextricably involved with the murder itself. Are there any patterns which recur that will help you in turning free motifs into bound motifs?

Absolutely. The ten strategies below, in roughly descending order of frequency, are the most common methods mystery writers use to fool the gullible reader/viewer. It's time to fight back!

1. *The dangling free motif.* Although the author is eager to protect the identity of the murderer, he is also aware that readers must feel, after finishing the story, that the selection of the murderer seems correct and not arbitrary. For this reason, the writer will usually treat the murderer differently from the other characters. Most often, he will surround the real murderer with a set of bound motifs that *seem* free. Other characters will be given free motifs, but these will be explained as the plot progresses. If a character's telephone conversation is interrupted by the tapping of a woodpecker, perhaps the incident is included only for atmosphere. But if this ostensibly irrelevant incident is repeated constantly, perhaps you should wonder if the damned woodpecker would be necessary unless it were a *bound* motif.

Often, these phony free motifs are sneaky attempts to

absolve the actual murderer from blame. In Agatha Christie's *Crooked House*, a murderer is at large. An "innocent" little girl is the only character attacked by the murderer. Because she was the only living character you see victimized by the killer, the little girl *can't* be the murderer. But, of course, she is. Forget whether the girl has any realistic motivation or opportunity to commit the murder—if she is the only character to have a dangling free motif associated with him or her, you've found your murderer.

All of the strategies below are more specific examples of how authors use seemingly free motifs to baffle unsuspecting readers.

2. *Time shifts.* Book editors and television and movie producers tend to dislike flashbacks. They think flashbacks needlessly confuse readers and viewers. And writers, all things being equal, usually like to tell stories in chronological order for one reason: It is easier to write a linear story.

So any time the plot's chronology departs from the story's, watch out! There is usually a good reason for the time distortion. Invariably, if only one time disruption occurs in the book, the event that precipitates the flashback or flashforward directs you to the murderer. For example, most of Erle Stanley Gardner's Perry Mason novels are simpler than their television counterparts. In one novel, *The Case of the Blonde Bonanza*, the plot is told with third-person narration in strict chronological order until Moose, one of Paul Drake's operatives, takes up several pages describing to Mason what he observed on his lookout.

Eureka! Moose must have been the murderer, for why else would Gardner not continue describing, simply, in the present tense, what Moose was telling Mason, clumsily, in the past tense? *Every time an author distorts time, there is a reason.* Sometimes, the writer's motive is to build suspense, but it is usually to hide a bound motif and disguise it as a free motif.

3. *A disproportionately long treatment of a seemingly free motif.* Actually, you could have discovered Moose as the murderer of *Blonde Bonanza* even without the story/plot discrepancy. For Erle Stanley Gardner, the most barebones and concise writer, took pages for Moose to describe what could have been told by third-person narration in a few paragraphs. *When a mystery writer seems to be wasting your time with what seem to be free motifs, he is probably trying to waste your mind.* A writer might describe the murder scene, for example, in more detail than you might want to know—chances are, he is trying to misdirect you from an obvious solution. But when an otherwise solid author suddenly begins boring you or saturating you with irrelevant trivia, keep in mind— why would a solid author waste his time by saturating you with irrelevant trivia?

4. *A character leaves abruptly or lingers too long. A character seems to be paid too much attention or not enough attention.* One of the perennial gimmicks of mystery stories is the "impossible murder." In the impossible murder, a person physically incapable of murder commits the deed. The most common alibi for the murderer is that he wasn't at the scene of the crime. The physical proximity of any character to the murder scene is totally irrelevant in solving the case. In fact, if a character suddenly disappears around the time of the murder (especially if it is clearly before the murder) and reappears after the dust has settled, you've got a prime suspect.

Similarly, when a character who doesn't seem to have a direct connection to the murder itself, or a particular reason for lingering, appears throughout the book, you've got another possible suspect. Look at it from the writer's point of view: Why would a writer bother with deadweight when he could spend his time misdirecting you toward one of the "real" suspects?

If only one character apparently did not have the means to commit the murder, he is often the perpetrator. Again, why would an author want to establish that an otherwise juicy suspect couldn't have done the deed? Beware of false gifts.

Occasionally, the reverse is true. A character with a good motive and a possible opportunity to commit the murder is not treated as a serious suspect, usually because his or her character is "beyond reproach." Although this hoary gimmick is still frequently used, it rarely fools the reader, who can see the author trying to bury the goody-goody character into the woodwork.

5. *Something seems funny or wrong about a character.* Trust your instincts here. Sit back and ponder: Why would the author undergo the inconvenience of providing dialogue for a prodigious stutterer if his speech impediment were irrelevant to the story? Why would the *Perry Mason* show cast an actress with a thick accent when her birthplace seems irrelevant to the story and you know, from seeing her elsewhere, that the accent is the character's and not the actress'?

There are traps in using this strategy. Many mystery writers delight in creating eccentric characters. Weirdness alone is not a criterion for labeling a character a suspect. But if the weirdness isn't established immediately, determine why you feel funny about the character. *If the reason has nothing to do with the murder*, ironically, *you've probably found your murderer.*

6. *The totally irrelevant character, or "The Butler Did It Theory."* The butler actually has "done it" less often than reputed, but the "butler did it" principle is a sound one. In solving television mystery reruns, you could do worse than just guess that the murderer is the suspect least connected to the murder in any obvious way.

The key, as always, is to look at the purpose of the character from the writer's point of view. Does the character serve any purpose? Butlers add atmosphere and a class motif to a story, but if the butler (or his equivalent) hulks around the story, included in scenes at which a butler's presence would be

inappropriate, wonder why an author would bother carrying
around the deadweight of an extra, unneeded character. Why
would a producer want to pay for an actor to portray an irrelevant character?

7. *Perfect symmetry*. Most mystery writers, such as the
fictional Hercule Poirot, are obsessed with symmetry. When
it is time to gather the suspects around the dining-room table,
the writer would like you to believe that any one of them was
equally capable of murder. One way of looking at a free motif
is as a blotch on an otherwise symmetrical world, a dangling
string in an otherwise perfectly wound ball.

But what if the fictional world of the mystery seems totally
symmetrical, with no loose ends, no obvious free motifs, one
where every suspect seems to have an equal opportunity to
commit the murder and an equally good (or bad) reason to
want the victim offed? When none of the above criteria seem
to fit, what is the solution?

After sitting through a bit of the movie, *Murder on the
Orient Express*, it became clear that the audience was presented with far too many free motifs, far too many suspects
to tie together logically. The clue lay in the plotting. The case
has twelve suspects—each of them initially lies when questioned by Poirot; each of them admits and partially corrects
his or her lie when confronted by Poirot; each has a strong
motive for murder; and each has an excellent alibi. The clues
are established so that any one of the suspects *could* logically
have been the murderer, but if any *one* of them were indeed
the murderer, you would have felt cheated. Nothing is more
awkward than a mediocre writer explaining why all of the
other suspects' motives were, in retrospect, totally different
from the perpetrator's. When all suspects are treated sym-
metrically, none of them committed the murder—or all of
them committed the murder.

8. *The ostensible mystery isn't the real mystery*. Often,
what seems to be the crucial murder in the book turns out to

be a red herring, serving as a Trojan horse for another mystery, usually another murder. In *Murder On the Links*, Agatha Christie knocks the reader for a loop by having her murderer murdered!

More often, however, an author will use this technique to divert your attention away from another, more important, mystery. In the Paul Newman film, *The Verdict*, the supposed mystery is: How did Newman's client die? And will Newman discover the truth? But very early in the movie, you realize that you are not about to be treated to a conventional mystery. Although it is Newman's job to ferret out the truth, the screenwriter lays out few free motifs, and thus no array of suspects to consider. You literally don't have a clue about how Newman's client died.

But there is another enigma in *The Verdict* that doesn't help solve the ostensible mystery but is treated with much more care: Who is this character played by Charlotte Rampling? Rampling suddenly appears in Newman's favorite hangout one night, and proceeds, on a subsequent visit, to make Newman think he is picking her up. Rampling refuses to tell Newman anything about her background (except that she is divorced and that her ex-husband is a lawyer) or explain what she is doing in Boston or how she spends her time when not with Newman. She is the second lead of the movie, yet she barely exists. You know so little about her and sense that Charlotte Rampling need not be hired and highly billed to play such a routine part, that by using Rule #4 you realize her character treatment is clearly a free motif.

In a subsequent scene, you see the villainous James Mason commiserating with a confederate, one who has sacrificed his or her ideals in order to squash Newman. The camera follows Mason, depriving you of the chance of seeing the identity of the traitor. The longer the scene drags on, without you viewing Mason's confederate, the more you realize that the unseen person must be a character you know, and that the camera's continuous one-shot of Mason is a glaring free motif. Since you know only two characters who are helping Paul Newman in the case, could it be the one without any glaring free motifs (Jack Warden)? Of course not. It must be the mysterious Charlotte Rampling.

The transformation of the free motif (i.e., you know nothing about this supposedly major character) into the bound motif (i.e., Rampling is a traitor) explains why the free motif was necessary in the first place and indicates how the free motif saves the writer time and trouble. In this case, without the free motif, a cover background would have had to be created for Rampling, detracting from the focus of the movie—Paul Newman's personal struggle.

9. *The narrator as tipoff.* Writers choose how readers gather information. With first-person narration, you are privy to a world filtered through one, possibly jaundiced, eye. Even so-called omniscient third-person narrations may or may not be feeding you the truth. You can bank on it that an author's choice of narration is highly significant. Be on the lookout for free motifs within narration: Agatha Christie made three of her narrators the murderers. If a particular narrative passage seems unduly long or different from the rest of the narration in the book, this is a tipoff that the passage is a free motif inextricably linked with the murderer. Why would the author change formats in midstream?

In television and movies, voiceovers occasionally serve as narrators (e.g., "Columbo" and "Harry-O"). More often, the camera itself acts as a narrator, censoring what you may or may not see. Although you hear Tony Perkins and his mother fighting violently, Hitchcock withholds the sight of Tony Perkins' sick mother from the audience in *Psycho*; at first, you might conclude that Hitchcock is postponing showing us a shocking effect. But at the end of the movie, when Tony Perkins comes running down the stairs with his mother, that famous overhead shot, again depriving the viewers of their look at Mommy, confirms to the sleuth what has already been suspected—that Tony Perkins and Mom are one and the same. Any time a narrator or camera in a mystery deprives you of the right to experience firsthand what the writer wants you to *assume*, you have your hands on a potent free motif.

10. *The title did it.* Surprisingly few titles of mystery stories yield real clues about the identity of the murderer. Most of the masters favor bland or descriptive titles. In several mysteries, the title can be viewed as a clue once the reader discovers who the murderer is (e.g., *Witness for the Prosecution, The ABC Murders, The Ladykillers*), but I have never seen a title act as the main free motif for a mystery, and my advice is not to attempt to use the title as a clue. Be suspicious only if the title of a book seems to be inappropriate for its content. If so, the title is probably leading you directly toward the murderer.

Of course, not all mysteries are primarily guess-along whodunits, nor is this kind of formalistic analysis the only way to solve all mysteries. The killer in most Agatha Christie novels is the suspect with the strongest motive and opportunity. But Christie uses the very tricks you've just read about to deflect you from realizing the obvious. In a well-written mystery, you should feel afterward not only that the author chose the "right" killer but that you had a fair crack at selecting him or her. These ten strategies occasionally might not work with hack writers (especially in television), who seem to be unaware of the conventions of mystery writing. But they usually will, for even the hack writer is likely to leave tracks while trying to hide the murderer.

All ten of these mystery devices serve the purpose of creating uneasiness in the reader by introducing some free motifs among a multitude of bound motifs necessary to solve the murder. Free motifs induce tension; readers share an instinctual need to make sense out of unfathomable material, to turn these free motifs into elements necessary to solve the mystery. When the murderer is revealed, and these loose ends are tied up, the extraneous is now integrated; the illogical, logical; and our anxiety, calmed.

We could turn to how-to books, biographies, exposés, cookbooks, and other genres of nonfiction bestsellers if we wanted an unfamiliar subject clarified or a complicated problem simplified. We read mysteries precisely because they *do* give us a hard time, forcing us to undergo this strange ritual of tension and release.

Mysteries are so delightful to the writer and reader alike because the story is so unimportant (and often arbitrary) that it liberates us from our usual concentration on content. We can forget the details of a mystery as soon as we finish it and still feel that we have had a worthwhile, even profound, aesthetic experience, because the mystery's lack of content liberates us to admire the beauty of its plot, its form. A still-life masterpiece does not triumph because its artist has selected a better bunch of fruit to depict than has the mediocre artist. The genius has succeeded by sharing his unique sensitivity and perception with us, forcing us to see a lowly apple in a brand-new way, as if for the first time.

Unraveling a mystery is perhaps the closest experience most readers will ever have to actually *writing* fiction. Becoming a super-sleuth will not ruin your enjoyment of mysteries. On the contrary, it will enable you to retrace the writer's steps, discovering the key decisions the writer faced, enhancing your appreciation of these magnificent constructions. Mystery stories were written to be solved, and you can't be a winner until you view a mystery as Hercule Poirot viewed his assignment in *Murder on the Orient Express*:

> I saw it as a perfect mosaic, each person playing his or her allotted part. . . . Every minute detail of their evidence was worked out beforehand. The whole thing was a very cleverly planned jigsaw puzzle, so arranged that every fresh piece of knowledge that came to light made the solution of the whole *more* difficult. . . . The case seemed fantastically impossible! That was exactly the impression intended to be conveyed.

# How to Win at Losing Weight

DESPITE THE *National Enquirer*'s weekly protestations to the contrary, there is a growing consensus that, in the words of one best-seller, diets don't work. Sure, it is not difficult for an overweight person to drop ten, twenty, or even fifty pounds or more while on a diet. But fewer than 5 percent maintain that loss for two years or more. Something must be terribly wrong with trying to lose weight by sticking to a diet.

### Why Diets Don't Work

1. *Diets force you to alter your natural weight.* Although physicians' weight charts might inform you that you are twenty pounds overweight, your body tells you something else. After you diet strenuously and shed those unwanted pounds, you are reasonably happy with the way you look and feel. You can now go off your diet. And you gain all the weight back.

The most curious element of this all-too-common syndrome is that you tend to return to exactly the same weight at which you started your diet. Could it be that your body is trying to tell you that your natural weight is your predict weight? Increasingly, doctors and nutritionists are saying "yes." Many conclude that it is next to impossible for dieting to permanently alter the body's natural weight or "setpoint." While your system allows you slight decreases or gains in weight, your body actually will wage a fight if you try to drastically alter your weight.

The setpoint serves an important biological function. It

monitors the amount of fat necessary for the body to fend off starvation. Unfortunately, the setpoint does not discriminate between starvation-level food intake and the food consumed during a weight-loss diet. When a diet does not provide enough calories for the body to maintain its natural weight, the setpoint tries to restore equilibrium by inducing hunger. When dieters are below their natural weight, they face constant hunger. Thin people trying to gain weight experience the same syndrome in reverse. Most can gain weight when put on a high-calorie diet, but they feel full constantly. As soon as they gain the weight they wish, they tend to lose weight when they go off the diet, because their setpoint tells them they are full even if they haven't eaten. The binges that dieters undertake after successfully completing a diet, then, can be seen not as indulgent lapses of discipline but rather as a natural response to weeks or months of what the body feels is starvation.

Many experts conclude that it is simply not worth the effort to battle a setpoint that is 5 to 15 percent over the weight you desire, and that the physical and emotional stress and strain is more damaging to health than the excess poundage. Indeed, one book, *Breaking the Diet Habit*, convincingly argues that dieting has been a far greater health hazard than obesity.

At the very least, the setpoint theory underscores one important point that most would-be dieters ignore. You simply cannot assume that passing the Special K pinch test or meeting an actuarial weight-chart goal is the same as arriving at your *natural* weight. Your natural weight is likely to be the number your scale gravitates to when you are neither actively dieting nor binging in anticipation of the next diet. Once you determine your setpoint, you can pursue a realistic goal: losing pounds in excess of your natural weight. The majority of dieters can never hope for more than this.

2. *Diets aren't natural.* People without weight problems seem odd to the overweight. Thin people eat when they are

hungry. If they are full, they don't finish their meal. Sometimes, they forget to eat. Some thin people don't even care much about food. What strange people!

Although dieting is something that most people choose to do to reach a normal weight, dieters eat abnormally. Most diets are extremely confining, often forcing dieters to eat when they are not hungry and then not enabling them to sate themselves when they are famished; people without weight problems wouldn't think of torturing themselves in this way. Most dieters are in a perpetual state of hunger, which teaches them that they can't use their body's hunger cues as a signal for when to eat. If they are confronted with a dietary program that forces them to eat specific things at specific times, they can often lose weight rapidly.

The Nutri-Systems' program, in which members eat only low calorie prefabricated meals, has helped many people lose weight. But what happens when the svelte graduate re-enters the real world? What happens when he is confronted with a choice of a salad or a bacon-cheeseburger? What happens when he decides to skip breakfast because he isn't hungry and then finds himself salivating in front of the pastry cart at coffee break? Most diets don't work because they involve a regimen that cannot be maintained throughout a person's life, through emotional hardship, through parties and Thanksgiving dinners. A normal person can gorge himself at Thanksgiving (although he is unlikely to binge quite as much as the overweight person, who continues eating long after his body has said, "Enough, thanks"). As Polivy and Herman put it in *Breaking the Diet Habit*, "people trying to fight their natural weight no longer eat in response to the signals that their bodies give; instead, they are at the mercy of the world around them."

Even worse, evidence exists that prolonged dieting can permanently slow metabolic rates. When you are dieting, your body compensates for the lack of nutrition by storing calories more efficiently. The body, a flexible and inventive mechanism, thinks you are trying to starve yourself when your caloric intake falls to unnatural levels and slows your metabolism.

Unfortunately, slow metabolism, which keeps you from keeling over from weakness when on a diet, serves you poorly when you are trying to maintain your newfound thinness. The slower metabolic rate makes it doubly hard to work off that indulgent piece of cheesecake.

3. *The what-the-hell effect.* All dieters know about this syndrome. Let's say that you have broken your Weight Watchers' diet by ordering a double-cheeseburger for lunch. "What the hell," you say. "As long as I've blown the diet, I might as well order a milkshake to go along with the sandwich."

Let me play Kreskin for a second. What day of the week did you start your last diet? Think about it? Ready? It was Monday.

Amazing, huh? I made this guess without calling your family, without remote-control devices or any other devious tricks. Let me make another bold statement. On the weekend before that Monday, you ate, shall we say, rather generously. In fact, you binged, did you not?

Obviously, it doesn't take a Kreskin to predict this most common syndrome of the compulsive dieter. The day before a diet commences, most people will eat enough for a family of four. Chances are, our schlep above who broke her diet by ordering the double-cheeseburger for lunch will fall off the wagon for dinner as well, reasoning "I've already blown my diet today. I'll start again tomorrow." If a transgression occurred on Friday, chances are she'll decide to start fresh on Monday. So she will binge for three days.

There is nothing wrong with having a fling before a protracted period of abstinence, but the alternation of binging and strict dieting leads most dieters into a dangerous either/or complex: Either I am a good boy and stick to my diet exactly or I might as well give up and eat as much of whatever I want.

Clinical experiments have proven that once overweight people break their diets, they lose self-control in much the same way that recovering alcoholics can return to uncontrolled drinking after one cocktail. In one experiment, two sets of dieters were given pudding. One group was told they were eating a low-calorie pudding; the others were told they were eating a fattening pudding. Scientists found that dieters who thought they were eating the high-calorie pudding ate more afterward than those who thought they were eating a dietetic pudding. The actual number of calories in the pudding had *no correlation* to how subjects subsequently ate. This study indicates that the fragile discipline of dieters can be broken not only by a transgression but by the perception of a transgression. Because the dieter is relying upon rules imposed by a book or a physician rather than hunger cues from the body when deciding what and how much to eat, one indiscretion is enough to send many dieters into a tailspin, wrecking the fragile resolve that enabled obedience up to that point.

Polivy and Herman believe that many eating disorders are preceded by, and probably produced by, alternating periods of binging and extreme dieting. Anorectics and bulimics, as well as "ordinary" dieters, learn to eat or to abstain according to external standards rather than according to the satiety cues of their body. If one slip off of the diet train can convince the miscreant that there is no use sticking to the diet for the rest of the day, until next Monday, or ever again, doesn't this indicate that either the diet itself is unrealistic or that the dieter will not have a chance to maintain the desired weight once he is off the diet and faced with the pressures and demands of everyday life?

4. *Diets turn food into an emotional and sensual reward.* Most of us tend to associate food with specific emotional states. During celebrations and holidays, we eat copious amounts of food. Part of the attraction of many fattening treats, such as pizza and cake, is the conviviality involved in sharing the food. When we are depressed, many of us bury our sorrows in a pint (or half-gallon) of ice cream or a frozen cheesecake. Food becomes a medicine to relieve depression or a treat to reward good behavior.

Dieting reinforces our emotionalization of food. Diets deprive us of our customary ways of using food to heal our psychic wounds. It is true that many people feel better about themselves when they are able to stick to a diet, but just as many feel that because they are overweight they don't *deserve* to eat good/fattening/rich food, at least until they lose weight. This kind of thinking is, of course, counterproductive. If the reward for successful dieting is the chance to eat foods that will make you gain weight, then the dieter will be on a binge-to-diet-to-binge cycle for the rest of his life.

Eating disorders simply aren't like other bad habits. It is tough enough for smokers or drinkers to remain abstemious. *Nobody* has the luxury of quitting eating altogether. Extreme anorectics feel guilty about eating *any* food—the logical consequence of this thinking is literally self-destructive. But even the dieter who wants to lose ten pounds is sowing the seeds of his own destruction if his method of motivating himself to stick to a diet is to dream about all of the emotional treats, in the form of food, that he will be allowed to have once he achieves his weight goal.

5. *It is difficult to lose, and next to impossible to maintain, a weight loss without vigorous exercise.* It is harder for most people to start a diet than to start an exercise regime. A jog around the park might be temporarily tiring, but it can't compare in torture to the constant hunger and omnipresent temptations you face on a diet. Yet most exercise regimens end up as failures as much as most diets.

There is mounting evidence that exercise might be more important than diet in keeping off unwanted pounds *permanently*. This argument seems to defy logic. If a long run around the park will only burn off the caloric equivalent of a banana, and leave us sweaty and panting besides, wouldn't it be easier just to skip the banana and the run? Yes, it would be *easier* to skip the run, but not more effective in controlling weight. Regular aerobic exercise actually can lower your setpoint. Not only does your setpoint adjust to a new level of calories required to maintain your lower weight, but it actually burns calories at a higher rate. Regular aerobic exercise, such as jogging, fast walking, or bicycling often can significantly speed up your metabolism.

And even if you would prefer to look as good in shorts as the jocks in your health club, isn't it nice to know that overweight people actually have an advantage in burning off calories through exercise: The heavier you are, the more calories you will burn off for the same exercise. Dr. William Bennett and Joel Gurin cite a specific example in *The Dieter's Dilemma*:

> In many activities, the caloric expenditure of a fat person is greater than normal, for the obvious reason that it takes more work to move a heavy weight. For example, if a man weighs 160 pounds, it costs him a hundred calories to run a mile in ten minutes. If he gained sixty pounds, it would cost him 136 calories. But if he remained the same weight and ran the mile in six minutes instead of ten, he would add only nine calories to his output. In other words, a heavy person moving relatively slowly may in fact be working far harder than a slender person who is moving much faster.

If the 220-pound runner ran only that one mile four times a week, he could be expected to lose almost ten pounds in a year without modifying his diet in any way. For most people, this is a far more dependable way of "counting calories" than trying to compute how many calories you have consumed.

6. *Many dieters aren't overweight even before they embark on their weight-loss program.* How can you determine what weight is safe for you? Ideal for you? These are really two separate questions. You might have noticed that the weight charts issued by insurance companies tend to be far more generous than physicians' charts, not only allowing for more weight but for far wider ranges in "normal" weight.

There is a simple reason for this phenomenon. Insurance companies are interested in weight only insofar as it correctly predicts mortality statistics. No proof exists that people who are mildly overweight, even if they exceed the suggested weights of physicians' charts, are any more of a health risk than people of "normal" weight. Polivy and Herman estimate that for 30 percent of the overweight population,

> Weight loss involves eluding the body's defenses of its natural weight, which seems to demand chronic semi-starvation. Not surprisingly, few of the juvenile onset, "naturally" overweight people are able to manage this constant vigilance and become dieting success statistics.
>
> For many such people, the penalties for defying their natural weights will be much more severe than can be offset by any benefits that may be derived.

Some people's natural setpoint lies in an unsafe zone, but these are the exceptions. For many more people, whose ideal weight is defined as that which will make them happy to stroll on the beach in a revealing bathing suit, the effort to reach the weight may cause severe physical and emotional problems.

With our greater affluence and more sedentary lifestyle, the average weight of the industrialized Western world has risen steadily in the last twenty years, yet our notion of the ideal physique has gone in the opposite direction. Would Mae West become a sex symbol today? She certainly wouldn't have the figure required to qualify as a "spokesmodel" on *Star Search*. Perhaps the discrepancy is not so much between what we *should* weigh and what we do weigh, but between what we *want* to weigh and what we do weigh. Since many of us, because of high setpoints, don't need to lose weight, and for practical purposes, can't lose weight permanently, any dieter who hopes to have long-term success must understand why he wants to lose weight. If the reason is *only* to "feel better about myself," perhaps the knowledge that it would be healthier *not* to try to become superskinny might allay some of the feelings of inadequacy. We can't do too much to change our society's obsession with weight, but we can give one hard look at whether dieting is really worth it.

If you think losing weight *is* worth it, I'll give you a strategy that has worked for me.

Let me tell you an inspirational story. In 1974 my favorite writer, Calvin Trillin, released a book about eating called *American Fried*. Although I had previously read many of its chapters in the *New Yorker* and *The Atlantic*, Trillin's humor and passion for "real" food was thrilling to me, as if I had met someone with my own perversion who had made my perversion not only legitimate but glamorous. *American Fried* is filled with references to the food in Trillin's hometown, Kansas City, Missouri. One of my favorite chapters is about Larry "Fats" Goldberg, a man who weighed 320 pounds and performed prodigious feats of binge eating. Goldberg was the kind of glutton who *"on the way downtown to lunch* [emphasis mine] . . . might stop at Kresge's and have two chili dogs and a couple of root beers." In one week of eating in his beloved Kansas City, Goldberg has gained as much as 14 pounds.

Through tortuous dieting, Goldberg managed to literally halve himself. By 1974 Goldberg, who now owned several renowned pizza restaurants in New York City, weighed a mere 160 pounds. It is exceedingly rare for those who have been fat throughout their childhood and adolescence to become and remain slim, but Goldberg accomplished the feat.

Goldberg's success lay in his self-insight. He realized that he was a compulsive eater and would always remain one. He knew that a life without the hope of an apple pie in the future was a bleak life indeed. Goldberg lost weight the old-fashioned way, with a sensible low-calorie diet. But once he arrived at his target weight, he maintained his slim physique by going on a program best described by the title of one of his books, *Controlled Cheating*. Goldberg has conceded that he can't eat in moderation. So five days a week, he maintains a strict, nutritionally sensible low-calorie diet. On those five days, he dreams about the other two days, when he can eat *whatever he wants*. Goldberg lets absolutely nothing verboten pass his lips on his five diet days. If he is invited to a dinner party on a diet day, he doesn't have even a taste of the chocolate cheesecake. But on his two free days—he has fun. Twice a year, Goldberg allows himself one-week vacations in Kansas City, where he runs amok among the transcendental barbecue, doughnut, fried chicken, and hamburger establishments that Trillin immortalized in *American Fried*. When he returns to New York, he goes back to controlled cheating, and reduces to 160 pounds, an indication that Goldberg has stabilized at his natural weight. Goldberg's system—turning disciplined eating off and on like a water faucet—requires more self-control than most people possess. If Fats Goldberg can lose his weight and keep it off, you've got a good chance of doing it yourself.

But you also need to face up to why you are overweight and whether you have certain fattening eating habits that you know you will never give up permanently. My system will allow you to eat buttered popcorn, for example, if that is your reason for living, but not without a little sacrifice somewhere else. To alter Jane Fonda's expression a tad: "No pain, no loss."

### Feldman's Assumptions About Permanent Weight Loss

1. *Any decent diet will help you lose the initial weight.* As Goldberg says in *Controlled Cheating*, "There are no secrets to losing weight and keeping it off." If you count calories and make up your own diet, you will lose some weight. Any sensible diet that your doctor advises will probably work as well. The success of long-term weight loss is much more likely to depend upon the strength of your resolve than the specific components of your diet. You can switch diets in midstream,

254            DAVID FELDMAN

forsaking Scarsdale for Weight Watchers. It really doesn't matter much in the long run, provided that your weight goal is realistic and not below your setpoint. I am going to be concentrating much harder on how to make your weight loss permanent.

2. *A successful weight-loss program must incorporate long-term goals.* The longer, the better. Most people diet until they lose that unwanted ten pounds. The moment they lose that tenth pound, whether it is two weeks or twelve months from the onset of the diet, they fall off the wagon and resume the same eating habits that fattened them up in the first place. Our system will involve not only weight goals but long-term time limits to reinforce the importance of permanent, rather than quick, weight-loss.

3. *A successful weight-loss program must eliminate guilt as a motivating agent.* Any diet induces guilt in all of us who inevitably violate it. This guilt triggers the dreaded what-the-hell effect which leads dieters to binge, rather than retreat, after eating a taboo food. That is why we recommend that there be *absolutely NO forbidden food on your weight-loss program.* If there is no forbidden food, then *you can't break this "diet."* If you can't break this diet, you will have no excuse for waiting until Monday to resume your diet. You need a weight-loss program that you can't get off of or out of no matter what you do.

## The Penalty System

In the past, I have fallen into all the diet traps described above. I woke up one morning in January 1985, after returning from a gourmet/gourmand fest in Los Angeles, and found myself perilously close to the two-hundred-pound mark. This time, I swore to myself, I was not only going to lose some weight but make my incremental losses easy to achieve and the goal not only to lose the weight but to keep it off as well.

How could I do this? I wanted the freedom, like Fats Goldberg, to have the right to go crazy once in awhile and eat to my heart's and stomach's content without feeling guilty, so I decided to set a weight goal for one year, ending not on December 31, but until the day of the first Christmas party to which I was invited (only Scrooge or stronger people than I can remain pure at Christmas parties). On that day, I would weigh 180 pounds or less.

In the past, I had dropped 18 pounds in four to eight weeks. I knew it would be harder for a compulsive eater like me to lose it in a year than in a month.

I decided to set interim weight goals every two months. On March 1, I would weigh 190 pounds or less. On May 1, 185 pounds or less. And on July 1, 180 pounds. As an experiment in terror, I decided that I would not have another official weigh-in until my final one.

I had never tried to lose weight so slowly, but I also had never committed to such a long program, either. I was strongly motivated to lose the weight, but I was frightened about one thing—what was going to force me to arrive at my weight goals? Then I hit upon what I thought was an ingenious idea: I would pay a penalty if I didn't reach any of my weight targets. If I didn't meet the goal, I would pay a rather large amount to my favorite charity. Although donating to charity could hardly be called an onerous penalty, the amounts I committed to were more than this struggling writer could afford. In the past, guilt, vanity, or shame had been my motivations for sticking to my diets. This time, I'd try a new one—fear.

Not until I researched for this book did I discover that my idea was not only not original, but that most of the same tactics were in a 1984 book, *The Blackmail Diet*. Actually, its author, John Bear, went much further in his scheme. He had to lose 75 pounds in one year and realized that he did not have enough discipline to lose it on his own. So Bear went to his lawyer and set up a binding trust. If Bear's physician did not inform the lawyer that he had lost the 75 pounds at the weigh-in at the end of the year, the lawyer was instructed to forward a check for $5,000 that had been made out to the American Nazi Party!

Bear strongly believes that the administration of the penalty (the ransom?) and the monitoring of the weight should be out of the dieter's hands. I didn't find this necessary, but then the stakes (the size of the check, the recipient of the check, the amount of weight to be lost) were much higher for him than for me.

Much to my surprise, I found that my modest amount of fear proved far easier to live with than guilt. Because I committed myself to weight goals but not to any specific diet, nothing I ate made me feel guilty. When I needed to lose weight (a born procrastinator, I found I always needed to drop several pounds the week before each deadline), I simply cut out the stuff—red meat, oils and butter, desserts, fried foods —that any sensible weight-loss diet would recommend eliminating. I ate huge salads and bowls of homemade soup with unbuttered bread, and the weight came off easily because, for all intents and purposes, this was more like the first week of my diet than the eighth or sixteenth or fifty-first. On December 17, three days before my first Christmas party, I hit 180 pounds, and stayed there. Although I went up a little before the end of the New Year, I found that because I hadn't been dieting stringently for months before the holidays, I didn't feel the need to binge either. I used to see diets as what I had to do to allow myself to eat as I pleased (i.e., binge). Once I accepted that I had to hit my weight goals (I literally couldn't afford not to!), I found tremendous flexibility with my system. During the entire year, I never was more than eight pounds above the last weigh-in weight. I knew that I was committed to a year-long effort, and that I did not want to go on month-long "diets": strong incentives to eating sensibly, or at least to go easy for a day or two after a binge.

Only you know what kind of penalty would be best for

you. You might find it best to pay a penalty to a friend, who would then be in charge of monitoring your weight. Perhaps, your penalty might not even be monetary. For 1987, for example, my penalty might be the humiliation of trying to promote a book that includes a chapter on "How to Win at Losing Weight" when I look like a blimp. John Bear believes it essential that your ransom be horrific if lost, but I'm not sure that his type of arrangement mightn't have paralyzed me.

The most important facet of the Penalty System or the Blackmail Diet is that the goals be long term and that the penalty be strong enough to prove a real incentive. It is also essential that your weight target be realistic. At 180 pounds, I am unlikely, in a bathing suit, to be confused with Greg Louganis. The ease with which I dropped weight when I ate sensibly proves that 180 pounds is at or above my natural weight. If your weight goal is below your setpoint, the Penalty System, like any other, will not work, but the Penalty System does answer all of the other objections we have raised about most diets.

- The Penalty System allows you to eat whatever foods you want as long as you are losing weight.
- The Penalty System never forces you to eat food when you are not hungry. You are free, then, to respond to genuine hunger cues. Most of the year, I ate many small meals, often at eccentric hours, rather than the usual "three squares."
- Food does not become the reward it does on other diets because you don't feel deprived: There are no forbidden foods.

What about the role of exercise in the Penalty System? I wish I could say I undertook a rigorous exercise regimen to accompany my weight-loss program, but I didn't. On the average day, the brisk couple of miles I walk is not aerobic training but rather my primitive mode of transportation. In 1986 I'm augmenting my Penalty System with an exercise regimen.

One woman I know uses a variant of the Penalty System. Rather than trying to reach a certain weight goal, she makes sure she fits into her sexiest dress. If she can zip herself up successfully (even if she has to hold her breath in), she treats herself to a new spring wardrobe. If she can't, she wears last year's rags. Her method (The Positive Reinforcement System?) might work better than weight goals for those people who are exercising along with changing their eating habits. As fat turns into heavier muscle, many people lose inches but not much weight. If fitting into that sexy dress is more important than the numbers on a scale, use that as your goal. As long as you have a realistic goal and fear—if only a little bit—the consequences of not reaching that goal, you have a great chance for success using the Penalty System.

**Note:** This chapter is designed for overweight but not grossly obese people. It is essential that anyone undergoing a new eating and/or exercise regimen consult a physician.

**For more information:**
*The Dieter's Dilemma*, William Bennett, M.D., and Joel Gurin (New York: Basic Books, 1982).

*Breaking the Diet Habit: The Natural Weight Alternative*, Janet Polivy and C. Peter Herman (New York: Basic Books, 1985).

These two books are not diet manuals. They ask fundamental questions, such as: "Are you really overweight?" "Do you want to lose weight because it is best for your health or because you have been conditioned to think that anything less than skinny is ugly?" "Should you go on a diet even if you do not need to lose weight?" and "If you go on a diet, what are your chances of keeping the weight off?"

Both of these books cover much of the same ground, emphasizing the importance of setpoints. Polivy and Herman's book is particularly strong in its treatment of the physical and emotional dangers of dieting. The discussion of their clinical experiments with dieters is fascinating. *The Dieter's Dilemma* emphasizes the sociological changes in the last century that have dragged many, reluctantly, into dieting. Bennett and Gurin's discussion of the importance of exercise in altering setpoints and keeping off weight is excellent.

Read at least one of these fine books *before* you embark on a diet. Either book may convince you it isn't worth the try. If you remain undaunted, you are probably resolute enough to succeed.

*The Blackmail Diet*, John Bear, Ph.D. (Berkeley, CA: Ten Speed Press, 1984). Although Bear's tactics are more radical than those described here, the principles are the same, and Bear offers many less extreme options to achieve weight loss.

*Controlled Cheating*, Larry Goldberg (New York: Doubleday, 1981). This unpretentious book has much padding but plenty of folk wisdom from one of the few heroes who has lost half his body weight and *kept* it off—and all the while working at a pizza restaurant! Recommended for those who genuinely love and are obsessed by food. Goldberg doesn't even try to condition you to seeing food as merely a form of fuel; he simply tries to convince you that you will live longer and more happily if you spend five-sevenths of your life looking forward to the two-fifths of your life when you can eat to your heart's content.

# How to Win at Solving Crossword Puzzles

IF YOU, LIKE ME, are a hack at solving crossword puzzles, there is one consolation: If you think solving the suckers is hard, try constructing them. Crosswords are tough to construct because every letter in a crossword is used horizontally and vertically and the required symmetrical pattern of black squares provides little flexibility.

One way to improve your crossword-solving ability is to learn more about the problems of constructing crosswords. For now, it is sufficient to remember that the technical requirements of fitting words into a symmetrical grid are so arduous that most puzzle-makers can't spend their time worrying about how to use the most obscure letters. Probably composers would love to use the lesser-used letters of the alphabet, *J*s, *K*s, and *X*s, but their worry about completing the puzzle with acceptable words leads them to favor the *E*s, *T*s, and *O*s. So when in doubt, it is more likely that a missing letter in an answer is a common one rather than a less usual one.

All puzzle constructors start by trying to fill a grid with words. Only after they are sure they can complete the grid do they bother composing clues. Many constructors *do* try to get tricky with their clues, for listing a series of synonyms gets boring for the solver as well as the composer.

After reading this chapter, you'll know more about some of the tricks of the composers' trade—how they fill the grid and how they disguise their clues to make answers harder to find. But the first few suggestions require only common sense.

## Starting Out

Your first step is to look at the set of clues. Try to find one clue whose answer you positively know. For this purpose, I seek out fill-in-the-blank clues, which are often the easiest, and usually the least ambiguous clues to solve. For example, if a *TV Guide* puzzle gives the clue

_____ Montalban

it doesn't take a nuclear physicist to figure out that the answer is "RICARDO."

When you first start out, try to answer the clues before you look at the grid to find how long the word or words are. If your guess fits the allotted space, you have more confirmation that your answer is correct. Even if you are sure of your answer, this self-test will alert you against misspelling the word.

It is important to start with an answer you are sure about, because any one answer, such as "RICARDO," will serve as an aid to solving—in this case—seven more words in the opposite direction. You will find it much easier to think of answers (and to check them for accuracy) when you know that the third letter in the word is a *C*.

Although you can't always manage it, try to start with an across answer on the top row or a down answer on the left side. This will make your next answer that much easier to conjure because the next words that intersect these answers will all *start* with a known letter. It is much easier to summon up an answer when starting with the first letter of the word instead of a middle letter (especially when the letter is a vowel; does anything come to your mind when asked to name a seven-letter word whose fifth letter is *A*?).

Now that you have at least one answer you are sure about, try to build on that answer. Many solvers make the mistake of trying to go down the clue list in order. If you are a genius who doesn't need prompting to supply answers, this is fine, but for the average person, it is much faster and easier to try to finish partly completed answers.

Even if you are stumped in a corner of the grid and can't arrive at any of the answers that intersect your "RICARDO," try to fill out answers adjacent to the area. Eventually, your answers will merge. The more letters you can fill in, the better the chance of getting both the across and down answers in one area.

What happens when you get stumped, and can't make progress in your "RICARDO" area? We asked this question of Stan Newman, the first United States Open Crossword champion and president of the American Crossword Federation. Newman, who has been timed at under three minutes for a daily newspaper crossword, doesn't ordinarily encounter this problem. When you get stymied, Newman recommends skipping the area altogether and letting your subconscious take over. Newman reports that many times after he has temporarily given up on a clue, he has returned to it and known the answer instantly. We are always told that we use only a tiny fraction of our brainpower. Perhaps a small portion of our unused brainpower is available for solving one crossword clue while we think we are working on another one.

Newman adds that crosswords are meant to be enjoyed. If you are totally frustrated even at the start, perhaps you should put the puzzle down and try later; maybe your subconscious will even work overtime for you. That's easy for Newman to say—his subconscious seems to be a lot smarter than mine.

## When You Get Stuck

Unless a crossword is extremely tough or extremely easy, most solvers can fill out many of the answers, but then they get stuck at some point. You may find yourself poring over the same clues, seeking inspiration anywhere. What techniques can prod you toward the solution? There are several tactics that won't work all of the time but that can often lead to one answer which will supply enough letters to unravel other answers. Here are some tactics that winning solvers employ:

1. *Many medium to difficult puzzles employ a theme.* This can either be a subject (e.g., many answers will pertain to flowers) or a particular eccentricity (e.g., many answers will be abbreviations). Often, puzzles become easy to unravel once you determine the theme of the puzzle. *If you are trying to solve a thematic puzzle, the longest words on the grid will invariably relate to the theme.* This is no accident. Because thematic puzzles are harder to construct, the puzzle-maker starts with the longest (thematic) words filled in and inserts the rest of the answers to fit in with these thematic clues. A constructor cannot decide to throw in a nine-letter answer into a puzzle he is half finished composing; the odds are stacked heavily against the constructor being able to reconcile a long word with a collection of other random letters.

2. *Many clues are models of how the answer is supposed to be expressed.* Crossword editors demand that clues be short. The only way the constructor can make the puzzle difficult but fair and stay within her space constrictions is by using the clues as shorthand to convey the form of the answer. If a clue is "hats," you can reasonably expect the answer to be in a plural form, and if you are otherwise stymied, you can speculate that the word ends with an S, insert the S, and see if that helps you figure out the word that intersects the S. Likewise, if the clue is expressed in the past tense, you can gamble that the answer ends in *ED*. If the clue is in the form of a participle or gerund, you can try an *ING* ending. If a clue is framed as a superlative (e.g., "mightiest"), it is worth the gamble to insert an *EST* at the end or a tentative *ER* when the clue is a comparison (e.g., "mightier"). Even an innocuous-looking abbreviation in the spelling of the clue might be

a signal that the answer is meant to be abbreviated. For example, if you see the clue, "A–1 at U.S.C.," you can be sure that the answer is in abbreviations (*BMOC*). A foreign word in the clue indicates a foreign word in the answer.

Assume that any modifications of a word in a clue are highly significant. Disclaimers like "sort of," "at times," or "type of" usually indicate that the clue is not a precise definition or is a joke or play on words. If a clue says, "Christmas, if you're lucky," you can be sure that the answer is not a synonym for Christmas but rather a word to describe *some* Christmases (in this case, *WHITE*). A question mark signifies a pun or other word play. Because it is so difficult to construct a crossword grid, puzzle-makers focus on making their clues hard rather than on making the words in the grid difficult. Most of the time when you encounter an obscure word in a puzzle, the constructor could find no other word that fit. He would much rather make your life difficult by inventing clever clues, as he is no doubt sick of simply supplying synonyms. Your best weapon in deciphering clues is learning the tricks of how puzzle-makers phrase clues.

3. *When you are missing just one letter or two in a word, try an alphabet scan.* In charades, when the actor signals "sounds like *hat*," the guessers might scan through the alphabet, changing *hat* to *bat*, *cat*, *fat*, *mat*, *pat*, *rat*, *sat*, and *tat* before arriving at the correct answer, *vat*. When you are searching for an elusive letter, simply scanning the alphabet in order can be of tremendous help in conjuring up the answer to what seems like a lost cause.

4. *Begin noticing that different letters tend to appear most frequently on certain areas of the grid.* For example, *E* and *S* seem to be the most popular word-ending letters. *S* is a most flexible letter, because it also starts so many words. Most of the vowels other than *E*, though, are comparatively rare as the last letter of words. For that reason, you find many

puzzles in which *E* is the only vowel on the right column vertically and the lower column horizontally. Because every letter in a crossword must be used in two words, and each of the letters in these two rows must end a word going in the opposite direction, constructors like to free themselves of the burden of trying to find words that end with an *A* or *U* in these two columns.

Conversely, you'll find that the top row reading horizontally and the left-hand column reading vertically have a disproportionate number of consonants and relatively few *E*s, since each of these letters must start a word going in the other direction. Relatively few words start with a vowel, and too many of them yield "crossword words," obscurities that aren't used in everyday life. These crossword words exist because of the constructor's need to find words with unusual letters to plug an otherwise unworkable hole in the grid. For example, it is not unusual to encounter the dreaded clue, "Belgian river." The answer, which only a crossword solver or a geography student from Belgium is likely to know, is *YSER*. *Yser* is a special word because all four letters are excellent word-enders: *D*, *W*, and *Y* are three relatively uncommon letters that are often found in a disproportionately high number of word endings.

Puzzle constructors must avoid inflexible letters, letters that will dictate their placement on the grid and dictate what letters must follow or precede them. *J* is a difficult letter, which is only good for starting words and is useless for ending them. *Q* must always be followed by *U*, and is also rare except as the beginning of a word. *Z*s and *X*s can be used in the middle of words but must invariably be sandwiched between vowels. Exceptions to these rules are rare, and most puzzle constructors don't tend to concern themselves with creative ways of using *Q*s. Crossword answers tend to exaggerate the letter patterns that already exist in English. The most common letters are represented in even greater numbers in crossword puzzles. Every time a constructor uses common letters that offer many different ways to intersect them, it makes her task easier. Once you recognize these patterns, it will make your job easier as well.

A few crossword letter patterns contradict typical English. Many more words in a crossword puzzle will alternate strictly between consonant and vowel, yielding a disproportionately high total number of vowels. If you try to construct your own crossword, you will see how much easier your life becomes if you try alternating vowels and consonants. The result is far more total vowels than written English usually provides. Vowels are much more flexible than consonants, and flexibility is what the constructor most cherishes in letter combinations.

The basic unit of the crossword puzzle is the word square, a section of the puzzle where all the horizontal and vertical words are of equal length. Notice the next time you solve a puzzle how many of these feature strictly alternating consonants and vowels. Here is a simple three-letter word square that occupied the upper-left-hand corner of a crossword I constructed.

```
D   O   N

A   R   E

S   E   T
```

Notice that in a three-letter word square with alternating vowels and consonants, it is necessary to insert at least two three-letter words with two vowels in them—these tend not to yield the most exciting clues or the most exciting words, but they make the constructor's job easy.

To continue the puzzle, I had to lengthen *SET* to the right and *NET* below. This alternating pattern of vowels and consonants consistently produces plenty of options for developing new and nonobscure words. In this case, this is how I extended these words:

```
D   O   N

A   R   E

S   E   T   (T   L   I   N   G)

    -W-

    -O-

    -R-

    -K-
```

Notice how many substitutions of vowels I could have used to change the word square completely. I could have changed the *ARE* to *ARI* (as in Onassis) and spelled *NITWIT* vertically if I needed a six-letter word or *NITRATE* for another seven-letter one. I could have changed *ORE* to a nefarious crossword word, *ORA* (the plural of *os*—never mind what *os* means), and extended the word to many different new ones—*SATIRIST* or *SATIABLE* among them.

If you are going to be a serious solver, you should probably do what I have never managed to do—learn those stupid short crossword words and be done with it. But even without such memorization, you can aid your alphabet scan by consciously recognizing the letter patterns and letter frequencies discussed here. No matter how tricky a crossword's clues are, when in doubt, always assume that missing letters are the more common or obvious ones rather than the tricky ones, for you can be assured that the constructor is more obsessed with arriving at any acceptable solution to her grid than she is in torturing you.

## When All Else Fails

There is no law against looking up an answer in a reference book. Do you really think you are an inferior human being if you don't know, off the top of your head, the name of that

Indian tree-dwelling mammal (colugo) or the archaic spelling of *nevertheless* (natheless)? As much as it hurts your pride, isn't it better to look up words that you don't know rather than to toss the crossword in the wastebasket? Expert solvers aren't shy about looking up a piece of information. Neither should you be.

My late editor, Eunice Riedel, had another tip that I've found to be helpful. If you get stuck in one area, chances are that you have made a mistake in the easiest word! Crossword constructors, sadists by nature, love nothing better than to give the solver a simple innocuous clue, such as "drag." If "drag" corresponds to a four-letter word on the grid whose second letter is *U*, the tendency would be to fill in *PULL* without giving it a second thought. But the answer could just as easily be *puff* (as in the drag of a cigarette). Solvers often forget that many clue words can be either noun or verb forms (words such as *drive, felt, swell*, etc.), leading to a false sense of confidence.

The last piece of inspiration is this. When all else fails, be aggressive. Fill in answers that you only have dim certainty about. Some solvers insert such guesses in lighter pencil (if you are solving crosswords with a pen, you probably didn't need to read this chapter in the first place) and others write in tiny letters.

Solving a crossword should not be an academic exercise. The more playful you become, the more daring you will be and the more likely you will be to place the pencil back on the coffee table, luxuriant in the knowledge that for once you have won at solving a crossword puzzle.

**For more information:**

*The Compleat Cruciverbalist: How to Solve, Compose and Sell Crossword Puzzles*, Stan Kurzban and Mel Rosen (New York: Barnes & Noble, 1981). This is the best all-purpose book about crosswords, although it is stronger on how to construct crosswords than on how to solve them. The authors give tips on how to solve and construct unconventional types of crosswords, including diagramless, cryptic, and humorous crosswords, as well as acrostic puzzles.

*How To Make and Sell Original Crosswords and Other Puzzles*, William J. Sunners (New York: Sterling, 1981). This book is designed primarily for would-be constructors, but by learning techniques for making the puzzles, you can learn quite a bit about how to solve them. The back of the book contains a word chart including all words between two to eight letters contained in the fifth edition of the *Merriam-Webster Collegiate Dictionary*.

*The Crossworders' Own Newsletter* (P.O. Box 1764, Murray Hill Station, New York, NY 10156). This newsletter is published by the master solver and president of the American Crossword Federation, Stan Newman, and is devoted to news and tips for crossword solvers. Newman, and his organization, are proponents of New Wave crosswords. Newman wants to banish crossword words and sees the existence of words such as *Yser* in crosswords as evidence of laziness on the part of both constructors and their editors. He would like to see such obscurities disappear.

Newman also believes that each clue in a crossword should be a puzzle in itself and not merely a synonym. An example he gave me illustrates the point. Why give "stereo equipment" as a clue for *AMP* when you could pose a cleverer "Band-Aid"?

Newman has edited four crossword books for the publisher Running Press called *Bulls-Eye Crosswords*, which exemplify the principles of New Wave crosswords.

# How to Win at Solving Cryptograms

IF YOU HAVE ENCOUNTERED cryptograms in crossword books or magazines, chances are you have followed the crowd by skipping the page and going on to the next crossword. The mystique built around World War II cryptographers, who spent months of tortuous work unraveling secret codes, has filtered down to the assumption that cryptograms are impossible to solve. Actually, decoding most cryptograms is rather easy, once you know a few simple techniques. If you have ever enjoyed solving a doublecrostic by figuring out letters that belong on the grid (and not just by answering the clues), you will find the same pleasure in deducing the patterns of letters that form words in a cryptogram.

A cryptogram is a simple substitution code. For any one puzzle, each letter of the alphabet substitutes for the same one other letter throughout that puzzle. *B* might substitute for *G*, *L* for *E*, etc. Most cryptograms are at least one sentence, often a witticism or proverb. You can count on the fact that the sentence, once decoded, makes sense. Let's work with one cryptogram:

OLMBJKINXC  BFKM  QPKM  NMRFLM  QZM

OLPTM  FR  XMIQZML  BACLFTAMQME,  NLPEMB

JBME  QF  QZLFG  FRR  QZMPL  LPYZQ  BZFM  IVE

RXPVY  PQ  IKPE  QZM  TFKOQPVY  ZFLEMB  FR

JVKILLPME  YJMBQB.

Note that punctuation is always included in a cryptogram. Sometimes an apostrophe will tip you off that the letter following it is a *T* or an *S*, but we have no such luck with this cryptogram.

It will help you understand this chapter if you get a piece of paper and use it as a worksheet. Your first step is to copy the cryptogram down on your worksheet quadruple-spaced, then count the frequency of each letter, using slash marks to keep a running total. When you are finished, arrange the letters in order of frequency. For this cryptogram, the tally is this:

| | | |
|---|---|---|
| M—20 | R—6 | A—2 |
| L—12 | I—5 | C—2 |
| Q—12 | J—4 | G—1 |
| F—11 | V—4 | D—0 |
| P—10 | Y—4 | H—0 |
| B—9 | N—3 | S—0 |
| Z—8 | O—3 | U—0 |
| E—7 | T—3 | W—0 |
| K—6 | X—3 | |

Five letters are not contained in the cryptogram at all. We can simply forget that they exist, and we are effectively searching only for twenty-one letters, but of course we don't know which twenty-one letters. Now you need to know a very important list: the most frequently used letters in the English language. Reading from most frequent at left to least frequent at right, they are:

E  T  A  O  N  R  I  S  H  D  L  F  C  M  U  G  Y  P

W  B  V  K  X  J  Q  Z

Although it is possible that any one sentence could have a totally skewed letter count, it is astonishing how consistently the frequency list can help you solve cryptograms. As you notice from your word count, the letter *M* appears much more frequently than any other letter. Let's assume, until we can prove otherwise, that *M* equals *E*. You will find that in most cryptograms of more than ten words or so, *E* will be the most common letter. On our worksheet, we will draw a line below each word and write *E* below each *M* that we find. We aren't positive that *M* equals *E*, but we certainly want to test the hypothesis. Your worksheet should look like this (we have numbered the words to make it easier for reference purposes):

OLMBJKINXC   BFKM   QPKM   NMRFLM   QZM   OLPTM

FR   XMIQZML   BACLFTAMQME,   NLPEMB   JBME   QF

QZLFG   FRR   QZMPL   LPYZQ   BZFM   IVE   RXPVY   PQ

IKPE   QZM   TFKOMQPVY   ZFLEMB   FR   JVKILLPME

YJMBQB.

    Although we still can't be sure, it looks very likely that the *M* is indeed the substitute for *E*. If *M* equals *E*, then *E* ends many of the words in the cryptogram, a characteristic not true of the other most common vowels, *A* and *O*. It is possible that *M* could substitute for *T*, a letter that ends many words. At this point, I like to use what I call the "THE Test." In a sentence as long as this cryptogram's, it is the rule that the word *THE* appears at least once. So once I think I know where the *E* is, I look to see if there is a three-letter word ending in *E* that might be *THE*. Eureka! Two of them. We still can't be positive we are right, but let's assume that *Q* equals *T*, and write this substitution down on our worksheet. If *Q* equals *T*, than we can assume *Z* equals *H*. We now have our first two words (#5 and #22) filled out. It is possible that our hypothesis is wrong, but we can quickly figure that out by looking at our worksheet.

    Look at Word #12. If *Q* equals *T*, then *F* must be *O*. *To* is the only common two-letter word starting with *T*.

    When you are stymied, always look for a word that is

missing only one letter. Word #17 looks interesting—a four-letter word ending in *HOE*. The word must be *SHOE*, so *B* must be substituting for *S*.

We've filled quite a bit of our worksheet and still haven't found the two other common vowels, *A* and *I*. Word #20 must be either *IT* or *AT* and therefore contain one of the two letters. Let's check *P* in a few other places where it occurs. Word #3 isn't of much help. We already have *T __ __ E* but the *P* could easily stand for either *A* or *I*, forming many common words such as *time*, *tale*, or *tile*. But try working on Word #15. *P* can't equal *A*, for we already have *T H E __ __* and there are no five-letter words starting *T H E A*. Therefore, *P* equals *I*. Once you know which letter represents *I*, then you can easily finish the blank in Word #15: *T H E I __*. *L* equals *R*.

At this point, finishing the puzzle is a snap. It doesn't take a genius to insert the right missing letters for words #4, #13, and #16 immediately, and you should be able to find the code for *A* rather easily (although if this cryptogram has any idiosyncrasy, it is that there are few *A*s in it). A few aggressive guesses, easily confirmed by trying your solution on other letters in the cryptogram, will fill in the missing letters in words #2, #3, #11 (doesn't this word have to be *USED*?— *ASEA* is rather unlikely), and #24.

Try to finish this cryptogram. The solution will be at the end of this chapter.

There are several other tricks of the cryptogram trade that will help you solve these puzzles more easily:

1. All words have one vowel. Any one-letter word is an *A* or an *I*. Occasionally, constructors will throw in a one-letter initial or abbreviation, but these should be punctuated with a period.
2. The importance of two-letter words cannot be emphasized enough, since each contains one vowel, but no two-letter word contains two vowels. Each vowel tends to appear in characteristic places.

The *A* is almost always the first letter (ha, ma, and pa are a few of the rare exceptions).

The *E* is almost always the second letter, with no common exceptions.

The *I* is almost always the first letter (unless you are solving a mathematical cryptogram (*pi*), a friendly cryptogram (*hi*), or a royal cryptogram (*di*).

The *O* is the most flexible letter. In fact, if you see a letter both starting and ending two-letter words in your cryptogram and you know that the letter is a vowel, assume that the letter signifies *O*. (Common examples are *of*, *to*, *or*, and *go*).

The *U* is invariably the first letter and is found in only two common words—*up* and *us*.

The *Y* is always the second letter, unless you are solving an Old English puzzle (*ye*). The only common uses are *by* and *my*.

3. Apostrophes are a gift from God, for they almost always precede the letters *S* or *T*. In two-letter words, they precede *D* or *M* (i.e., *I'd* and *I'm*).

4. When in doubt, look for vowels first. When you are totally in the dark, assume as I did in the example that the most frequently repeated crypt signifies *E*.

5. Double consonants must be preceded by a vowel (e.g., _ _ *T T* _ _. The second letter must be a vowel).

6. In a word with a double consonant that is followed by a blank and then an *E*, the blank usually stands for *L* (e.g., *little*, *waddle*, and *bubble*).

7. When there is a double letter in a four-letter word, the doubled letter is almost always a vowel (e.g., *seen*, *boot*, and *deer* but not *ally*). It follows, then, that the first and last letters are usually consonants.

8. When the first and last letters of a word are identical, the letter often, but not always, stands for *S* (e.g., *sets*, *says*, *suds*).

9. Relatively few words in the English language start

with three consonants, although there are plenty of exceptions (e.g., *strength, chrome,* and *screeched*).

10. Be on the lookout for series of commas or a colon followed by a series of commas. These might signify a list. If you see a combination such as:

- - - - - - - - - - - - - - - - -, - - - -, - - - - - - - - - -.

you can bet that the fifth word is a conjunction, either *BUT* or *AND*.

11. When in doubt, be aggressive. Guess away. You are not being graded on the neatness of your worksheet. The joy of solving cryptograms lies not so much in the solution of the puzzles—at a certain point, it becomes trivially easy—but in testing hypotheses by a trial-and-error method. You will stumble upon the underlying patterns and principles that rule our crazy language's syntax and spelling. Unlike crosswords, which must often fall back on using the same words over and over again in order to make a puzzle work, every cryptogram is different. Most cryptograms are easier to solve than the crosswords you would find, say, in the *New York Times.* You now have the tools to decode them.

The solution to the cryptogram is:

PRESUMABLY SOME TIME BEFORE THE PRICE OF

LEATHER SKYROCKETED, BRIDES USED TO THROW OFF

THEIR RIGHT SHOE AND FLING IT AMID THE COMPETING

HORDES OF UNMARRIED GUESTS.

**For more information:**

There aren't too many reference works available on cryptogram strategy. The best is:

*Fun with Cryptograms*, Joseph Verner Reed (Walker and Co.: New York, 1968).

If you can't locate the Reed book, you might want to send for a free two-page leaflet published by Dell, the publisher of the biggest-selling puzzle magazines. Although this leaflet is short on strategy, it will show you how to set up a worksheet and takes you through the solution of one puzzle. Enclose a legal-sized self-addressed stamped envelope to:

> Have Fun With Cryptograms
> Dell Publishing Co., Inc.
> 1 Dag Hammarskjold Plaza
> New York, NY 10017

# How to Win at Choosing the Right Checkout Line in a Supermarket

FRUSTRATION AT THE SLOWNESS of checkout stands is the number one consumer complaint about supermarkets. The only thing that is worse than paying exorbitant food bills is having to wait for the privilege. Supermarkets are aware that slow checkouts are a crucial problem, and spend, on average, between 2.5-to-3 percent of their total sales revenues on checkstand help, their largest single labor expense.

Truth be told, the slowness of my own checkouts are a gnawing but secondary frustration for me. I am more concerned about why everyone else seems to be moving faster than I am. I seem to have an uncanny knack for always choosing the wrong checkout line. While I seemed to have an instinct for the proper strategy in most of the other subjects in this book, nature has deserted me on this topic, so I resolved to try to figure out how to select the right checkout line.

I have no easy answers. I can honestly say that it is harder to select the right checkout line in a supermarket than to win in the stock market. But since I've conducted some book research and more crucial field research, my track record has improved to the point where I can, more than half the time, choose the right line.

I haven't minded sharing any of my other proprietary se-

crets, but I hope that you disregard this chapter as being simply too frivolous to take seriously. I don't want more competition in the supermarket.

## *Criteria for Selecting the Right Checkout Line*

1. *How many shopping baskets are in line?* Notice that the criterion is not how *long* the line is. You cannot always tell how many people are in a line by measuring the length of the line. The number of shopping baskets is a better indicator than the number of people in line, because couples and children share one basket and can deceive nonreaders of this book into thinking the wait for their line will be longer in time simply because their line is longer in distance.

2. *How many items do those waiting in line have in their baskets?* One person waiting in line with eighty items is likely to take longer to process than two customers with fifteen items each. Be aware, however, that there is a certain amount of incremental time spent setting up for each new customer: Cash registers must be cleared; greetings are usually exchanged; new shopping bags must be snapped open; change must be made. Each new customer represents a potential threat to bog down the checker with cashing a check, returning bottles, or fumbling for change. It is thus always preferable to stand behind one customer with forty, or even fifty items, than to risk following two shoppers with twenty items each.

Stores measure their own efficiency by counting not how many customers are processed per hour, but how many "rings per hour" are achieved at each register. You should measure your wait more by how many rings on the cash register your line will generate than by how many people are in line.

3. *How many employees are working at the checkstand?* Any shopper with pretensions toward being a scientific line-waiter notices the first two criteria, but this point might go

undetected and is just as important. In his book, *Modern Supermarket Operation*, Dr. Edward A. Brand cites a Food Marketing Institute study, conducted before the use of optical scanners, on the effect of different checkstand teams on time taken to process customers.

| Checkstand Team | Customers Per Hour | Customers Per Employee Per Hour |
| --- | --- | --- |
| Checker | 24.7 | 24.7 |
| Checker plus bagger | 43.3 | 21.65 |
| Checker plus 2 baggers | 45.6 | 15.2 |
| Checker plus 2 baggers plus changemaker | 77.6 | 19.4 |
| Checker plus bagger plus changemaker | 72.0 | 24.0 |

From this study, Brand logically concludes that two baggers do little to speed up the line, but that, surprisingly, using a separate person to ring up and make change, to check the items, and to bag the groceries is actually cost efficient for the supermarket (since the team of three can dispatch 24 customers per employee per hour, compared to 24.7 by the checker alone) and much, much faster for the customer. I have never seen this configuration, but have many times seen two baggers in one line. Simply throwing in more employees at a checkstand doesn't necessarily increase productivity. As we can see, the checker plus two baggers plus changemaker team barely beats the team without the second bagger and is obviously not cost-efficient.

Clearly, if all other factors are equal, always choose a line with a bagger, even if it has more customers. The presence of one bagger will ensure the line moving 50 to 100 percent faster than the checker bagging alone.

Baggers are of crucial importance with optical scanning equipment, as well. According to an article by Robert E. O'Neill in the January 1986 edition of *Progressive Grocer*,

"How to Coax Greater Productivity From the Front End," the best configuration for the average checkstand is to have the checker use the scanner and to have a separate bagger. With this setup, the grocery store can expect to ring up seven hundred items per hour.

The next best strategy, according to O'Neill, is to have the customer bag the items himself, a system used more often in warehouse stores. With the customer bagging, a checker can expect to ring up about six hundred items per hour. Stores would usually prefer not to have customers bag their own goods, because they use many more sacks than the stores' baggers would, usually routinely doublebagging and putting fewer items into each bag.

When the cashier works alone but bags each item immediately instead of passing it along the checkstand, the average is four hundred and fifty rings per hour, quite a bit slower than with a bagger. An employee can't be nearly as fast bagging with one hand, and the hand used for scanning can work much more quickly than the hand used for bagging. Not all items can be bagged in the same order they are scanned, either, further slowing this technique.

Still, the scan-and-bag technique is faster than the cashier scanning, passing all of the items along the counter, and then bagging himself. This most common type of checkout service can be expected to yield only three hundred rings per hour.

That's right. One cashier with an optical scanner and one bagger (seven hundred rings per hour) are usually more than 100 percent faster than a cashier forced to bag by himself. The presence of a bagger in one line and no bagger in the other is the single most common reason for lines moving at unequal speeds.

4. *What types of items are in the carts?* Not all rings on the cash register are created equal. In particular, watch out for vegetarians! Nothing can slow a line down longer than waiting for the cashier to weigh twenty-six plastic bags of indeterminate produce (particularly nonpackaged produce,

which is unlikely to have a marked price, leaving the cashier to memorize correctly how much each type of produce costs per pound). But do not be afraid to stand behind someone with eighty-three cans of the same cat food. Incremental time is saved when the checker processes many of the same item. Usually, each item need not be scanned separately, nor prices hunted by checkers without scanners.

5. *Does anyone in line look as if they are going to cash a check?* Supermarkets differ in their check-cashing policies, but one thing you can be sure of. If someone ahead of you cashes a check, it will slow you up. Some stores require an okay from the manager for every check cashed, often resulting in long waits. Even without a manager check, time will be consumed verifying IDs or logging the check.

Unfortunately, most customers who intend to use a check will not reveal their checkbook until after you take your place in line. (Indeed, most won't take out their checkbooks until their order has been processed, a discourtesy to others waiting behind them.) The only hint I can offer is that when in doubt, watch out for women, especially if they have their purses clutched. For some reason, relatively few men pay their supermarket purchases with checks (perhaps because so many supermarkets demand a check-cashing card and married men tend not to take care of major shopping expeditions). Of course, if your store has separate no-checking lanes, gravitate toward them.

6. *Is your checker fast?* Just as horse handicappers note the idiosyncrasies of each horse, so should you note how fast your checker is each time you shop. If you are in a new store or have never bothered to discern the work habits of the different checkers, it is worth a few seconds before committing yourself to one line to observe the different checkers or checker-and-bagger combinations. If a checker seems to be dozing with one customer, he is unlikely to change by the (long) time

you get to the front. Individual checkers can vary by hundreds of rings per hour on a regular basis.

7. *Does the store have an express lane?* Stores have various policies for their express lanes, usually allowing only customers with eight, ten, twelve, or fifteen items or less to pass through. In most cases, customers are not allowed to cash checks or return bottles in the express lane.

The classic problem, when you have fewer than the necessary twelve items, is whether to enter the express lane, which has eight people already, or to stand in one of the regular lanes with fewer customers waiting but with many more items per shopping cart.

The six criteria above should stand you in good stead for making this momentous decision, but there are a few factors you should be aware of.

Is your supermarket strict about enforcing the twelve-item limit on express-lane fudgers?

Does the checker in the express lane bag the items himself? Just because he has fewer items to bag doesn't mean that a lack of a separate bagger won't slow the line down.

Is the express line well enough equipped to allow the checker to process items quickly? Many express lines in otherwise well-equipped stores do not have optical scanners and are truncated in size. The reason the counter of many express lanes is smaller is to discourage people with too many items from crashing the express lane, upsetting the crasher and the legitimate standees behind him. Unfortunately, the small size of the checkout counters in many express lanes serves to slow down the checker, especially if there is not adequate room to pass items after they have been checked or not enough room for the next customer to place his items on the belt while the shopper in front of him is being processed. Criterion #2 reminds us that the start-up time for each new customer processed by the checker will serve to slow down the line, and this is never truer than in the express line, which contains many customers with relatively few items per basket.

One pleasing psychological note about the express line, however, is that while it might be longer than any other line, it also moves faster than any other line. If you are in the express line, you are likely to receive envious stares from sufferers in other lines, who thought they were clever in thinking that the shortest line would provide them with the shortest wait.

8. *Is anyone in the line likely to desire any special services that might cause delays?* In general, the more items in a shopping cart, the more likely the patron might require an additional service, particularly check-cashing. In areas where most customers do not use a car to get to the store, large orders often mean deliveries, which can slow down the processing of the order. Bottle returns, which you should be able to spot with a cursory glance at the carts in front of you, can be particularly nettlesome, since the checker must often not only count bottles but process the deposit separately from the rest of the order and then lug the bottles away.

9. *Are there some lanes with scanners and others without scanners?* Scanners have received a mixed reaction from consumers. But there is no doubt that scanners have speeded up the checking-out process. If you are in a store that has converted only partially to scanners, or more likely, has a few scanners on the blink, always choose the line with scanners, all other things being equal.

Is it worth all of this intellectual investigative work to save a few minutes in the checkout line? For people like me, yes. In fact, I'd rather spend an extra few minutes determining the right line than using the same time waiting, flipping through the latest issue of the *National Enquirer*. Finding the right line is no longer an issue of saving time, but of saving pride and self-respect.

# Help!

REMEMBER, we only promised you that we could make you win at *just about* everything. We'd like you to win at everything.

If you have other winning approaches to the subjects in this book, we'd love to hear about them.

If you are a frustrated, consistent loser at some area in your life, we'd like to know about it. Perhaps we can solve your problem.

If you would like to comment on this book, or ask a question about its contents, please write. We thrive on your input.

David Feldman
Box 28415
Los Angeles, CA 90024